Feelings 102: Bible Studies for LIVING God's Written Word, Volume 1, 3rd Edition

(Trials from Adam & Eve to Abraham & Sarah)

by

William J. Clark, Jr.

With

CH(COL) William J. Clark, Ret.

Keys To Understanding Life Series

Feelings 102: Bible Studies for LIVING God's Written Word, Volume 1, 3rd Edition
5th in the *Keys To Understanding Life Series*

www.KeysToUnderstandingLife.org
www.Feelings102.com

ISBN 13: 978-0-9900193-4-3
ISBN 10: 0-9900193-4-9

Cover Design:
Practical Photography & Publishing
and
Innovo Publishing

Printed in the United States of America
U.S. Printing History
First Edition: February 2013 – Innovo Publishing
Second Edition: October 2013 – Keys To Understanding Life Series
Third Edition: July 2016 – Keys To Understanding Life Series

Feelings 102 is dedicated to the Lord
and to those of you who study His written Word
for the high purpose of seeking to let Christ live through you,
making you godly, Christ-like doers in in your trials.

May your study help you improve in recognizing God's keys to
understanding life. May you allow Christ to use them
to transform your heart and renew your mind during your trials.

These godly tasks are key to diligently doing our part
in submitting to God,
to resisting Satan during our trials,
and in LIVING God's Written Word.

CONTENTS

CONTENTS iv
INTRODUCTION TO FEELINGS 102: BIBLE STUDIES FOR LIVING
  GOD'S WRITTEN WORD..1
  WHAT IS POIEOLOGY?...2
  OVERVIEW OF THE POIEOLOGICAL BIBLE STUDY 5
  FOUNDATIONS FOR FEELINGS 102...6
  FEATURES FOUND IN FEELINGS 102 8
OVERVIEW OF THE BIBLICAL BASICS OF TRIALS........................11
  WHAT IS A TRIAL? 12
  WHAT IS OUR IDENTITY IN CHRIST, AND WHY WE DON'T
  ALWAYS ACT ACCORDING TO THAT? 13
    Our Human Spirit is United with Christ..............................13
    Characteristics of Our Identity in Christ 14
    Our Soul's Identity Can Be Fleshly Or Godly 16
  WHAT IS THE HEART? 17
    What did God Design Our Hearts to Do for Us? 20
    What is a Heart Disturbance?...23
    Characteristics of Fleshly Identity – Lying Beliefs.................24
  WHAT IS THE PEACE OF CHRIST? 25
  WHAT IS A DISCIPLE; WHAT IS DISCIPLESHIP? 27
    Real-life Discipleship...28
    Discipleship is About God Making Us into a Vessel for Him 29
  WHAT IS THE HOLY SPIRIT'S ROLE IN OUR TRIALS? WHAT IS
  DISCERNMENT?...30
    Discernment..31
    What Does the Holy Spirit Seek to Reveal to Us During Trials?
   32
  HOW TRIALS WORK (THE BIBLE'S A,B,C,DS OF TRIALS)........36
HOW TO PARTICIPATE IN A POIEOLOGICAL BIBLE STUDY 39
  HOW TO GET STARTED WITH THE BIBLE STUDY 39
    The Overall Focus of the Bible Study 40
  GOALS, RECOMMENDATIONS AND "RULES" 41
    Overall Goals of the Poieological Bible Study 41
    Recommendations for the Poieological Bible Study...............43
    "Rules" for the Poieological Bible Study............................45

POIEOLOGICAL BIBLE STUDY TEMPLATE 48

EXPLANATION OF THE PARTS OF THE TEMPLATE 49

LESSON 1: GENESIS 2:15-3:7 SPIRITUAL WARFARE FROM THE VERY BEGINNING (EVE)...63

LESSON 2: GENESIS 2:15-3:7 CHOOSING BETWEEN GOD AND MY WIFE… THIS IS GONNA HURT (ADAM) 71

LESSON 3: GENESIS 4:1-8A TEMPTATION AND MASTERING SIN (CAIN) 76

LESSON 4: GENESIS 6:3-21 WHAT WILL MY FAMILY THINK? (NOAH)...83

LESSON 5: GENESIS 12:1-4 TIME TO MOVE! (ABRAM) 89

LESSON 6: GENESIS 12:1-4 TIME TO MOVE? (SARAI)...................95

LESSON 7: GENESIS 12:10-20 HORRIBLE HUSBAND! (SARAI).....100

LESSON 8: GENESIS 13:1-11 YOU DECIDE (ABRAM) 108

LESSON 9: GENESIS 15:1-16:3 WHO WILL GET MY ESTATE? (ABRAM) 115

LESSON 10: GENESIS 16:1-6 WHY WOULD YOU WANT ME IN THIS UNHEALTHY ENVIRONMENT, LORD? (HAGAR) 121

LESSON 11: GENESIS 17:1-18 GOD REMINDS US, AND OFTEN HE CHALLENGES US TO MORE FAITH (ABRAM) 127

LESSON 12: GENESIS 18:1-15 IT'S BEEN SO LONG, I DOUBT GOD REALLY SAID THAT (SARAH)...134

LESSON 13: GENESIS 18:16-33 YOUR WILL IS FOR ME NOT TO HELP MY FAMILY? (ABRAHAM) 140

LESSON 14: GENESIS 19:1-8 TAKING THINGS INTO OUR OWN HANDS "TO PROTECT GOD'S INTERESTS" (LOT)...................147

LESSON 15: GENESIS 19:30-38 THERE'S NO WAY I'M NOT HAVING KIDS (LOT'S DAUGHTERS) 155

LESSON 16: GENESIS 20:1-13 I'M STILL RELUCTANT TO TRUST GOD (ABRAHAM)..161

LESSON 17: GENESIS 21:1-11 HOW DO YOU WANT TO DEAL WITH MY WIFE'S DISSATISFACTION, LORD? (ABRAHAM)...............169

LESSON 18: GENESIS 21:1-16 UNLOVED, USED, AND DUMPED (HAGAR) 177

LESSON 19: GENESIS 21:22-32 SOMETIMES THE UNBELIEVER CHALLENGES US TO OWN OUR STUFF (ABRAHAM) 182

LESSON 20: GENESIS 22:1-10 DON'T TAKE AWAY WHAT I HAVE EARNED THROUGH MY PATIENCE (ABRAHAM) 189

LESSON 21: GENESIS 22:1-10 WHAT ARE YOU DOING? YOU DIDN'T CONSULT ME! (SARAH)...197

LESSON 22: GENESIS 23 BEING KICKED WHEN YOU'RE DOWN (ABRAHAM)..205

LESSON 23: GENESIS 24:1-16 A BIG, PERSONAL TASK TO TAKE ON FOR THE BOSS (CHIEF SERVANT OF ABRAHAM)...............213

APPENDIX 1: FACILITATING A POIEOLOGICAL BIBLE STUDY 219

APPENDIX 2: INTRO TO THE AUDIO PART OF THE STUDY.........223

APPENDIX 3: AUTHORS' EXAMPLES.................................229

  LESSON 1: GENESIS 2:15-3:7 (EVE) 229

  LESSON 2: GENESIS 2:15-3:7 (ADAM) 233

  LESSON 3: GENESIS 4:1-8A (CAIN) 237

  LESSON 4: GENESIS 6:3-21 (NOAH)................................241

  LESSON 5: GENESIS 12:1-4 (ABRAM) 244

  LESSON 6: GENESIS 12:1-4 (SARAI) 249

  LESSON 7: GENESIS 12:10-20 (SARAI) 251

  LESSON 8: GENESIS 13:1-11 (ABRAM) 256

  LESSON 9: GENESIS 15:1-16:3 (ABRAM) 260

  LESSON 10: GENESIS 16:1-6 (HAGAR)............................264

  LESSON 11: GENESIS 17:1-18 (ABRAM) 267

  LESSON 12: GENESIS 18:1-15 (SARAH) 270

  LESSON 13: GENESIS 18:16-33 (ABRAHAM) 274

  LESSON 14: GENESIS 19:1-8 (LOT)................................277

  LESSON 15: GENESIS 19:30-38 (LOT'S DAUGHTERS) 281

  LESSON 16: GENESIS 20:1-13 (ABRAHAM) 283

  LESSON 17: GENESIS 21:1-11 (ABRAHAM) 287

  LESSON 18: GENESIS 21:1-16 (HAGAR) 289

  LESSON 19: GENESIS 21:22-32 (ABRAHAM) 292

  LESSON 20: GENESIS 22:1-10 (ABRAHAM) 295

  LESSON 21: GENESIS 22:1-10 (SARAH) 299

  LESSON 22: GENESIS 23 (ABRAHAM) 304

  LESSON 23: GENESIS 24:1-16 (CHIEF SERVANT OF ABRAHAM)..307

REFERENCES 311

OTHER TITLES BY THE KEYS SERIES AUTHORS.......................312

ABOUT THE AUTHORS 314

Special Consideration:

Each lesson has a 6-10 minute AUDIO piece associated with it. The AUDIO is NOT an introduction to the lesson, but a piece you will listen to partway into the study. The role of the AUDIO is discussed further in the "How To" chapter. Each lesson in this book tells you at what point in the study to listen to that lesson's AUDIO.

Each lesson's AUDIO is an MP3 recording and is free (and no sign-up required) from *Keys To Understanding Life*. You can download and save the AUDIO, or simply play it at the appropriate time during your study directly from the website using a smart phone or other internet capable device. Go to www.Feelings102.com to download or play any lesson's AUDIO.

INTRODUCTION TO FEELINGS 102: BIBLE STUDIES FOR LIVING GOD'S WRITTEN WORD

2 Timothy 3:16-17 says that *all* Scripture is useful for teaching and training in righteousness. This means that even the stories and trials of the Old Testament are useful for training us in how to be transformed by the Lord during trials. Studying trials from the Bible can have a big impact in preparing us to do our part in submitting to God during our trials. Offering training and preparation in this area is the primary goal of the *Feelings 102* Bible Study lessons.

Learning more about God and our trials can be an enjoyable experience using *Feelings 102*, either on your own or in a small interactive group (3-10 people). Learning more about God and how He works to change us through trials doesn't have to feel like studying for a Master's Degree. To that end, *Feelings 102* is rewarding, fun and interactive as it helps us learn more about how to get ourselves out of the way so Christ can live through us.

Many of us are familiar with the stories presented in Genesis, including Adam and Eve, Cain and Abel, Abraham and Sarah, Jacob and Rachel, and the classic rags to riches story of Joseph. While it is good that we are familiar with these age-old stories, the very fact that we know the outcome of the stories can sometimes make it hard for us to deeply relate to and learn from the trials themselves. *Feelings 102* will give you a fresh look at some of these stories.

With any Biblical story of a person's trial, it is important to be able to relate to the person's perspective in the trial. Why? The people in the Bible struggled in their trials, just like you and I do! *Feelings 102* speaks to aspects of your relationship with Christ to help you experience Him more and to help you follow Him as He sorts out the confusion of trials for you. Each lesson will help you with this.

The lessons in *Feelings 102* look at Biblical people's "failures" in trials apart from the Lord, as well as their "successes" in the Lord. We can learn from trials in which the Bible indicates a person chose to act independently of God – not good! Like those who acted independently of God, sometimes we too miss the mark when trials hit us fast, or when they are confusing or complex. We are often tempted to handle things on our own while praying that God will help us do so. The idea is to let the Lord grow us in being dependent on Him. The lessons in this book will help you work on that. Again, *Feelings 102* gives you practical lessons which prepare you to respond better to the Lord in your own trials by working with others' trials in the Bible.

WHAT IS POIEOLOGY?

The authors of *Feelings 102* call its particular form of Bible Study a Poieological Bible Study. Don't worry though, the word Poieology is the only challenging word you will come across in this book. So, what does it mean? Poieology comes from the Greek word, ποιέω, which means "to do" or to act.[1] This word appears in verses like James 1:22.

> *James 1:22* "But prove yourself **doers** of the word, and not merely hearers who delude themselves." (**Bold** added)

Poieology comes from the Greek word ποιέω, or *poiéō*, is a masculine verb meaning "to make, or to do."[2] The Greek word ποιητής, or *poiētēs* (poy-ah-tace), basically means "a doer. One who makes something, a doer...a doer, keeper of a law or precept."[3] (This Greek word for "doing" is used particularly in James 1:22, 23, 25; 4:11).

So, what is a Poieological Bible Study? Simply put, it is a study of what we allow Christ to "do" through us in a trial.

To be clear, the letter God's Spirit inspired James to write is not trying to imply that WE are the doers. Were we to take such verses out of the context of the whole New Testament, then we might mistakenly conclude that we are the doers, and that we are to simply pray to God for help in the times when we need an assist to do whatever we do. Let's not forget that the Holy Spirit inspired Paul to remind us this...

---

[1] Zodhiates, Spiros: *The Complete Word Study Dictionary : New Testament.* electronic ed. Chattanooga, TN : AMG Publishers, 2000, c1992, c1993, S. G4160
[2] Ibid., G4160
[3] Ibid., G4163

2

> ***Galatians 2:20*** "I have been crucified with Christ; and it is no longer I who live, but Christ lives in me…"

Again, the *Feelings 102* lessons are designed to help you examine what you allow Christ to do through you in a trial. The lessons will assist you in discerning what the Holy Spirit would reveal to you about keeping yourself out of the way, so the Lord can do His works through you.

As we know, trials don't just involve us and God. Satan, his evil and the power of sin work to make it hard to sort out what God wants to do through us in trials. Temptation is present in trials, and while God seeks to build us up through trials, everything that is against God works to pull us down. This can be seen in the many trials the Bible records for folks like Abraham, Sarah, the nation of Israel, and Peter, just to name a few.

One of the uniqueness's of the Poieological Bible Study lessons builds on the fact that Satan often attacks us according to certain patterns. The Spirit of God works to reveal to us the patterns Satan uses against us personally. The Holy Spirit can do this to help us to better understand the steps of faith needed for the Lord to live through us in the trial. However, while the power of God's own Spirit seeks to reveal need-to-know information to us, we have to be open and sensitive to discerning that which He desires to reveal to us.

So what do we mean by "patterns" in Satan's attacks? The patterns Satan uses against us are not simply patterns in the external circumstances of our trials. Satan's attacks can include patterns that cause us to have certain fleshly desires. There are patterns in the way the power of sin tempts us to be unresponsive and fearful of the changes the Lord seeks to make in us. Satan's attacks can include patterns in getting us to interpret our feelings (or lack of feelings) as though they were facts indicating things about us, God or how God would seek to respond to the trial through us. Patterns in Satan's attacks can also be seen in the fleshly responses we often make in similar kinds of trials.

Whether or not you recognize all this works at this point, you will come to understand how these things work together as you progress through the *Feelings 102* lessons.

If we do not see how trials work, it is much easier for Satan to deceive us in our trials. The result is that we may end up doing things independently of God when some of our trials come up. The lessons will help you better discern what God's Spirit would reveal to you about Satan's attacks against Christ in you during trials.

With these things in mind, whether a person lived in Old Testament times, New Testament times, or today, **everyone's trials share a number of things in common**:

1. A person's trials represent a spiritual battle between God and Satan that involves the person in a personal way.

2. Satan, his evil and the power of sin work together to attack us. This evil goal works to influence us to act independently of God in response to our trials. When we act independently of God, we are acting in sinful or fleshly ways.

3. In a trial, God's Spirit is seeking to reveal to us how the Lord is working to transform our hearts and to overcome Satan's influences.

4. In a trial, there are often any number of ways we might act in the flesh and sin (when we act on our own). And, often there is one main attitude and action (or inaction) that God seeks to live through us.

5. In trials we make decisions, whether we think about them or not. We have to discern between what God wants to do or not do through us versus what Satan wants us to do on our own. God's Spirit works to reveal to us which is which, and discerning this is "easier" in some trials than in others.

6. In a trial, one challenge is that fleshly thinking offers us reasons to justify why it is "OK" to do what we want or think we must do when our hearts are feeling unwanted and troubling feelings. Our thinking is influenced by how we feel or what we want while the peace of Christ is escaping us. This means that regardless of where a person is on the human timeline, submitting to letting God respond through us in a trial involves allowing Him to change whatever is in our hearts. This God-directed heart-change involves renewing the mind (Old Testament: lean not on your own understanding – Proverbs 3:5; New Testament: transform, or renew, the mind – Romans 12:2).

These common characteristics of trials, along with our God-given ability to use our hearts to connect with people's trials recorded in the Bible, led the *Feelings 102* authors to create the following dictionary style definition of poieology (for those who like that sort of thing!).

Poieology (poy-eh-**ology**). *n*. A branch of theology that is concerned with the study of spiritual "doing" (godly action or inaction) in trials presented in Scripture where "an aspect of God's will is clear" (for more on this, see the **Special Consideration** on page 42); in the study the participant works to experience the trial in order to learn about discerning whatever the Holy Spirit seeks to reveal about both God's and Satan's involvement in the trial; the participant works to gain personal insights and revelation on what to anticipate God may seek to do through the participant to change and transform the participant's heart in his/her own trials; [From Greek word ποιέω, *poiéō* (poy-**eh**-o), meaning to make, do, or act (express action) either as completed or continued; figuratively spoken of a state or condition, or of things intangible and incorporeal, and generally of such things as are produced by an inward act... (described in James 1:22-26).[4]] **1.** *Godly doing*. Living dependently on the Lord in life in general or in a given trial; living God's written Word by submitting to God living through the individual; walking with God (Micah 6:8); walking in the light (1 John 1:7); being a slave to obedience (Romans 6:16); being slaves to God (Romans 6:22); walking in the Spirit; living by the Spirit and being led by the Spirit (Galatians 5:16-18); keeping in step with the Spirit (Galatians 5:25). **2.** *Ungodly doing*. Living independently of God in life in general or in a given trial; failure to incline one's ear to God (Jeremiah 7:24); being a slave to sin (John 8:34); being in the flesh – fleshly beliefs and/or behaviors (Romans 8:5); being deluded (James 1:22); walking in darkness (1 John 1:6); living according to a sinful nature or fleshly nature (1 John 2:16) – poieological (poy-eh-o-**logical**) *adj*.

OVERVIEW OF THE POIEOLOGICAL BIBLE STUDY

Let's take a quick look at what you'll be doing in the lessons.

The first part of a Poieological Bible Study lesson involves looking at a trial and its Biblical context.

---

[4] Ibid., G4160

In the second part of the lesson you will put yourself in the person's shoes in order to observe what **you** might experience if you were in that trial. In this part of the lesson, you will practice discerning what the Holy Spirit seeks to reveal to you about how the flesh is working against you, about how to connect to your identity in Christ and experience His peace, and about the step(s) of faith God might ask of you in the lesson's trial situation.

FOUNDATIONS FOR FEELINGS 102

1. Spiritual warfare is both an Old and New Testament concept.
   a. The New Testament affirms that the spiritual conflicts and battles we experience are part of the spiritual war that began before mankind was created (John 8:44; Luke 10:18; 2 Peter 2:4; Jude 6).
   b. Spiritual warfare was the setting in which mankind was created in the Garden of Eden (Genesis 3:1-4; James 1:13-15).
   c. "Spiritual battles" is another name for trials.
2. Even though Satan (devil, evil one, deceiver, etc.) is not specifically mentioned in every Bible story involving trials, Satan's involvement is implied (though often underappreciated). Why?
   a. Satan is the Tempter, and his evil and the power of sin is involved in every trial we experience (Matthew 4:3 and James 1:13-15).
   b. When we sin in a trial, we are following the flesh (acting independently of God) in that moment (1 John 3:7-8).
   c. In any trial we experience, Satan, evil, and/or the power of sin is seeking to drive us like slaves (Romans 6:16).
3. God is also involved in each trial, seeking to change us, to counsel us and to lead us in how He wants to handle the trial through us (John 10:3-5).
   a. Whether in the Old or New Testament times, God disciplines those He loves (Psalm 119.75; Hebrews 12:6).
   b. We must discern between what God wants of us versus what Satan wants of us (1 John 3:19-24). This involves hearing God's voice with our spiritual ears (John 8:47; 10:3-5).

    c. God's Spirit is seeking to guide and teach us in every trial we face (John 16:12-13; Galatians 5:17, 25).

    d. The Holy Spirit was given to us permanently by the Father as a result of the sacrifice Jesus made on our behalf (Ephesians 1:13-14).

    e. The Holy Spirit, The Teacher, seeks to reveal need-to-know information about what God seeks to do through us in our trials (John 16:14). In the Holy Spirit, we have access to the same source of power that raised Jesus from the dead (Ephesians 1:15-21).

4. Every human being is fully accountable for their fleshly actions regardless how much knowledge of the Bible they may have:

    a. This is demonstrated in many Old Testament stories, (Judges 2:1-5; 2 Samuel 12:7-14).

    b. This is specified in the New Testament (Romans 1:18-20).

5. If a person desires for God to work through them during a trial, that person can expect to have to take steps of faith, regardless of where one is on the "human" timeline.

6. Having and exercising faith, whether in Old or New Testament times,...

    a. ...involves submitting to and being trained by the Lord's discipline during a trial (Hebrews 12:4-13).

    b. ...is not always desirable from a worldly point of view (Hebrews 11:24-26).

    c. ...is often difficult, as Christians, when our sense of identity is bogged down in the flesh as opposed to embracing our true identity in Christ (Galatians 5:17).

7. Poieology (the Scriptural study of spiritual doing or action in trials) involves seeking to observe the involvement of God, Satan, and ourselves in trials from Scripture...

    a. ...so that we may, by God's Spirit, better discern between God's influences versus Satan's.

    b. ...so that we may study the feelings, desires and challenges we would experience in a trial described in the Bible, thereby learning more about what God seeks to do through us in our trials.

FEATURES FOUND IN FEELINGS 102

1. <u>Overview of the Biblical Basics of Trials</u> Chapter. This was added in this 3rd edition of the book. Prior to this, it was a handout we used when working through the lessons. We highly recommend that you acquaint yourself with this material prior to moving on to the "How To" chapter. It lays a strong foundation for getting a good grip on several key Biblical concepts relating to trials. If you are working with a small group, this chapter will also help you ensure the participants are on the same sheet when it comes to trials.

2. <u>"How To" Chapter with Poieological Study Template</u>. Explains the goals and objectives of a given lesson, and answers questions about how to do the study.

3. <u>Context Information</u>, <u>Historical Information</u>. This is provided in each lesson. Simple-to-understand, interesting and relevant. Some lessons also look at <u>Patterns</u> that can be observed in a particular person's trials.

4. <u>6-10 Minute AUDIO</u>. The Bible Study approach has an accompanying AUDIO piece for each lesson. It is played partway through the study to help participants "get into the shoes" of the person whose perspective is studied in a given lesson. **The lesson tells you when to listen to the AUDIO.** Each lesson's audio is free (no sign-up required) from KeysToUnderstandingLife.org. Download and save the AUDIO, or simply play it during your study directly from the website using a smart phone or other internet capable device. More info on the AUDIO is in Appendix 2 – page 223.

5. <u>Key Words</u> in their original language (Hebrew/Greek) are examined at critical points in some lessons. The footnote references provide a Strong's Identifying Number with its source.

6. <u>Discussion Questions</u> are raised at critical points in certain lessons. These questions are particularly poignant when it comes to examining issues that can influence how we view a given trial.

7. <u>Special Considerations</u> are highlighted throughout the book in order to point to cautions, pitfalls and often-overlooked, key points. A few lessons direct your attention to optional lessons that you could look at from another Biblical person's perspective. There are seven of these optional lessons. They

    add to the number of lessons presented in this particular volume of *Feelings 102*.

8. <u>Information for Teachers/Facilitators</u>. If your small group wants to designate a facilitator, this useful information is in Appendix 1 – page 219.

9. <u>Authors' Examples</u> are provided in Appendix 3 – starting on page 229. The examples are a sampling of sentiments others expressed when studying the lessons with the authors. These are *examples*, NOT answers; your responses don't have to be the same as these examples. Authors' Examples are provided in order to help you get the gist of the kinds of things we may observe in the course of studying the Bible's trials.

We've been blessed by and are thankful for those who participated in our small groups as we conducted these Bible Studies. It was an exciting, interactive and dynamic experience. We are thankful to God for the opportunity to present the lessons to you. We hope that you will experience the rewards and benefits of gathering in small groups to study God's written Word, as part of your own training for letting Christ LIVE through your lives.

God bless you,

William and William Clark

Overview of the Biblical Basics of Trials

Growth Step 1:

To understand our true identity in Christ and how it relates to trials.

Growth Step 2:

To understand how God designed our hearts to work and how that relates to the peace of Christ, and trials.

Growth Step 3:

To understand what discipleship is and the Holy Spirit's role in it.

Growth Step 4:

To get a really good snapshot of how trials work (The Bible's A,B,C,Ds of Trials).

The *Feelings 102* Bible Study lessons are all about helping you understand not only how trials work, but to help you get a better grip on how to submit yourself to the Lord so that HE lives and works through you in your real-life trials.

Let stick what sticks as you work through the book and particularly this chapter. The goal here isn't to memorize everything.

To that end, the Lord helped us (the authors) discern that it would be useful to talk to a few concepts about our relationship with Jesus Christ. The point for laying out some of these Biblical concepts to you in this initial chapter, before the lessons proper, is so that you can gain a better understanding of how those concepts come together in trials. It is our prayer that you will take these Biblical concepts to heart, and that the Lord will use them to help you orient on Him in your trials.

Again, the point isn't to memorize everything here. Simply try to get a sense of how these Biblical concepts mesh together. With that…

WHAT IS A TRIAL?

The Bible refers to trials in different ways – spiritual battles, tribulations, times of temptation, etc. Trials are often the tough times in life, whether we consider them a biggie or just a little annoyance. Usually, trials are times we don't like. They are times that, when they happen, cause us to feel something that is often uncomfortable. If you've had a bad day – that's about trials. When you are struggling to figure out what decision to make, that's a trial.

The Greek word for *trial* is πειρασμός. It means, "to make a trial of, to try, or to tempt."[5]

While God permits us to experience trials, His purpose is NOT to tempt us or cause us to stumble. As a believer in a trial, God gives you the opportunity to let Him transform your heart and mind to reflect your true identity in Christ. He offers this opportunity completely out of His love for you.

However, God isn't the only one working on us in trials. Satan, his evil and the power of sin work on us too. Satan specifically intends for us to act independently of the Lord in our trials. Satan and the power of sin seek to draw us away from God, to misunderstand God and not to live according to our true identity in Christ. Satan's goal is to reinforce and strengthen the lying beliefs that can draw us into fleshly behaviors with a fleshly sense of identity.

In EVERY trial, God seeks to change you even though Satan wants you to stumble. God uses Satan's ill-will for the purpose of working to sanctify our souls and bodies so they are in alignment with our united spirit with Christ (we'll look closer at all these things in this chapter). The point is that we need to see how trials are spiritually significant events behind what we often view as "normal life stuff."

When you face a trial during your day, regardless what it is about externally, God's Spirit is a key part of that trial too. The Holy Spirit works to reveal to you how to live according to your identity in Christ. Of course Satan knows this. So, in those same moments of trial, Satan seeks to get you to do *anything* other than what God would have you do to let Christ live through you. Satan seeks to deceive you so that

---

[5] Zodhiates, Spiros: *The Complete Word Study Dictionary: New Testament.* electronic ed. Chattanooga, TN: AMG Publishers, 2000, c1992, c1993. G3986

you do not pick up on what the Holy Spirit tries to reveal to you! And, all of this is specifically focused on an issue of... identity.

WHAT IS OUR IDENTITY IN CHRIST, AND WHY WE DON'T ALWAYS ACT ACCORDING TO THAT?

Our sense of identity drives everything we do or avoid doing. While we don't usually think about that very much, when it comes to our relationship with Christ, identity is extremely important. Let's touch on some basics about our identity so we can then see how it relates to our trials.

Our Human Spirit is United with Christ

By entering into a relationship with Christ, your identity fundamentally and radically changes. The passage below indicates that your spirit's identity changes and is united with Christ.

> *1 Corinthians 6:17* But the one who joins himself to the Lord is one spirit *with Him*. (*Italics* are part of translation)

> The Greek word for *spirit* is πνεῦμα. The Bible speaks to "a distinction between the two immaterial aspects of man's soul and spirit. The spirit is man's immaterial nature which enables him to communicate with God, who is also spirit." [6]

Romans 6:6 says the "old you" was crucified with Christ. Galatians 2:20 says that because you were crucified with Christ, you aren't supposed to be thinking that it's YOU who lives, but rather it is CHRIST seeking to live through you.

When we enter into a relationship with Christ, the fleshly identity that characterized our human **spirit** is actually replaced by an identity of truth, i.e., the identity of Christ. God made this possible because we recognized our need for Jesus and the sacrifice He made on our behalf. God the Father sees us as a new creation. God the Father sees our spirit's new, true identity in Christ, and condemns us no more. While

---

[6] Ibid., G4151

you are forgiven for sin by entering into a relationship with God through Jesus Christ, God seeks to grow and transform you so that Christ lives THE LIFE through you.

> ***John 14:6*** "Jesus said to him, 'I am the way, and the truth, and ***the life***; no one comes to the Father but through Me.'"
> (**Bold** and *italics* added)

There is no sense of lack, aloneness, deficiency or chaos in our identity in Christ. Our new identity in Christ is perfect! This change in the identity of our spirit is one of God's many acts of grace.

> The Greek word for ***grace*** is χάρις. It means "unearned and unmerited favor."[7]

However, when we are in a trial, the trial usually starts with us feeling some sense of lack, aloneness, deficiency or chaos. Why is that? Well, when God created us, He created us with a body and soul in addition to a spirit. God created us so that the human body is tied to our soul. In turn, the soul is able to connect to our spirit. BUT, our soul can only connect with our spirit, which is in Christ, when we submit to God's intervention in the trial.

Characteristics of Our Identity in Christ

Some of the Bible's truths about our identity in Christ can be found from words Jesus said Himself. There are a great number or characteristics of this identity listed throughout the New Testament, but we'd like to boil them down to four key characteristics.

1. IN CHRIST, I am good enough.

> ***Matthew 5:14-16*** "You are a light of the world. A city set on a hill cannot be hidden; nor does anyone light a lamp and put it under a basket but on the lampstand, and it gives light to all who are in the house. Let your light shine before men in such a way that they may see your good works, and glorify your Father who is in heaven."

---

[7] Ibid., G5485

2. IN CHRIST, I am NOT alone.

John 14:23 "Jesus answered and said to him, 'If anyone loves Me, he will keep My word; and My Father will love him, and We will come to him and make Our abode with him.'"

3. IN CHRIST, I have enough.

Matthew 6:19 "Do not store up for yourselves treasures on earth, where moth and rust destroy, and where thieves break in and steal."

Matthew 6:31-34 "Do not worry then, saying, 'What will we eat?' or 'What will we drink?' or 'What will we wear for clothing?' For the Gentiles eagerly seek all these things; for your heavenly Father knows that you need all these things. But seek first His kingdom and His righteousness, and all these things will be added to you. So do not worry about tomorrow; for tomorrow will care for itself. Each day has enough trouble of its own."

4. IN CHRIST, I can be at peace with how He wants to live through me.

Special Consideration: in most every trial, we don't feel peaceful. So be aware, this characteristic of your identity in Christ assumes that at the start of the trial you already know how He wants to live through you – i.e., the trial you are facing is a reoccurring trial for you AND He made it clear to you how to respond before this trial even came up. So, if you haven't yet discerned that, then expect that one of the other characteristics of your identity may deal with the root issue of identity.

John 14:27 "Peace I leave with you; My peace I give to you; not as the world gives do I give to you. Do not let your heart be troubled, nor let it be fearful."

Matthew 11:28-30 "Come to Me, all who are weary and heavy-laden, and I will give you rest. Take My yoke upon you and learn from Me, for I am gentle and humble in heart, and YOU WILL FIND REST FOR YOUR SOULS. For My yoke is easy and My burden is light." (CAPS are part of translation)

Special Consideration: If you would like to remember just one thing from this chapter, remember this: when your heart really feels the truths we've listed above, it is an indicator that in the moment, you are connecting to your identity in Christ. When your heart struggles to feel any of these things, all isn't lost, it just means you are in a trial and it is time to really work to turn your attention back to the Lord.

So, here is an important question: if our spirit is united with Christ and experiences no sense of lack or whatever, then why is it that sometimes we don't feel the truths above in a trial?

Our Soul's Identity Can Be Fleshly Or Godly

The Greek word for *soul* is ψυχή. The soul means "the mind and feelings [the heart]."[8]

"The soul is the aspect of [a person's] immaterial nature that makes him aware of his body and his natural, physical environment. The difference between soul and spirit is not one of substance but of operation."[9]

Special Consideration: From now on in this book, when we talk about our *hearts and minds*, we are talking about our soul as God designed it. Similarly, when we use the word *soul*, we are talking about our hearts and minds.

God created us such that our hearts and minds function in relationship to one another. On the one hand, they are capable of functioning in sinful or fleshly ways, which is in response to Satan, his evil and the power of sin. On the other hand, the heart and mind can also function in godly ways, but ONLY in response to the Holy Spirit, and Christ living through us.

---

[8] Ibid., G5590
[9] Id., G4151

Our hearts and minds are capable of functioning according to a sense of identity that is independent of our human spirit and of God. This is what happens when we embrace a fleshly sense of identity. Or, our hearts and minds can function out of dependence on Christ. This is what happens when we embrace our true identity in Christ.

So again, why don't we consistently act according to our true identity in Christ? This is because the soul's sense of identity is by default a fleshly sense of identity – because we were first born into sin (Romans 5:12).

The sense of identity of the soul is often a fleshly sense of identity because it is based on what we learned from our life as experienced by our hearts and minds... *independent* of God. This is true for all of us, regardless how young or old we are when we entered into a relationship with Christ. So, it is a sense of identity that is of death – independence/separation from God. It is one that thinks functioning dependently on God is about being in a relationship with Him and then using our own minds to think of solutions to solve our problems – that is actually one way "acting independently of God" can look! A fleshly sense of identity is one that is based on beliefs we are drawn to embrace about the world, God and ourselves in relationship with Christ, but which are UNtrue beliefs based on lies, i.e. Lying Beliefs. You know who is responsible for cultivating that junk in us – you got it, Satan, the deceiver.

Our true identity in Christ doesn't automatically replace the fleshly identity we are used to living by (the one often relied upon by our **soul**). Our hearts and minds, and the fleshly identity to which they are used to clinging, must be changed by the Lord, one trial at a time. The truth is that we are completely incapable of changing our hearts and minds on our own, though we have a relationship with God through Jesus Christ.

Only out of dependence on God will He enable our soul's fleshly sense of identity to connect to our true identity in Christ, and again, this happens one trial at a time! Now we are getting to the heart of things.

WHAT IS THE HEART?

In *Feelings 102* we sometimes use terms like *painful experiences, challenges, trials, tribulations,* and *spiritual battles.* Again, all of these terms describe trials. They describe experiences that are accompanied by desires, as well as emotions (feelings). Desires and feelings are things that come from the heart.

> **Romans 5:3-5** "And not only this, but we also **exult** in our tribulations, knowing that tribulation brings about perseverance; and perseverance, **proven character**; and proven character, hope; and hope **does not disappoint** because the love of God has been poured out within our **hearts** through the Holy Spirit who was given to us." (*Italics* and **bold** added)

In Romans 5:3-5, the Greek word for **exult** is καυχάομαι. It means "to glory in or boast in (as in a godly, Christ-like way)."[10]

Paul is telling us that we can **exult**, or glory, in our trials! How often do our hearts feel that DURING our trials?

Everybody, including non-Christians, lives through trials as long as they don't kill us. But as Christians, we are not supposed to just tolerate trials. Romans 5:3-5 indicates that, by the Holy Spirit, "the love of God" is "poured out within our **hearts**" in a trial. So why don't we feel more of that? Let's look more at the heart.

You know, we often interpret *heart* far too loosely. In America today, "taking something to *heart*" means to really understand something. It might mean to listen very closely. To "get to the *heart* of the matter" means we must really know what is at the core of an issue. Knowing something "by *heart*" often means we have memorized something.

In these ways, our use of *heart* often refers to the mind or to mental knowledge. Knowing something and understanding something is done with the intelligence of the mind. The way we often use the word *heart* really refers to thinking about something very carefully and seriously. The mind is part of the soul just like the heart is part of the soul, but it is important not to confuse the heart with the mind, or vice versa. They work in relationship, but they serve two different functions.

Sometimes we use the word *heart* to emphasize how we feel. For example, "you broke my *heart*" is a way of saying you did something that caused me to feel bad. "My *heart* aches" means "I am feeling

---

[10] Ibid., G2744

18

wounded or hurt." "My *heart* aches for that poor person" means "I can feel something because of how someone else might feel."

Let's go back to the concept of the love of God pouring through our hearts in trials (Romans 5:3-5). Given how we often use the word *heart*, some think that means...

1. ...we should be careful to love God in the midst of life's tough times (trials). And of course we should do that.
2. Or, ...we should be careful to do things while *remembering* we are to love God and defend His Truth. That is true. We typically defend God's Truth by *knowing* His Truth in our minds (from the Bible) and *thinking* about it.[11]

Those two ways of looking at things are definitely important. But, they are not what *heart* in Romans 5:3-5 means.

The Greek word for **heart** is καρδία. It means "the seat and center of human life; the desires, feelings, affections, passions, impulses."[12]

Isn't that interesting? The heart is viewed as the seat and center of human life. This means the heart is the seat and center of the human **soul**, NOT the human **spirit**. In trials, God seeks to use the heart to help us connect with our identity in Christ because the heart involves feelings, motives, desires, etc. These are things which influence us to do the things we sometimes do, either independently of the Lord or out of dependence on the Lord. The heart is felt.

In creating us with a soul, God designed an intricate relationship between our hearts and our minds. As the center of our soul, the heart has the potential to change our minds for better or for worse depending on whether we let the Lord work through our hearts, or not.

Recognizing this stuff about heart is very different compared to how we view the heart today. While thinking is important, early Christians understood that clear thinking with a mind open to the Lord during a trial begins with a heart that is transformed by the Lord.

---

[11] *Feelings 101: Pain to Peace 2nd Edition*, William J. Clark, Jr. with CH (COL) William J. Clark, Ret., 2013, Keys To Understanding Life Series, pg. 26, modified with permission.

[12] Zodhiates, Spiros: *The Complete Word Study Dictionary: New Testament*. electronic ed. Chattanooga, TN: AMG Publishers, 2000, c1992, c1993. G2588

Romans 10:10 "...for with the heart a person believes...."

Here is an interesting tidbit for you. The word *believe*, or *believing*, is mentioned 244 times in the New Testament alone. In other words, this critical function of the heart is mentioned a lot – just shows how important the role of the heart is in letting the Lord connect with us.

The heart can experience any number of feelings, desires and beliefs, and each of those reflects something that we believe or something that we are starting to believe – for better or worse.

What we will look at next is how God also designed our hearts to be a "spiritual indicator" of sorts to tell us about what is actually influencing us at a given moment in a given trial.[13]

What did God Design Our Hearts to Do for Us?

1 John 3:18-24 "Little children, let us not love with word or with tongue, but in deed and truth. We shall know by this that we are of the truth, and shall **assure** our **heart** before Him, in whatever our **heart condemns** us; for God is greater than our **heart**, and knows all things. Beloved, if our **heart** does not **condemn** us, we have confidence before God; and whatever we ask we receive from Him, because we keep His commandments and do the things that are pleasing in His sight. And this is His commandment, that we believe in the name of His Son Jesus Christ, and love one another, just as He commanded us. And the one who keeps His commandments abides in Him, and He in him. And we know by this that He abides in us, by the Spirit whom He has given us." (*Italics* and **bold** added)

In these verses, again we see καρδία, the Greek word for **heart**. Remember we mentioned that God designed a relationship between the heart and mind? John says the **heart**, can condemn us or **assure** us. This means God designed the **heart** to function like an alert system that indicates whether or not we are **thinking** with fleshly

---

[13] *Feelings 101: Pain to Peace 2nd Edition*, William J. Clark, Jr. with CH (COL) William J. Clark, Ret., 2013, Keys To Understanding Life Series, pg. 27, modified with permission.

thoughts that will lead to action in sin IF we were to act on them.

Special Consideration:
Let's be really clear about the heart and mind. The heart feels and desires. The mind thinks. It is true that when we feel something the mind helps us express what we are feeling. The mind also helps us express what we desire in our hearts. And, the mind gives us reasons for why we feel or desire certain things. But, the mind is not the seat and center of the soul; the heart is. Again, it is with the heart that we believe. It is with the mind that we express what we believe and why. When the mind needs to be "renewed" (Romans 12:1-2) from fleshly thoughts, it can only happen when we are open to letting the Lord transform, or change, our hearts.

The heart, as the seat of the soul, can change the mind. Again, God designed this heart and mind relationship when He created us way back in the beginning with Adam and Eve. By opening our hearts to the truth of our identity in Christ (pg. 14), God helps us by changing the mind's thinking.

In John 3:18-24 (previous page), the Greek word for ***condemn*** is καταγινώσκη and means "to blame, or to detect something bad about."[14]

Let's take that and put it together with what we know about how the heart and its relationship to the mind.

"Our ***heart condemns us***," can be rephrased like this: When a person's heart isn't peaceful, the person's heart is responding, the way God designed it to respond, in order to tell us something that our thinking thinks is true, but which is actually UNtrue, i.e., something in our thinking is a problem.

This fault isn't a fault in the sense of meaning you've already sinned. So, what "fault" or problem would God possibly want to warn

---

[14] Zodhiates, Spiros: *The Complete Word Study Dictionary: New Testament.* electronic ed. Chattanooga, TN: AMG Publishers, 2000, c1992, c1993. G2607

us about during a trial? God is warning us about Satan and/or the power of sin as it works to influence us to act on fleshly thinking in a trial. The fault is information about the activity or presence of the flesh seeking to drive our actions. The ***heart condemning us*** means God designed our hearts to warn us when the power of sin is pulling at us. This is one way God always reaches out to help us in trials.

When our hearts warn us, God wants us to look for the fleshly tendency, discern it by His Spirit, and let THE LORD change it!

While the feelings and desires of our hearts may correspond externally to someone else's actions, the accurate way to view the heart is as an indicator of what is going on spiritually in us during a trial. 1 John 3:18-24 indicates that while someone else may be sinning or have a problem, the things you or I feel and want are specifically about *a temptation* being presented to us. [15]

> The Greek word for ***assure*** is πείσομεν. It means "to persuade another to receive a belief, meaning to convince; [AND HERE'S THE KICKER]... **to quiet an accusing conscience.**"[16] (**Bold** added, words in [BRACKETS] added)

When our ***heart assures*** us, it means our hearts and minds are responding to the Lord such that He is connecting our soul with our spirit's true identity in Christ. It is normal that when our ***heart assures*** us, we feel differently from when our ***heart condemns*** us.

The transition from our ***hearts condemning us*** at the start of a trial to our ***hearts assuring us*** is a transition only God can make when we depend completely on Him in the trial. That transition ONLY happens when we open our hearts to the truth of our identity in Christ so He can change us and center our soul in union with Christ in our spirit. When we submit to the Lord and He transforms us, even just a little bit; the Lord lives the rest of 1 John 3:21-24 through us. In short, through us He enables us to "keep His commandments and do the things that are pleasing in His sight."[17]

---

[15] *Feelings 101: Pain to Peace 2nd Edition,* William J. Clark, Jr. with CH (COL) William J. Clark, Ret., 2013, Keys To Understanding Life Series, pg. 30-31, modified with permission.

[16] Ibid., G3982

[17] *Feelings 101: Pain to Peace 2nd Edition,* William J. Clark, Jr. with CH (COL) William J. Clark, Ret., 2013, Keys To Understanding Life Series, pg. 30-31, modified with permission.

What is a Heart Disturbance?

Special Consideration: As we mentioned, trials often start with us feeling uncomfortable feelings. In other words, our hearts are not experiencing the peace of the Lord. The peace of Christ is something our hearts feel when our hearts are assuring us. We (the authors) call these **non-peaceful** feelings and desires, **"HEART DISTURBANCES."** You will see this term over and over in the book.

Just so you know, because our feelings play a key role in alerting us to trials, and because we usually haven't a clue what to do with them, the first part of this book's title is *"Feelings...."* Again, just an FYI.

Part of each lesson in *Feelings 102* involves identifying heart disturbances that you might experience were you in the trial you are studying. Below is a list of examples of heart disturbances. When you are doing the lessons, you'll be referred to this page to help you express the heart disturbances you might experience. You may add others to the list if you like.

FEELINGS THAT DESCRIBE HEART DISTURBANCES

anguish, adrift, aloof, anger, annoyed, anxious, bored, burdened, cheated, concerned, confrontational, depressed, despair, disappointed, disconnected, discouraged, disgust, dispassionate, distraught, distressed, dread, empty, envy, fear, frightened, frustrated, grieved, guilt, hateful, haunted, heavy-laden, humiliated, hopeless, inadequate, insignificant, jealous, justified (in an angry way), lack, left-out, lost, manipulated, melancholy, mocked, overwhelmed, passionate, powerless, rage, regretful, repulsed, resentful, resistant, sad, scared, shame, skeptical, stressed, suspicious, tense, torn, troubled, unappreciated, uneasy, unloved, upset, unsupported, useless, vengeful, victimized, vulnerable, weary, worn-out (emotionally), worried, worthless, etc.[18]

---

[18] Ibid., pg. 8, modified with permission.

Those are lots of different kinds of non-peaceful feelings we might experience from time to time. They are all simply different ways our hearts tell us a fault about some very basic fleshly thinking. Below are the kinds of fleshly thinking that hides beneath our other thoughts in a trial.

Characteristics of Fleshly Identity – Lying Beliefs

I am good enough the way I am.
I don't need anyone or anything from anyone.
I am a failure.
I'm not good enough.
I'm alone.
I don't have enough.
I can't be at peace with God's plan for living through me.
I really work at being a good person and that is good enough.
I'm not a good person.
I can't do this (whatever *this* is).
This (whatever *this* is) isn't what I wanted with my life.

All of the above are not true when it comes to your identity in Christ. But, when a trial begins, we are being tempted to think they are true (with the mind) and then believe they are true (with the heart). They are lies, or lying beliefs of the flesh. From now on, let's call them, "**Lying Beliefs.**"

Special Consideration: At the start of a trial, our focus is usually on the external. We have to set the external down in order to discern the Lying Beliefs like what are shown above. God's Spirit will be helping you with this (we'll talk more about how that works in a bit). Nevertheless, to discern the Lying Belief, simply ask yourself, "**How does this situation reflect on me as a person.**" Then, let your mind answer that question. If the answer doesn't look like one of the above, continue asking that question. It won't take long before the answer drills down to one or more of those kinds of Lying Beliefs. This is a very simple exercise, but our thinking tends to resist it. Make sure you discipline yourself not to start getting into why you think what you think. Just keep asking and answering that question. Try this only when you are in a trial.

Now, let's take a look at what we can experience in Christ during a trial, when we allow the Lord to connect our hearts to our true identity in Christ.

WHAT IS THE PEACE OF CHRIST?

Colossians 3:15 "Let the peace of Christ rule in your hearts, to which indeed you were called in one body; and be thankful."

The Greek word for the ***peace of Christ*** is εἰρήνη. It means "the tranquil state of a soul assured of its salvation through Christ, fearing nothing from God and consequently content with its earthly lot – whatever it is. God's peace is independent of outside conditions."[19]

The peace of Christ is something the heart can feel, but ONLY when we are open to embracing the changes the Lord seeks to make in us.

It is important to remember that the peace of Christ can sometimes come on powerfully when we feel our true identity in Christ (pg. 14). BUT, then it can be replaced by uncomfortable feelings soon after. This is normal when we are still working on letting God center our hearts and minds (soul) with the truth of our connection and union with Christ in our spirit. The peace of Christ slips from our hearts when the fleshly tendencies of the soul are trying to kick in again.

When the thoughts (in the mind) are UNtrue and of the flesh, then God's design of the heart doesn't permit it to feel the peace of Christ. As is to be expected, the heart then reverts back to alerting you to a fault, i.e., alerting you to fleshly thinking. This back and forth thing can happen at any time after you've experienced the peace of Christ in a trial. Remember, when the peace of Christ slips away, it is simply a warning, an alert to fleshly thinking, which means it is again time to submit your heart to being open to your identity in Christ.

---

[19] Zodhiates, Spiros: *The Complete Word Study Dictionary : New Testament.* electronic ed. Chattanooga, TN : AMG Publishers, 2000, c1992, c1993, S. G1515

Let's look more about the words in Colossians 3:15.

Paul told the Christians in Colosse to "let the peace of Christ rule." This is a command.

The Greek word for *rule* is βραβευέτω and means 'an umpire, a director or arbiter in Greek public games.'[20]

Colossians 3:15 says the peace of Christ is to act as an umpire. In sports, where this Greek word comes from, an umpire blows the whistle when a foul is committed. The umpire calls attention to the foul. The umpire has the authority to stop the game and address the foul to ensure the game is played appropriately.

The Greek terminology is interesting. It indicates that a disturbance of peace in your heart is supposed to do the same thing for us as Christians. However, it isn't just about your heart....

It is important to understand that the Holy Spirit is also called the Comforter, the Helper. God's Holy Spirit works in conjunction with the peace of Christ. John 16:14 says that the Holy Spirit "takes of Mine (Christ) and will disclose it to you."

When our sense of the peace of Christ slips away, the Holy Spirit is blowing the whistle to call attention to a spiritual problem – an issue of the flesh working on us, not somebody else – **even though externally it might look that way!**

We must let a disturbance of the peace of Christ within our hearts have the authority to redirect our attention from our thinking to our hearts. In short, we have to pay attention to when that peace is slipping away – we have to notice and pay attention to the heart disturbance that arises in its place.

Like an umpire briefly halts a game to deal with a foul, the uncomfortable feelings in the heart are to redirect our attention long enough to discern the fleshly thinking the Holy Spirit seeks to reveal. But, we have to submit to that redirection. The purpose of the Holy Spirit working with our heart is to enable us to let Christ handle the trial appropriately through us, and to transform us.

Let's be clear. The peace of Christ does not automatically rule our hearts (feelings, desires, motives, etc.) Remember, we have freewill to choose to whom we will open our hearts. Paul says, "**LET** the peace of Christ rule...." The subject of that sentence is YOU. "You have to let the peace of Christ rule," this is the sentiment Paul is expressing.[21]

---

[20] Ibid., G1018

When your heart is disturbed, the Spirit of the Lord is seeking to reveal to you some things He wants to change in you, but you have to surrender to being open to the Lord.

Your heart can feel the peace of Christ when the Lord helps you connect to your true identity in Himself. Peaceful is how it feels when we let the Lord connect our soul to the truth of our spirit in Christ. This is different from the mind just thinking about peace.

The words below express feelings our hearts can experience AS A RESULT of being at peace. They are NOT substitutes for feeling the peace of Christ; they can accompany it.

FEELINGS THAT CAN ACCOMPANY PEACE OF CHRIST

relieved, confident, safe, secure, grateful, humbled, unencumbered, free, light, released, burden-free, trusting, certain, comfortable, relaxed, strengthened, connected, composed, trusting, encouraged, serene, unfettered, assured, blessed, accepting, clear-minded/steady-in-heart, calm, still, patient, loved, pleased, protected, tranquil, placid, unruffled, unperturbed, satisfied, joyful, tolerant, thankful, understood, valued, honored, lifted up...[22]

So, how does the Lord help us open our hearts to Him? How does the Lord help us discern what changes He wants to make in us in a trial? Well, this is where discipleship comes in.

WHAT IS A DISCIPLE; WHAT IS DISCIPLESHIP?

Discipleship is a process by which the Lord seeks to open and change our hearts and minds so that they reflect the true identity of our spirit, which, as a believer, is united with Christ.

In Matthew 28:19, Jesus says we are to make disciples. When we enter into a relationship with Christ, we become His disciples. To understand what it means to "make disciples," it helps to understand what being a disciple of Christ means.

---

[21] *Feelings 101: Pain to Peace 2nd Edition*, William J. Clark, Jr. with CH (COL) William J. Clark, Ret., 2013, Keys To Understanding Life Series, pg. 125-126, modified with permission.

[22] Ibid., pg. 161-162, modified with permission.

The Greek word for *disciple* is μαθητεύω and it means "not only to learn, but to become attached to one's teacher and to become his follower in doctrine and <u>conduct of life</u>. It is really not sufficient to translate (being discipled) as 'learning' but as 'making of a disciple.'"[23] (Words in parenthesis are added; <u>underlining</u> added to the definition for emphasis)

Many believers think the word disciple is simply an older, Latin word for student. That is an inadequate view. A disciple learns things like students, but a disciple also takes on the task of learning to live the lifestyle of the master, as the master directs. As believers, our Master is the Lord Jesus Christ, and we cannot live His lifestyle on our own. He must be allowed to live it through us. The differences between student and disciple may seem like subtle distinctions; on the contrary, they are huge and important!

Real-life Discipleship

It is important to realize that the Lord's discipling of us doesn't happen just in a classroom, although we can grow there too. It mostly happens in real-life, particularly when we are experiencing trials.

Being a disciple of Christ isn't so much about US studying our way to embracing the lifestyle Christ would have of us. Although studying the Bible is vital, being discipled isn't *just* about gaining more Biblical knowledge. Also, being a disciple of Christ isn't about US trying to do all the "right" and "godly" things in order to reflect THE life only Christ can live. Being a disciple of Christ is about allowing the LORD to live THE life (John 14:6) through us in real-life by opening our hearts to Him.

Being discipled is about allowing the Lord to change who we are… even in smoothing the rough edges off of our personalities where He sees fit.

Learning to allow the Lord to live through us involves the Holy Spirit revealing to us how to allow Christ to live through us. Bear in mind, the Holy Spirit knows His job. He is quite skilled at working to reveal to us the things we need to submit to in order for Christ to live

---

[23] Zodhiates, Spiros: *The Complete Word Study Dictionary : New Testament.* electronic ed. Chattanooga, TN : AMG Publishers, 2000, c1992, c1993, S. G3100

28

through us. For us, part of being discipled involves being open, discerning, and seeking out what the Holy Spirit would reveal to us. This is how we yield our freewill to the Lord.

James 1:22 tells us not to just listen to the word, but to do it. But, as you might have figured out by now, that doesn't mean WE are the doers. In Romans 7:18, Paul says that he often has the desire to do good, but he cannot carry it out on his own. When "we" do God's good will, on the outside it appears we are the doers, but only because on the inside we are opening our hearts for Christ to live through us. Again, this is how we submit our freewill to Christ in a trial.

God did not design us to be capable of freewill just to override it later! Remember, we are united with Christ in spirit. When we submit our freewill to Him in a given trial He will live through not only our human spirit, but our hearts, minds and bodies in that trial. This means we are simply to open our hearts to being instruments of Christ; we are to be the vessels. As we become vessels allowing Christ to live through us, God helps us become imitators of Christ, a.k.a., imitators of the Lord (1 Corinthians 11:1; 1 Thessalonians 1:6) and imitators of God (Ephesians 5:1-2).

Discipleship is About God Making Us into a Vessel for Him

Being the vessel through which the Lord lives THE life involves changing, but not under our own power or by our clever thinking and good, godly ideas. *The Lord* changes *our hearts and minds* as we respond to the Holy Spirit's revealing. The Lord transforms us, one trial at a time.

As is to be expected, the Lord works to disciple us in real-life, all the time. But, just because God loves us does not mean being discipled is easy. It is not by chance that the words disciple and discipline come from the same basic root word.

Hebrews 12:4-11 show us that trials involve being disciplined by the Lord as He is showing us our need to open our hearts to Him. This can be hard because we are so used to living according to the ways of the flesh. But, these verses also say that trials WILL bring joy and peace *IF* we submit to being trained by God's Spirit during them.

The Bible shows that every decision and every experience can involve the opportunity to respond to the Lord's desire to live through us. Each is a discipleship opportunity. Each experience involves the possibility to be personally discipled *beyond the basics*, i.e., in real-life (Hebrews 6:1-2 tell us what some of the "basics" are).

WHAT IS THE HOLY SPIRIT'S ROLE IN OUR TRIALS? WHAT IS DISCERNMENT?

1 Thessalonians 5:23 speaks to the importance of being sanctified, not only in spirit (which actually was completed when you entered into a relationship with God through Jesus Christ), but also in soul and body.

> The Greek word for *sanctify* is χάρις and it means "to set apart, to make holy, to purify."[24]

The process of discipleship and being discipled is one of sanctification. Discipleship offers the opportunity, particularly through trials, to allow the Lord to change, or sanctify, our hearts and minds so that we live according to our true identity in Him not only in spirit, but in soul and body during a trial. As God works to sanctify us, He provides us His Holy Spirit to help us. Let's touch on that.

In Ephesians 1:17, Paul prays for the people of Ephesus. In this particular part of the prayer he prays that they may receive "a spirit of wisdom and of revelation of the knowledge of God" and His will for them.

> The Greek word for *revelation* is ἀποκάλυψις. It means "to reveal; a revelation, uncovering, unveiling, a disclosure."[25]

This revealing by the Spirit of God plays a critical role in our being discipled. As disciples of Christ, a big part of being discipled is about being sensitive to the Holy Spirit revealing to us how to keep ourselves out of the way so Christ lives through us.

Discernment

1 Corinthians 2:14 But a natural man does not accept the

---

[24] Ibid., G5485
[25] Ibid., G602

things of the Spirit of God, for they are foolishness to him; and he cannot understand them, because they are spiritually appraised.

In this verse, the Greek word for *appraised* is ἀνακρίνω. It means "to discern."[26]

The dictionary defines discernment as "the quality of being able to (perceive), grasp and comprehend what is obscure (or concealed), to see or understand a difference; to detect; a power to see what is not evident to the average mind...."[27]

Because of the key role the Holy Spirit plays in aiding us during trials, our trials require discernment on our part, but don't take this to mean we can do it on our own without the Lord.

Now, it is one thing to discern the relationship between the temperature of a part of the ocean and the weather which forms above it! It is one thing to discern the movement of the sunlight and various shadows and conclude that the earth must be round! It is one thing to discern that there must be a relationship between an apple falling from a tree and a law called "gravity!" However, it is a completely different thing to discern God's Holy Spirit Who seeks to reveal guidance to us during trials!

In 1 Corinthians 2:14, "what is translated 'natural man' in the Greek [means] the soul of man."[28]

Discernment is not something that WE do with our brains or minds. As the paragraph above indicates, the soul level of our being CANNOT discern squat that is of a spiritual nature... unless we rely on God through His Holy Spirit. Discernment involves opening your heart and being sensitive to the Holy Spirit's guidance as He works to reveal to you how to let Christ live through you in the trial at hand. The Spirit seeks to reveal to you how to let Christ "call the shots" for the trial.

---

[26] Ibid., G350

[27] Merriam-Webster, I. (2003). *Merriam-Webster's collegiate dictionary.* Includes index. (Eleventh ed.). Springfield, Mass.: Merriam-Webster, Inc.

[28] Zodhiates, Spiros: *The Complete Word Study Dictionary : New Testament.* electronic ed. Chattanooga, TN : AMG Publishers, 2000, c1992, c1993, S. G4151

What Does the Holy Spirit Seek to Reveal to Us During Trials?

God's Spirit seeks to reveal a number of things to us from the moment a trial arises. Chances are that you have actually discerned each of these in one trial or another. These might be discerned more easily in some trials than in others. The key is that each of these is need-to-know information in a trial, and God knows you need it.

(We bolded this next part so you really pay attention to it.)

It is important that you understand that what follows is NOT a "formula" of some sort. It is about a conversation, from God to you. Think of any person that you are really close to. Think of a person you've been around for a long time, perhaps a parent or a spouse. Chances are that when some issue arises, you have a pretty good idea what aspect(s) of the issue are very important to them. You probably have a good idea how that person is going to respond to that issue.

Well, the Bible has a lot to say about how God views the flesh, temptation, and how important it is to Him to have a really strong relationship with you. The more you become familiar with the Lord's concern for transforming you during life's trials, the more you will have a really good idea of what He's going to want to talk to you about from the moment the trial first pops up. So, keep in mind, what follows is a general outline of a conversation He will seek to have with you, regardless of the external circumstances of the trial. What you won't find below are the specifics of what He will say to you – that's between you and Him. However, what follows will certainly help you stay focused on the conversation itself.

With that being clear, let's look at how God's Spirit works to help you follow the Lord's conversation with you....

1. **The Holy Spirit seeks to reveal the temptation/deception in a trial. This includes revealing fleshly tendencies that arise for you in a trial, and the Lying Belief that Satan offers for you to believe is true about your identity, pg. 24.**

Here's the deal. Because your heart is troubled, you know that the flesh is trying to pull you into acting in response to the trial. Here's where you try to discern *how* the flesh is trying to get you to respond. In this phase of the trial, let your heart continue feeling whatever it feels. It may be a bit uncomfortable, but it's OK because God is using your heart to help you see WHY YOU NEED HIM!

Special Consideration: The idea, at the start of a trial, is to open yourself to the Holy Spirit and **DISERN FLESHLY TENDENCIES**. Write down what you discern. First, does the current trial remind you of a past trial? The Spirit might bring to your mind a past trial – trust that whatever pops in your head is the Spirit helping you out. How did the flesh try to get you to act? If nothing comes, just be honest before the Lord and continue to be open to discerning the fleshly tendencies working against you in the trial. Ask these questions and write down what the Spirit reveals to you.

- How is the flesh making you want to deal with the situation?
- What's your motive?
- Are you wanting to speak up, say nothing, what?
- When you feel troubled like you do, how would you normally try to handle it?

Chances are that your answers will reveal how the flesh is tempting you. Even when your answers sound "godly," they are being tainted in some way. Write your answers down as you look for influences of the flesh in terms of how you are being tempted to respond to the trial.

Once you've discerned and made notes about that, then next, you want to open yourself to discerning some specifics about the Lying Belief you are being tempted with. To discern the Lying Belief, use the exercise found in the **Special Consideration** on pg. 24. When you are finished with that, continue on….

2. **The Holy Spirit seeks to reveal how to open your heart to the Lord and feel your true identity in Christ. Refer to pg. 14 and use your heart.**

To connect with God's Spirit in this phase of a trial, simply look at the Lying Belief He helped you discern. Now, using your heart let the

Spirit help you discern which of the four characteristics of your identity in Christ runs counter to that Lying Belief. Refer to the examples starting on pg. 14. Select the one that seems to fit the best.

It is normal that sometimes there might be more than one of those characteristics that fit. Don't get caught up in trying to reason which fits. Trust that God's Spirit is working to reveal it to you – just use your heart. Don't overthink it.

Once you discern that, let your heart feel the truth described in the verse(s) associated with that characteristic. Focus on the verses that quote the Lord. Feel what He was saying about who you are. Let yourself sit with that for a few moments. Be still (Psalm 46:10, 131:2). As the Lord connects you with the truth, your heart will begin to feel different. This is the peace of Christ coming on! Let the Lord work in your heart. (Just so you know, as this happens, the Lord is connecting your soul to your spirit, which is united with Him.)

Let God put the peace of Christ in your heart then ask "how is the Lord trying to change me through the trial at hand?" Continue on....

3. The Holy Spirit seeks to reveal what change(s) God seeks to make in you so that your thinking is renewed with thoughts based on your identity in Christ.

For the Lord to shift your heart from being troubled to experiencing the peace of Christ (in 2 above), you had to be ***open*** to Him to changing something in you. Now the Spirit of the Lord will help you discern that change(s). Ask what the Holy Spirit is trying to reveal to you about changing any of the areas listed below so that God will continue to connect your heart to your identity in Christ... and you'll continue experiencing the peace of Christ. Look to discern changes in...:

> **behaviors** (internal too, not just external), **attitude,
> preferences, opinions, thinking, point of view,** or **sensitivity**
> (i.e., more Christ-like sensitivity to others/self or less fleshly
> sensitivity to others/self, etc.).
> Write down the changes you've discerned from the Spirit, then
> continue....

4. The Holy Spirit seeks to reveal steps of faith that, if you take them, allow the Lord to live through you.

This is when the Holy Spirit works to reveal the specific steps of faith that the Lord wants you to take in the trial at hand. Isn't that awesome?! Now it's time to discern how the Lord wants you to show your faith.

The steps of faith the Holy Spirit works to reveal constitute the "how to" for letting Christ live through us in a given trial. The Holy Spirit works to reveal exactly what steps of faith the Lord wants to you to take. Seek to discern what Christ wants to do and not do through you in the trial at hand. Leave the outcome of the trial to the Lord. Make notes about what the Spirit reveals to you in terms of steps of faith God wants you to take, then take them.

As the Holy Spirit grows your discernment, you'll "hear" Him (with your spiritual ears) telling you, "Christ wants to do this and this through you. Christ doesn't want to say that through you. And, Christ doesn't want to do that and that through you."

You might be thinking, "Hey, that's cool! If I only knew exactly what He wanted to do through me, I'd be happy!" Well, not necessarily; the flesh has a way of creeping back up on us. So though the Spirit can help you discern what the Lord wishes to do through you, everything isn't always "peachy!" You see, the ways of the Lord will definitely go against your soul's old, familiar fleshly ways and habits. The flesh will be competing in your soul against the Lord's will until you've actually walked a while with a real (from God's perspective) dependence on Christ.

One of the big, reoccurring steps of faith in many trials will be about completely embracing the change(s) God seeks to make in your heart and mind through a given trial. And, you will have to allow Him to change you in order to move through the trial with love and the peace of Christ in your heart.

You might be thinking, "Boy, this is a lot!!" Well, in Mark 12:30-31, Jesus provides us the overview, or what we (the authors) call the short, short version for how to handle everything in life, including trials.

MARK 12:30-31 "'AND YOU SHALL LOVE THE LORD YOUR GOD WITH ALL YOUR HEART, AND WITH ALL YOUR SOUL, AND WITH ALL YOUR MIND, AND WITH ALL YOUR STRENGTH.' The second is this, 'YOU SHALL LOVE YOUR NEIGHBOR AS YOURSELF.'

There is no other commandment greater than these." (CAPS are part of translation)

Jesus wasn't saying that the rest of the truths in the New Testament, including the Biblical concepts we've pointed out, are unimportant. He's saying, "You'll get it if you love Me." Oh by the way, love is a heart thing.

It is very clear that, in trials, our love of Christ is essential. So, how often do we feel love in our trials? In other words, how often do we feel love and the peace of Christ during a trial, before the outcome is decided? Anyone can feel peace and love after a trial if the outcome is what they want.

Disciples of Christ can experience God's love in and through them, during a trial, even when the outcome doesn't go the way we would normally expect it will to go.

The heart of a believer is not to be one of continuing chaos, frustration, etc. during trials (1 Corinthians 14:33), although each trial will start out that way. Through discipleship and being discipled, God seeks to grow you so that He can regularly walk through you with everything you've read so far… in a single fluid experience, trial after trial.

With these things in mind, let's boil everything down (trying not to oversimplify things) and look at the Bible's A,B,C,Ds of trials.

How Trials Work (the Bible's A,B,C,Ds of Trials)

1. **Attack (The temptation)** – A trial, big or little, starts with Satan's ATTACK (James 1:13-15; 1 Peter 5:8; Ephesians 6:16). The Holy Spirit seeks to reveal Satan's ATTACK to you to help you DISCERN how the flesh is working against you. God designed you to be able to DISCERN the Spirit's warning by using your heart.

   a. 1 John 3:18-24 – When your heart "condemns you," you WON'T be at peace, i.e., you have a **heart disturbance**.

   b. When this happens, God is warning you that evil wants you to sin so that fleshly behaviors and a Lying Belief will be strengthened (Romans 6:15-16).

   c. When Satan ATTACKS, you are being tempted. There WILL be some kind of deception at work. You cannot see through it on your own. Satan's deception is designed to make it hard to

DISCERN what the Holy Spirit seeks to reveal about the temptation/deception, so you'll sin.

d.   PRAY! However, don't pray that God will help you. He's already trying to do that. Thank Him for His help. Pray that you'll be open and sensitive to DISCERN how He's trying to help – there is a difference.

e.   Your part in this is to open yourself to DISCERNING what the Spirit would reveal to you about…
   •   how the flesh wants you to respond to the trial (pg. 33).
   •   the Lying Belief you are tempted to embrace (pg. 24).

2.   **Bond (The Connection)** – In trials, BONDING with the Lord in your heart involves DISCERNING what the Holy Spirit would reveal to you about opening your heart to the truth of your identity in Christ. BONDING with Christ involves embracing the truth of who you are in HIM.

a.   BONDING with the Lord involves HIM transforming your heart disturbances to peace and love (Romans 5:3-5; Colossians 3:15; John 14:27).

b.   BONDING with the Lord isn't *just* about prayer and then reading the Bible, although these are part of it. Part of BONDING with the Lord in a trial involves opening your heart for the Lord to connect you with the truth of who you are in Christ.

c.   Take the Lying Belief you DISCERNED earlier and DISCERN which aspect of your identity in Christ is the closest to going against that (starting on pg. 14). After you've selected the closest one, let the Lord connect your heart to the truth so that you feel it. Don't just read the truth and associated verse – meditate on how feels. Sit with the peace of Christ which follows.

d.   The next step in BONDING with the Lord is to be open to DISCERN the change(s) the Lord wants you to embrace. As you do, ensure you remain centered in the peace of Christ. Changes can be in terms of behaviors (internal too, not just external), attitude, preferences, opinions, thinking, point of view, or sensitivity (i.e., more Christ-like sensitivity to others/self or less fleshly sensitivity to others/self, etc.).

3. **Complete (The Response)** – You will always COMPLETE a trial by action or inaction in the flesh or in Christ (Romans 6:1, 1 Peter 1:13-16). The point is to allow the Lord to COMPLETE the action(s) through you, and not to act independently of Him. You'll know you've DISCERNED the steps of faith God asks of you when you remain at peace while doing so (1 John 3:18-24), even if that sense of the peace of Christ only lasts for a short while.
    a. Based on what changes the Lord seeks to make in you to center your heart in His peace, DISCERN the steps of faith God seeks so that Christ lives through you in response to the trial.
    b. Take the step(s) of faith the Holy Spirit revealed to you. And give *thanks*!

4. **Discernment (The Awareness)** – It is important to DISCERN all that the Holy Spirit works to reveal to you in a given trial. Proverbs 14:33; Philippians 1:9-11.
    a. The Holy Spirit has to assist you in DISCERNMENT (John 16:12-14). DISCERNMENT isn't just about you coming up with your own smart ideas.
    b. In a two-way relationship with God through Christ, it is important to be open to being discipled by DISCERNING the guidance of God's Spirit, especially during trials.

Well, that's it for this "overview" chapter. Again, don't try to memorize everything. Each lesson will refer to key pieces of this overview as you go along. Each of the lessons is going to help you connect with the Lord and so He can help you live these Biblical truths about your relationship with Christ. In turn, this will help you connect with the Lord in whatever real-life trial you may face.

If things ever start to get a bit hectic for you, just remember that God loves you. He designed your body, your heart and mind (soul), and your spirit so that He could reach out to you no matter where you go or what you face.

Now that you've absorbed what you could with this overview, let's look at how to participate in the Poieological Bible Study itself.

HOW TO PARTICIPATE IN A POIEOLOGICAL BIBLE STUDY

Growth Step 1:

To identify how to get started, and some of the overall goals, recommendations and "rules" of a Poieological Bible Study.

Growth Step 2:

To specify the parts of a Poieological Bible Study, i.e., the template.

Growth Step 3:

To clarify the goals and challenges of each part of the Poieological Bible Study template.

The lessons use trials or situations from the Bible in which we'd likely experience a trial if we were in the situation. In these situations there aren't really any questions about what God sought to accomplish through the men and women in the stories. The lessons will help you use the Bible's records of these events in a way that you learn how to open yourself to the Lord, His Spirit and all that He wants do through you in your own trials.

HOW TO GET STARTED WITH THE BIBLE STUDY

Here's the best way we recommend to get started, particularly with a small group. Even if you are doing the study on your own, you can use this same step-by-step approach.

1. At your first session, walk participants through the Overview of the Biblical Basics of Trials chapter (starting on page 11). Use this first session to make sure that everyone is generally familiar with how their relationship with Christ relates to trials. Make sure everyone understands that the goal isn't to memorize everything in that Overview, but simply to be familiar with basic Biblical

concepts relating to trials.

2. One option is to have everyone read this chapter on their own before the second session. However, the way we usually handled this was to talk to certain parts of this chapter at the second session, based on our assessment of the group's needs. We did not require participants to read it unless they just wanted to on their own.

3. At your second session, discuss this "How To" chapter. Talk about what you've learned about the study approach, and make sure you are all on the same sheet of music as far as how the lessons work.

4. Also at the second session, set some time aside to designate someone in the group to be prepared to play the AUDIO associated with each lesson. Each lesson tells you when to listen to it. The AUDIO piece is a 6-10 minute MP3 recording; the length varies by lesson. The AUDIO is free from KeysToUnderstandingLife.org (no sign-up required). You can download and save the AUDIO, or simply play it at the appropriate time in your study directly from the website with a smart phone or other internet capable device. Go to www.Feelings102.com to get each lesson's AUDIO.

5. Before your third session, have everyone, on their own, read the intro to Lesson 1 (starting on page 63), the Scripture passage for the lesson, the CONTEXT, WHO IS INVOLVED, DECISIONS, and KNOWLEDGE sections – **these parts of a given lesson are what we refer to as the "read-ahead" for a lesson**.

6. At your third session, do a short review of the read-ahead. Let everyone share their thoughts about the passage and trial. Then, move everyone on to answer "What was Eve's Heart Disturbance." After that everyone is ready to put themselves in Eve's shoes by listening to the AUDIO… and you are on your way.

The Overall Focus of the Bible Study

There are three parts to a trial:
1. The *before* part that leads to the trial,
2. The *during* part we experience both externally and internally in the trial,
3. And the *after* part, i.e., the outcome.

The Poieological Bible Study lessons focus heavily on the *before* and *during* parts of trials that are described in the Bible. Focusing on these two parts in particular helps increase our sensitivity to discerning what God's Spirit is revealing to us on how to let Christ live through us throughout the trial. This, in turn, helps us to submit to the Lord and take the steps of faith God seeks for us to take in response to the trial, even when we are not able to see the outcome, i.e. the *after* part of the trial.

The challenge of trials is that Satan works to get us wrapped up in worrying about what might happen in the *after* part of a trial. It is important that we surrender the outcome of trials, the *after*, to the Lord. The outcome is His. If you truly believe God's will is perfect and sufficient, then by bonding with the Lord *during* a trial you can be assured that He will live through you, especially when you are not able to control the outcome, or *after* part, of a trial.

To help us learn more about our part in the *before* and *during* parts of trials, **the Poieological Bible Study has two basic parts**:
1. The part where we look at the Scriptural trial from the perspective of a particular Biblical person in their situation.
2. The part where each Bible Study participant works to put themselves in that Biblical person's *situation*.

Making the transition between the two parts can be challenging. So, with these things in mind, let's look at…

GOALS, RECOMMENDATIONS AND "RULES"

Overall Goals of the Poieological Bible Study

1. To become better at discerning what the Holy Spirit can reveal about both God's and Satan's involvement in trial situations found in the Bible.
2. To gain a greater appreciation for the fact that no matter how much we may know about the Bible and God's will, that knowledge is not consistently sufficient to ensure we *always* will let Christ live through us in response to our own trials. (i.e., we can't *think* our way through the process of transforming our *hearts* during trials – God has to transform us.) The only real choice we make in a trial is whether we will find our rest in the Lord.

3. To study, in a very intentional way, how it is that godly living during trials is really about submitting to God as He works to change and transform our hearts and minds during a trial.
4. To gain insights into patterns in Satan's attacks on us personally and to examine the difficulties we sometimes have in submitting to God transforming us during our trials.
5. To recognize that some of the things that Christ seeks to do through us in trials can be far more challenging to submit to than we typically care to think.
6. To partner with fellow believers in a practical Bible Study. To encourage each other to focus on real-life applicability of the Lord living through us, as we study trials found in the Bible.
7. To strengthen the bonds of spiritual family between the Bible Study participants by being open, by sharing in spiritually intimate ways, and by respecting God's presence behind the unique lessons each person discerns from studying a trial.

Special Consideration:

For the most part, the trial you will study in each lesson is one where God's will is clear. This means we can figure out God's will in terms of any of the following for the person experiencing the trial (the person whose perspective we study in a given lesson):
1. God challenges the person to take specific steps of faith in response to the person's trial.
2. God seeks to transform the person's heart, and the person has to submit to that process to experience the following:
   a. The peace God offers.
   b. The godly attitude and mindset God seeks to develop.
   c. The best possible chance of creating harmony with their spouse, family member, or other person(s) by allowing God to do what He deems best through the person in terms of responding to the trial.
   d. Letting God live through the person in light of the role they have, as God sees that role (which can be different from how a person sees their role)

Recommendations for the Poieological Bible Study

1. **Be familiar with the Poieological template and its parts.** It can really take away from the participation in the study when the discussion gets bogged down or even goes in a counterproductive direction simply because there is confusion over how to use the Bible Study template effectively (we'll get to the template used in each lesson shortly).

2. **Each participant in the study should have a copy of *Feelings 102*.** This is important so each participant can quickly refer to the descriptions of the template (presented in this chapter) without disrupting the flow of the discussion. It allows each participant to be able to refer to the Authors' Examples (in Appendix 3) whenever they want or need to during the study. Finally, it allows each participant to confidentially write responses directly in the spaces provided in the book.

3. **Have each participant read the lesson's Bible passage and the notes provided in the first part of each lesson *before* getting together as a group.** There will be more time for group study and interaction if, in advance and on their own, everyone goes through a given lesson's passage and the notes provided at the start of the lesson. Take time to digest this read-ahead and to identify questions to bring up in the group. If the group chooses not to do this, some lessons may take more than an hour to get through. If your group study time is limited to less than an hour, some of the lessons may carry over to the next time you meet.

4. **Consider having everyone use the same version of the Bible for the study.** This can help everyone to keep up better when certain verses are being read aloud in the group.

5. **Do the lessons in order.** The lessons are designed to be done in order because nearly all the trials flow from one to another in terms of the overall spiritual war behind the human events. Though not always, many times a Biblical person's action or inaction in a trial impacts not only that trial, but the ones that follow, even for many generations. Remember that the goal of the poieological study is to focus on the *before* and *during* parts of the trial. These parts influence the outcomes (the *after* parts) of trials in terms of whether we are actually letting God live through us in the trial.

   Feelings 102 lessons are designed to help you reflect and introspect in order to discern patterns in how Satan trips us up in the *before* and *during* parts of trials. The Holy Spirit works to reveal these to us. So if you decide to study the lessons out of order, you can miss out on seeing how Satan often does this to persons in Scripture. You may miss critical information and need-to-have insights that can only be fully appreciated by working the lessons in order. In short, if you don't do the lessons in chronological order, then one of the key things that may remain unappreciated is a Biblical character's fleshly patterns. This is seen best through the flow of his/her trials, just like in our own lives.

6. **Refer to Appendix 3: Authors' Examples as needed**. As mentioned in the Introduction, the Authors' Examples (starting on page 229) are provided to augment your own study experience. They are designed to assist you. They are NOT "THE ANSWERS" that you are to strive to get. The best part about the Authors' Examples is that they can give you the gist of the direction in which a lesson can take you. The responses you find in Appendix 3 vary. This is appropriate because each participant was seeking to discern from the Spirit whatever He would reveal to that participant. Each person's heart and experience of trials are different. God is the only unwavering constant.

7. **Use butcher paper, chalk board or dry-erase board**. It adds a helpful dimension to the experience if someone writes group responses down for all to see. It helps everyone to keep up and remember points brought out in the study. These tools can also facilitate an easy, quick refresher when a lesson takes more than one session to complete.

Special Consideration About Confidentiality:
Due to the nature of parts of the Bible Study, participants may express some personal feelings and thoughts. This is useful, but it is probably important to safeguard or destroy any group notes later as part of respecting confidentiality. If your group elects to use butcher paper, a chalk board, or to have someone write up study notes for everyone, do so in a way that respects each participant's confidentiality.

"Rules" for the Poieological Bible Study

1. **Everyone participates**. Everyone must be encouraged and allowed to participate. Everyone should join in the study with the intention of participating. Participants with lots of Scriptural knowledge must watch that they don't get carried away with sharing their knowledge. In this kind of study, while knowledge is important, what is more important is working to be sensitive to discerning the Holy Spirit's revelations to you personally. Specifically, you are looking for what the Spirit will say to you about how the flesh seeks to drive your heart and mind. The lessons will point to the things you need to know in order to approach the study from a theologically sound perspective. *Feelings 102* works to ensure that even groups with minimal theological knowledge and background can profit greatly in being open to the Lord and His Spirit within. The challenge is to participate in each lesson with a focus on sharing what you learn from the Lord by putting yourself into the trial situation.

2. **Everyone respects confidentiality**. This is the corollary to "everyone participates." The point of the study is to recognize and share one's experience with the Biblical trial situation, as well as observations one may make about patterns in his/her life. While this is very practical and helpful, it can be personal. Everyone needs to be able to <u>trust each other not to share each other's stories or experiences outside of the group</u>.

3. **Don't judge or argue**. The study challenges everyone to share in confidentiality and in an environment of mutual respect. It is your own heart you must watch if you find yourself tempted to comment on, or "correct," what others experience as they put themselves in to a trial. Be cautious before trying to teach each other personal lessons; this can enable Satan to get involved and lead to arguments. The goal of the study is, in part, for each participant to become more sensitive to the Spirit of God, Whom Jesus secured for us through His love and sacrifice. The other part is to seek out how to simply let the Lord live through you in a trial. Encourage each other to introspect and share lessons you each learn about what God is saying to YOU in the study.

4. **Study the spiritual dynamics behind your own trials, not someone else's**. Each lesson is designed to aid participants in recognizing their own challenges in trials, and to examine how

God is seeking to transform their hearts and minds accordingly. Don't slip into telling someone else what they are feeling, thinking or whatever. Part of the goal is for each person to work on discerning and then expressing those kinds of things for themselves.

5. **Focus on learning about the challenges of being transformed by God, not on quoting Scriptures that say we must transform or change.*** Quoting or referencing various Scriptures that speak to God's guidance about being transformed can be a helpful part of dealing with trials. However in the Poieological Bible Study lessons, the idea is to voluntarily refrain from doing so until the final part of the study. The goal is to challenge ourselves to focus on the trial by using the knowledge that the Biblical person in the trial may have had, according to what we read in the written Word. By doing so, you will gain a greater appreciation for how to observe the ways in which *you* experience different trials, including God's ways of seeking to transform you.

6. **Don't refer to or draw on Scriptural knowledge that isn't specifically mentioned until later in the Scriptures.** Since the lessons in *Feelings 102, Volume 1* deal with trials in Genesis, essentially you will want to refrain from focusing on Bible passages that come after that. After all, it is information the "Biblical characters" didn't have. While this may be different, try it. Again, for example, you'll need to refrain from referencing "the Law," Psalms, Proverbs, or anything else written after the book of

---

* In the Poieological Bible Study, it is NOT wrong, but rather helpful, to refrain from quoting Scriptural truths that God presents later in the human timeline, i.e., after the person whose trial you are studying. This includes things Jesus or His Disciples may have said. In each Scriptural trial you study, it is likely you can figure out how God would have the Biblical person respond to the trial. And, each person in the Bible, whether godly or not, apparently had enough knowledge of God to be accountable for whether they let God transform them and live through them or not! We know God was just looking for them to be in relationship with Him and to simply let Him handle the situation! So, the idea is to focus more on approaching the trial based on what the person in the trial knew and experienced! This approach will open you to the deeper challenges of *allowing the Lord to transform your heart and renew your mind* during a trial. By identifying what you would have felt or wanted were you in the trial, you are in a better position to study the challenges of being transformed and of discerning the actual steps of faith God would have for you. Sometimes that is "easy;" sometimes it is flat hard! Nevertheless, doing so is part of LIVING God's written Word.

Genesis. Basically, this study challenges you to "face the Biblical person's trial" with whatever knowledge that person would have. <u>Keep in mind that from God's perspective, the person had enough knowledge available for God to hold the person accountable.</u> The Poieological Bible Study lessons challenge us to briefly limit ourselves to that same knowledge. Remember, Poieology is about getting better at discerning our fleshly patterns, discerning God's will for us in a given trial, and examining the challenges of surrendering to God as He works to transform our hearts and minds *during* the trial.

The study will definitely help you come to appreciate other Bible passages you've studied. It is important to note those insights, but refrain from focusing on the other Bible passages until you come to the end of the DISCERN/OBSERVE portion of the study – we'll talk about this again on page 61.

Having said that, there are few necessary exceptions to the practice of not referring to information that comes later in the Bible. These exceptions are due to how the Bible is written. Occasionally key information about a trial isn't recorded until a few verses later, or in the next chapter. When these exceptions apply, they are mentioned in the CONTEXT part of the study.

7. **Talk about a leader/facilitator.** A small group doesn't have to have a leader/facilitator to do the study as a group, but a good facilitator can increase everyone's experience in the study. Each group decides for themselves. See Appendix 1 (page 219) for more about facilitating the Poieological Bible Study lessons.

POIEOLOGICAL BIBLE STUDY TEMPLATE

SCRIPTURE SUMMARY:

CONTEXT: (includes *Patterns* and *Other Relevant Information*)

WHO IS INVOLVED IN ___'S TRIAL (Main Players Only)?

WHAT DECISION(S) MUST ___ MAKE?

WHAT KNOWLEDGE OF GOD COULD ___ HAVE HAD TO ASSIST HIM/HER TO ACT AS GOD WANTS?

WHAT WAS ___'S HEART DISTURBANCE?

DID ___ LET THE LORD TRANSFORM HIS/HER HEART AND MIND SO THE LORD COULD LIVE THROUGH HIM/HER?

PUT YOURSELF IN ___'S "SHOES" – LISTEN TO THE AUDIO (Go to www.Feelings102.com to get or play the AUDIO)

WHAT WOULD YOUR TYPICAL HEART DISTURBANCE BE IF YOU WERE ___ IN THIS SITUATION OR ONE LIKE IT?
I'd feel _____ because _____.
I would/would not want _____ because _____.

DISCUSSION QUESTION(S):

DISCERN/OBSERVE:
Discern Fleshly Tendencies.
Discern the Lying Belief.
Discern and Feel the Truth of Your Identity in Christ.
Discern What The Lord Would Seek to Change in You to Transform Your Heart Disturbances So You Experience the Peace of God.
Discern Possible Steps of Faith; Observe Things About Your Life, Spiritual Battles, and What to Expect in Trials.

EVENTS AFTER THIS LESSON AND BEFORE THE NEXT:

SCRIPTURE SUMMARY:

1. The Scripture Summary is a short overview of the trial on which a particular lesson focuses.
2. To start the study, read the short introduction to the lesson (the paragraphs above the Scripture Summary) and then read through the lesson's text from Scripture.

Special Consideration About The Bible Texts:

Often times the selected text for a lesson *excludes* the verses that tell the actual outcome of a trial (the *after* part). This is usually critical to the Poieological Study. Remember, the focus of the study is on the challenges we experience in the *before* and *during* parts of the trial. Sometimes we do not learn as much about the challenges of trials when we rush to see the outcome of the person's trial in the Bible. Each Biblical person in a trial had to deal with not knowing the outcome, just like we often must do in our lives. Again, the idea is to leave the outcome to God, and to get a better idea of how to experience that. Still, Satan was often successful in causing Biblical persons to act independently of God due to fear and worry about the outcome. This is why the *before* and *during* parts of the trial are parts from which we learn a lot. You will look at the outcome of a trial in a couple lessons, but most focus is on the *before* and *during* parts of the trial.

CONTEXT:

The CONTEXT part deals with a couple of important perspectives. We provide information in this section, but you and your small group may add to it as you like.

1. *Patterns*: You will see this feature regularly when you get to Abraham and Sarah. It recaps events and/or *previous* trials revealing possible patterns in Satan's attacks against them. This is discussed more in Lesson 7.
2. *Other Relevant Information*: This provides useful information about the Biblical person or their trial. It can include a variety of information: distances people traveled, Hebrew Key Words, etc.

<u>**Special Consideration on CONTEXT:**</u>
As the lessons are designed to be completed in order, each lesson is important to the CONTEXT of the lessons that follow.

WHO IS INVOLVED IN ___ 'S TRIAL (Main Players Only)?

God and Satan are always included as "main players" in the trial. Sometimes we don't always think about God and Satan being part of trials because we get caught up in focusing on the external aspects of a trial. The same can happen in our own real-life trials when we get caught up in the external aspects too. The purpose for always listing God and Satan as participants in each trial we study is to remind ourselves that each trial is fundamentally a spiritual battle between God and Satan. Each is seeking to influence us – God from His love for us; Satan from his hate for God. We are the battlefield! In each trial, God and Satan are both involved, whether the Bible specifically mentions them each time or not. The point is to discern whatever the Spirit of Christ will reveal to you about their involvement.

WHAT DECISION(S) MUST ___ MAKE?

This section of the study identifies decisions related to the Biblical person's trial. The decision(s) listed always relate(s) to an action that the person might, or did, consider. Sometimes decisions relate to actions that the person wanted to avoid taking. And, sometimes people got focused on making a decision that wasn't the decision God sought to make through them. By observing the decisions people faced in the Bible's trials, we can get better at seeing the importance of submitting to the Lord's decision-making in our own real-life trials. Add to the decision list if you like.

WHAT KNOWLEDGE OF GOD COULD ___ HAVE HAD TO ASSIST HIM/HER TO ACT AS GOD WANTS?

This section lists relevant knowledge of God, and His will, that could have been available to the person whose trial you are studying. The goal Is to identify how much or little of this knowledge the person had available to make the decision(s) identified in the previous section.

As you will discover, trials in the Bible demonstrate that no matter how much knowledge one had about God or what He wanted to do through the person, that knowledge *alone* was **NOT a consistently reliable factor** in enabling the person to avoid acting independently of God in a trial. Knowledge of the Bible is important; however, as the Bible's trials show, Satan was often able to seduce people away from letting God live through them in the way their own knowledge indicated He desired (and this sometimes happens with us too). One of the things the lessons help us to see is that letting God live through us in a trial ALWAYS requires that we allow Him to transform our hearts, that we allow Him to transform our perspective, and that we take the specific steps of faith God lays out for us. As we let the Lord change our hearts, our minds will "think on things above" (Colossians 3:1-2).

Many of the lessons also show us that the Bible often indicates very little about what a person might have known about God in a specific trial. This omission may imply that while knowledge of God and His will is very important, it may not be the sole factor in serving God during our trials. The Poieological Study helps you to decide for yourself.

No matter how much knowledge *we* can discover from the Bible, we can never know the total amount of knowledge that a Biblical person actually knew when facing his/her trial. So, there are basically two ways to approach this "knowledge" section of the study:

1. *Assume that knowledge is more or less cumulative for persons in Scripture.* In other words, you might choose to assume that because Hagar lived in Abraham's household, then Hagar's knowledge of God could have included being exposed to what Abraham knew of God. You could assume this includes any knowledge that Adam, Eve, Cain, Abel and Noah had. If you assume that, then an approach to this section of the study for Hagar would likely involve going through the Scriptures that precede her trial and identifying every truth one can find that would remotely relate to guiding Hagar in her trial.

2. *Assume that while some knowledge may have been passed down to individuals, it is useful to identify whatever knowledge the Bible directly indicates the person had, if any.* This is the approach we use in the lessons. It involves identifying the knowledge a person had based solely on the knowledge the Bible records that they personally had. So when it comes to what knowledge Abram had when he lied to Pharaoh to save his skin, in Genesis 12:10-20, there is a short, but important list. The list includes God's Promises

to Abram, Abram's awareness of having a relationship with God, and that Abram had a concept of serving God, which included differences between acting dependently on or independently of God. When it comes to Hagar, we see that basically there isn't a list of what she knew about God. Still, she, like every human being, was still accountable and was not out of the loving reach of the Father or the Holy Spirit.

As your small group studies the lessons, realize that participants might not agree on what knowledge the Biblical person could have had. Regardless what knowledge anyone in the group believes the person may have had, each participant will have to face the fact that when the Bible is conspicuously vague on the subject, the person was still accountable before God! This seems to imply that even when a person's knowledge of God is not great, the fact that *every* person has the God-given opportunity to connect with Him through the heart is sufficient for accountability. Satan knows we are accountable. Satan's goal is to make it hard to trust God and incline our hearts to Him and His desire to transform us.

WHAT WAS ___'S HEART DISTURBANCE?

This is the first part of the study that you will work to fill out completely on your own. (You can see how others responded to the rest of the lesson's questions starting with this part of the template, by referring to the pages we'll provide to you at the start of this section.)

Remember, heart disturbances can include desires and/or feelings (emotions). To review what we mean by heart disturbances, see pg. 23. In this section of the study, the goal is to note what the Bible says about how the person felt or what the person's strong desires were. You will discover that a person's heart disturbance is not always recorded in the Bible. This is not a problem as the Poieological Study ultimately focuses on you identifying what your heart disturbance would be were you the one in the trial. Herein lays one of the values of using the poieological approach to study trials.

Be aware that some of the trials examined in *Feelings 102* are not always immediately recognized as trials until we are really working to put ourselves in the Biblical person's situation. We can study some of these harder-to-recognize trials based on what we know God directed or wanted and based on how *we* might react to a similar situation.

For example, in Genesis 12:1-4 (Lesson 5) God tells Abram to move, but God doesn't tell Abram exactly where to go. The Bible says nothing to indicate that following God's directive in this situation involved a trial for Abram or his wife. When we look at the situation, we see that God basically tells Abram to start walking and He will tell Abram when to stop. Maybe it wasn't a trial for Abram and Sarai. However, it doesn't take a big stretch of the imagination to realize that were a husband to come home and tell his wife, "We're moving, but I don't know where we're going," a potentially heated discussion could easily ensue! The bottom line is that the lesson will show you how this is a likely trial and that it is worth studying using the poieological approach.

DID ___ LET THE LORD TRANSFORM HIS/HER HEART AND MIND SO THE LORD COULD LIVE THROUGH HIM/HER?

This question deals with whether the person's knowledge of God helped him or her to submit to the Lord's desire to transform the person's heart and mind.** You may be surprised to discover that many trials in the Bible demonstrate how often a person had significant *knowledge of God and what He wanted*, yet that knowledge wasn't sufficient to enable the person to submit to God transforming their hearts. Satan can deceive and influence us regardless of how much we know about God and His will for us. Our part is to allow God to change our hearts and renew our minds.

DISCUSSION QUESTIONS:

1. DISCUSSION QUESTIONS are intended to help you focus on important spiritual issues underlying a given trial. Some of these questions are vital to recognizing the challenges of letting ourselves be transformed by the Lord, and to discerning the Spirit's

---

** This question can usually be answered based on what the Bible records. However, there are a few situations where the Bible doesn't make it clear one way or another whether the person experienced a trial and, if they did, whether the person's heart was transformed. In these situations, we (the authors) simply state (in Appendix 3: Authors' Examples) that the Bible doesn't say one way or another.

revelations on ways of thinking that are influenced by the flesh, ways of thinking which God wants to change in us.

2. DISCUSSION QUESTIONS sometimes center on Key Words from Hebrew. Information on these words is provided.

3. DISCUSSION QUESTIONS may appear in different places within the study process, and sometimes there aren't any for a lesson. The responses to a lesson's DISCUSSION QUESTIONS, listed in Appendix 3: Authors' Examples (starting page 229), are sentiments expressed by the participants of our small group studies.

PUT YOURSELF IN ___'S "SHOES" – LISTEN TO THE AUDIO

The "Biblical character," you study in a trial was a real person, just like you. In this section you will try to deeply identify with his/her situation, and not just read and think about it intellectually.

To help you "get into the person's shoes," you will listen to a 6-10 minute AUDIO MP3 recording when you get to this part of a lesson.[***]

The AUDIO section ties into the next section, i.e., the "WHAT WOULD YOUR TYPICAL HEART DISTURBANCE BE…" section. While you listen to the AUDIO, put yourself in the trial and write down your heart's disturbances in the blanks, in the WHAT WOULD YOUR TYPICAL HEART DISTURBANCE BE…" section.

Some people may want to listen to the AUDIO on their own before doing the lesson as a group. We do not recommend doing this. It definitely takes away from the study, and you'll tend to lose the impact if you listen to the AUDIO before doing it as a group. Listen to the AUDIO during the study when the lesson prompts you. Pause the AUDIO, if necessary, to let participants write down their heart disturbances.

Success with the AUDIO portion involves identifying your own heart disturbances as if were you in the trial yourself.

The AUDIO is designed to help you use your God-given imagination to get past any external differences you may have with the person in the trial. Focusing too much on these differences can tend to

---

[***] For more information on the AUDIO, see Appendix 2: Intro to the AUDIO Part of the Study. This is extra information. Each lesson's AUDIO piece, and an AUDIO excerpt of Appendix 2, are free (no sign-up required). Go to www.Feelings102.com to download or play a lesson's AUDIO.

block us from experiencing what it must have been like to be in that person's trial. Specifically, it limits the opportunity to look at the challenges that would arise in our own hearts and minds were we in a similar situation. In turn, that limits how much God can use the study of the Bible's story to speak to how He's trying to change and transform us.

When you put yourself in the trial situation while listening to the AUDIO, it is normal to feel a bit conflicted! On the one hand, you may be aware of the reality of the deception and temptation Satan presents in that trial situation. On the other hand, you may recognize the evil behind Satan and the power of sin and be able to see through it. This is normal because the trial isn't actually happening to you; you are reading *about* it in the Bible. However, many times when our own trial is happening to us, we don't actually detect the deception, and we feel justified in feeling the way we do and wanting what we want.

While listening to the AUDIO, do not dismiss the part of your heart that can detect the "tug" of the flesh on you. When this happens, realize that you are discerning the Holy Spirit, Who is seeking to reveal that stuff to you. If you move away from what you feel in your heart, you'll miss out on becoming more sensitive to how the Holy Spirit works with you to reveal the pull of the flesh. This experience is very useful. Every soldier, even the Christian soldier, needs to know the enemy. The Lord knows this. In helping you be more aware and alert to the lure of the enemy's deception/temptation, the Spirit of the Lord is helping us understand our NEED for submitting to the changes God wants us to make in us when we *are* in our own trials.

While putting yourself in the person's shoes, what you feel or desire may be the same or different from what the Biblical person experienced. That's OK. What *you* feel or desire during the lesson can help you to learn about how Satan attacks *you* in trials. This is true even though your trials may or may not be the same as those of the Biblical person. Externally trials can differ. Internally we all experience heart disturbances in response to our trials. This is not a sin, as Jesus experienced heart disturbances too (Matthew 26:36-44). Satan's attacks create heart disturbances within us. While heart disturbances can differ, each of us has to deal with whatever disturbances come up for us. They are a normal part of the spiritual war. It involves surrendering to the Lord as He works to transform your heart disturbances to peace during the trial, regardless of the outcome of the trial.

WHAT WOULD YOUR TYPICAL HEART DISTURBANCE BE IF YOU WERE ___ IN THIS SITUATION OR ONE LIKE IT?

At this point in the study, avoid focusing on what the Biblical character *should* have felt, wanted or done. Again, get into the trial situation and write the heart disturbance(s) you would experience by filling in the blanks as you listen to the AUDIO. Imagine the trial actually happening to you. **Identify your own heart disturbance in order to transition from the Biblical character and focus on how Satan would attack you were you in the trial.**

1. We (the authors) have found that making the effort to verbalize heart disturbances clearly, at least to ourselves, helps train us to be more aware of them in a trial. Again, this part of the lesson is "fill in the blank." The formats provided help you to verbalize the connection between your inner heart disturbance and the external aspects of the trial. (The format we use for expressing heart disturbances is very similar to how Jacob responds to Laban in Genesis 31:31.)

   a. *Identify feelings: I'd feel _____ because _____.*
   b. *Identify desires: I would/would not want _____ because _____.*

2. Each person should write down their own heart disturbance(s). If your group has a facilitator, the facilitator can write one from each participant (as they are willing) on a board or butcher paper. Write the person's name or initial by the heart disturbance they shared. This will help you when working through the DISCERN/OBSERVE section later as a group.

3. When it comes to heart disturbances you **feel**, we recommend you reference the list of feelings (on page 23) to help you express these. Additionally, many times we don't say, "I feel...." People sometimes don't like to use the word *feel,* maybe in part because it can seem so unintelligent, immature, or emotional. So, we often express ourselves by sayings things like, "I am ___ (mad, sad, etc.)." We might say, "If that happened to me, I'd be ___ (upset, etc.)."

   Regardless of how we express ourselves in terms of heart disturbances, the fact is we experience them and they influence us greatly in trials. The key is first to discern them, and then (later in the lesson) let God work to transform them to peace. When trying to identify what is going on in your heart during the lessons, discipline yourselves to stick with the example formats provided.

4. When working to express heart disturbances involving **desires**, you simply have to be honest with yourself before God about what you would want or not want in the trial. Remember, Satan tries to get us to deny, even to ourselves, what we want and don't want. Use your heart to discern what the Spirit indicates to you about those denials.

5. Appendix 3: Authors' Examples (starting on page 229) lists heart disturbances that different participants (including the authors) shared when going through this part of the study. The examples are intended to give you an *idea* of the direction of this part of the study. Again, your heart disturbances may be the same, or they may be different. Write down your own so that later in the lesson you can work to open yourself to what God's Spirit will reveal to you about patterns in *you* when Satan is trying to tempt you in your trials.

6. Finally, while you actually work to verbalize the heart disturbances *you* might experience in the trial, don't judge or analyze them right now. Just state them clearly. Later in the DISCERN/OBSERVE part of the study you will be challenged to work on discerning what steps of faith God would want you to take as He works to change and transform you through the trial situation.

DISCERN/OBSERVE:

This final half of the study template is the piece that focuses both on practicing discerning God's Spirit and making observations about your trials. Everyone in your small group must have the opportunity to share what they come up with, as they are comfortable.

Again, use Appendix 3: Authors' Examples (starting pg. 229) as needed. All the lessons we (the authors) studied were accompanied with lively and rewarding discussions; we hope you experience this too.

The DISCERN/OBSERVE portion has a couple parts:

1. *Discern Fleshly Tendencies.* In part you will use the questions in the Special Consideration on pg. 33. The goal is simply to open yourself to discerning this from the Spirit. When you do, write down any thoughts, actions or inactions that the trial brings up for you, but which are likely of the flesh in some way.

2. *Discern Lying Belief.* In this part you will be using the exercise on pg. 24. The idea is to use that exercise to assist you in discerning the Lying Belief, which will look like one of the simple statements listed above that exercise on the same page. Don't be surprised if the same one or two Lying Beliefs come up over and over for you as you go through the lessons. This is actually normal. You will find that each person tends to get tempted by just one or two primary Lying Beliefs. As you go through the lessons, in time one of the things the Spirit will help you discern is a pattern in Satan's attacks against you.

3. *Discern and Feel the Truth of Your Identity in Christ.* Your identity in Christ is already true; the point is to *feel* it with your heart! Detach yourself from the external situation long enough to focus on the Lord and who you are in relationship to Him.

    Look at the Lying Belief the Holy Spirit revealed to you. Now, using the four characteristics of your identity in Christ (starting pg. 14), select the one characteristic which seems to be the key one that God is trying to help you embrace in the trial. Don't overthink it or reason why the one you're thinking of picking is "THE Right One!" Just use your heart to discern which one you feel the Spirit is pointing you to.

    Again, don't be surprised if the same one comes up over and over for you as you go through the lessons. This too is normal. Just as there are patterns of the flesh, there are corresponding patterns in God's guidance to us.

    Describe feeling who you are in Christ using names and pronouns describing *only* you and the Lord.
    - **What it _doesn't_ look like**: "Lord, I know You will help me say the right thing to ___ (whoever)," or, "I know I am not alone because the Bible says so."
    - **Also what it _doesn't_ look like**: "I know that I am good enough in You and You will support me in getting __ (whatever)."

AN EXAMPLE OF FEELING IDENTITY IN CHRIST

I feel calm because You are working in me. I feel unencumbered because I know You want to transform me. I feel strengthened because in You I have everything I need. I feel calm because there is nothing that I can do that You cannot do with greater power and love through me. I feel protected and accepting because You have a plan to use me in this trial.

Each lesson offers examples of feeling one's identity in Christ. You can find these in Appendix 3 (starting pg. 229).

4. *Discern What The Lord Would Seek to Change in You to Transform Your Heart Disturbances So You Experience the Peace of God.* Work to open yourself to the Holy Spirit so He can reveal to you what God would seek to change and transform in you. Discern what the Lord seeks to change in you based on what you wrote in the "DISCERN FLESHLY TENDENCIES..." part of the study.

To work on this, look for the change or transformation God would be trying to make in you were you the one in the trial being studied. Areas of change can include[29]:

- Change your behaviors (primary internal, not just external)
- Change your attitude
- Change your sensitivity (more Christ-like sensitivity to others/self or less fleshly sensitivity to others/self, etc.)
- Change your preferences
- Change your opinions, thinking, or point of view

Special Consideration: When you are opening your heart to discerning what the Holy Spirit would reveal to you about how the Lord seeks to change you, be careful. You don't want to fall into thinking that the purpose of embracing how He seeks to change you is just to make your problems go away. The purpose is to change and transform you as part of connecting you to your true identity in Christ, regardless of how the trial turns out. Embracing the way God works to transform you is part of how you surrender to letting God live through you. It is how you let God connect you to Him as your Source. This does not, in any way, guarantee that the Lord is going to eliminate the problem you face. One of the things I try to remember is this: if God

---

[29] *Feelings 101: Pain to Peace 2nd Edition*, William J. Clark, Jr. with CH (COL) William J. Clark, Ret., 2013, Keys To Understanding Life Series, pg. 163, used with permission

doesn't deliver me from a situation, then His desire is to sustain me and live through me in that situation… the issue is whether I'll let Him transform me so that He can do so. Always leave the outcome of the trial to Him; remember, He sees more than we see. This is handled best by inclining your heart to Him, out of love for the Lord.

5. *Discern Possible Steps of Faith; Observe Things About Your Life, Spiritual Battles, and What to Expect in Trials.* This part starts by discerning the step or steps of faith that you discern God would want of you, were you in the trial.

When you are seeking to discern possible steps of faith, it is really important to remain centered in your identity in Christ. So, if a heart disturbance arises while you are trying to discern the steps of faith, take a pause and go back to feeling the truth of your identity in Christ. When your heart disturbance is replaced by His peace again then continue here.

WRITE DOWN POSSIBLE STEPS OF FAITH YOU DISCERN FROM THE HOLY SPIRIT

Below are some good questions to ask while seeking to discern the following about God's steps of faith for you:
- Is God's Spirit revealing to me that I allow Christ to live through me by **listening** to someone else, by **asking** questions, by **clarifying** something, by seeking to **learn** something I need to learn, by **apologizing**, by **stating** something, and/or by **doing** something?

The steps of faith God has for you will challenge you to demonstrate your willingness to embrace the change(s) He seeks to make in you. There is a relationship between the changes He seeks to make in you and the steps of faith you should take. Look back at the change(s) you discerned that God seeks to make in you, with that in your heart, ask yourself:

- How does God want me to show my willingness to embrace this change in the trial?

If the trial situation involves a step of faith where you might have to speak to someone, ask yourself this:

- How does the Lord want me to handle the situation if the other person does not receive/accept what I say, do or avoid doing?

FINAL OBSERVATIONS

The last part of this section involves looking for insights into your experience of the trial you studied. The Holy Spirit may also give you insights into trials in general. Think about what your study of the trial reveals to you about your life and trials, about the nature of your trials, or about what you can expect to face when Satan attacks you in trials. There are two ways to do this:

A Common and Accurate Observation
(but not the kind you are seeking in this kind of Bible Study)

EXAMPLE: Abraham lied (sinned) out of fear that Abimelech might kill him.

A More Personal and Practical Observation
(basically just try to express your insights as they relate to you)

EXAMPLE: Sometimes I act in the flesh when I cling to fears or other heart disturbances. Fleshly behaviors come out when I resist how God wants to transform me during my trials. I must pay attention to my heart and allow the Lord to change me during trials.

EVENTS AFTER THIS LESSON AND BEFORE THE NEXT:
This final part of a lesson is pretty straightforward.
- It is a summary of the main events, recorded in the Bible, which happen between one Bible lessons' text and the next.
- The summary may tell the rest of the story for the trial you studied. Refrain from referring to this information *during* the study as it describes events that happen *after*, i.e., that haven't happened yet for the people whose trial you are studying.

- If there is some particularly key information in this summary that relates to the next lesson, it is typically reiterated in the CONTEXT section of the next lesson. However, to ensure a more fluid experience from one lesson to the next, we recommend you read this summary as part of preparing for the next lesson.

LESSON 1: GENESIS 2:15-3:7 SPIRITUAL WARFARE FROM THE VERY BEGINNING (EVE)

For a step-by-step approach to getting started
with this first Bible Study lesson, refer to page 39.

Let's briefly summarize what is recorded in the Bible prior to the first recorded trial for mankind:
1. Genesis 1 – First six days of creation.
2. Genesis 2:1-2 – The seventh day of creation.
3. Genesis 2:3-14 – A more detailed account of God creating man and planting "a garden in the east, in Eden;" also includes a description of the rivers within the garden.

The Garden of Eden is sometimes compared to heaven. A big difference between the two is that Satan was in Eden, but he won't be in heaven! Still, God's creation was "good." A theme that begins in this lesson, and which is reiterated throughout the other lessons, is that God created us in the midst of the spiritual war between Him and Satan. God's intent was NOT that we should sin or fall to sin. It was, however, God's will for us to be exposed to the deceptions and temptations of Satan (the flesh), starting in the Garden of Eden.

No matter how great or small, every single trial we face takes place in the context of the greater spiritual war between God and Satan. This means that our decision-making processes must be accompanied by a recognition that God's idea of what is *best* is not based on what is always safe and secure, or which ensures we are always going to live "the American dream." Our challenge, as children of God, is to discern His will for us in a given trial, and to love Him enough to let Him respond to the trial through us, even when doing so goes against what the flesh would want or desire.

Eve is the first recorded person to have to deal with the powerful and hard-to-see deceptions of Satan. To us, Eve's trial may seem easy to recognize because God's will was pretty clear. Let's NOT assume Eve was an idiot, or that she acted independently of God because she didn't care. Let's assume Eve did care, that she was smart, but that Satan's deceptions were actually quite deceptive to Eve.

It is important to notice the spiritual dynamics within Eve. Temptation, her heart's disturbances, and her reasons and chain of reasoning are examples of those dynamics. We've experienced similar stuff in our own trials too! The things we experience at the onset of our trials influence us. Our interpretation of those experiences will be based on Satan's deceptive logic, unless we stay dependent on the Lord. We have to submit to Him as He works to transform our hearts to peace during the trial. While Eve's trial may seem "simple," remember that Satan's deception is always the hardest to recognize for the person who is experiencing it!

SCRIPTURE SUMMARY: Genesis 2:15-3:7 – God puts man in the Garden of Eden to work and take care of it; instructions are given not to eat of the tree of knowledge of good and evil; God has Adam name the birds and beasts; God creates Eve; the serpent (the deceiver Satan) tempts (attacks) Eve (the first recorded human trial); Eve eats of the tree of knowledge of good and evil; Adam also eats.

CONTEXT:
Other Relevant Information:

In Genesis 3:6 there are three Hebrew Key Words related to Eve's heart disturbances (her desires and emotions).

> ***Genesis 3:6*** "When the woman saw that the tree was **good** for food, and that it was a **delight** to the eyes, and that the tree was **desirable** to make *one* wise, she took from its fruit and ate; and she gave also to her husband with her, and he ate." (**Bold** added)

1. The first Hebrew Key Word טוֹב is translated as **good** and can be understood to mean the fruit had good value as a food. [30] The word **good** can also mean the moral opposite of evil, meaning that in and of itself, the fruit was not evil.[31] The word

---

[30] Swanson, James: *Dictionary of Biblical Languages With Semantic Domains: Hebrew* (Old Testament). electronic ed. Oak Harbor: Logos Research Systems, Inc., 1997, G3202.
[31] Ibid.

good is not about Eve feeling good. Rather, it is simply a thought. However, this thought becomes part of the chain of reasoning Satan uses to trip Eve up as her trial progresses.[32]

2.   The Hebrew Key Word תאוה is translated into English as **delight**. It means "a longing, desire, craving, i.e. the state of having a wish or want for something for the pleasure it brings. It can be selfish or proper."[33] This **delight** is a thought followed by a feeling. This heart disturbance is a warning that Eve was being tempted. It indicates that Eve felt good; the fruit was a delight! She wanted the fruit in part because of how it made her feel. If Eve thought about NOT eating the fruit the feeling would change. She would have felt less pleasant. This indicates that her mind is also interpreting the good feeling as meaning that eating the fruit would be a good thing. So, not fulfilling her good and delightful desire would make her feel like she is accepting a "bad" situation. This is fleshly thinking at work.[34]

3.   The third Hebrew Key Word חמד translates into English as **desirable** and is a feeling.[35] Similar to **delight**, this heart disturbance tends to feel good the more a person's thinking justifies the **desirable** action! Eve saw the fruit as desirable for the purpose of making her wise. However, the idea behind "making one wise" inferred she lacks some degree of wisdom. Maybe she did, but Satan's deception was deeper. Eve's mind interpreted having a lack of wisdom as meaning who she was, as a person, was lacking. This Lying Belief was aimed against her deeper sense of identity as a child of God (she was already perfect and without sin).

Having wisdom isn't necessarily sinful; however, in Eve's trial, the real issue was about how she perceived herself as God

---

[32] *Feelings 101: Pain to Peace 2nd Edition*, William J. Clark, Jr. with CH (COL) William J. Clark, Ret., 2013, Keys To Understanding Life Series, pg. 112, modified with permission.

[33] Swanson, James: *Dictionary of Biblical Languages With Semantic Domains: Hebrew* (Old Testament). electronic ed. Oak Harbor: Logos Research Systems, Inc., 1997, G9294.

[34] *Feelings 101: Pain to Peace 2nd Edition*, William J. Clark, Jr. with CH (COL) William J. Clark, Ret., 2013, Keys To Understanding Life Series, pg. 112, modified with permission.

[35] Swanson, James: *Dictionary of Biblical Languages With Semantic Domains: Hebrew* (Old Testament). electronic ed. Oak Harbor: Logos Research Systems, Inc., 1997, G2773.

created her! Again, Satan's deception involves the feeling that not fulfilling her "good" desire would be the same as accepting a "bad" situation. Accepting that she might not "be wise" wouldn't feel as good to Eve (or us for that matter) unless something in her changed! Therefore, God transforming her heart and mind was required in order to avoid sin. The main point here is that Eve's desire for wisdom is built on fleshly thinking and a Lying Belief: the idea that she is less or that she lacks in something. Eve slipped into believing she was lacking as God created her, probably without discerning God's truth about her. Eve was not lacking (and in Christ we aren't lacking either)! Satan lured Eve into acting independently of God by influencing her thoughts.[36]

WHO IS INVOLVED IN Eve's TRIAL (Main Players Only)?
God, Satan, Eve

WHAT DECISION(S) MUST Eve MAKE?
1. Obviously Eve has to make a decision of whether to eat or not eat the fruit of the tree of knowledge of good and evil in the Garden of Eden.
2. However, to make that decision, Eve will first decide whether to attempt to handle the situation on her own (independently of God), or whether to seek out God for clarification and help (remaining dependent on God).

WHAT KNOWLEDGE OF GOD COULD Eve HAVE HAD TO ASSIST HER TO ACT AS GOD WANTS?
The Bible doesn't record whether Eve's knowledge of God was being passed on to her by Adam, or whether God personally reiterated some things to her. Still, she does say certain things which indicate she did know certain things about what God wanted.

---

[36] *Feelings 101: Pain to Peace 2nd Edition*, William J. Clark, Jr. with CH (COL) William J. Clark, Ret., 2013, Keys To Understanding Life Series, pg. 112, modified with permission.

1. V. 3:2 – God implied they could eat of the tree of life, although apparently Adam and Eve had not done so.
2. V. 3:3 – Eve knew that God said don't eat of the tree of knowledge of good and evil.
3. V. 3:3 – Eve knew that God said that if they did eat, they would die.
4. Eve probably knew she was a helpmate to Adam.

WHAT WAS Eve's HEART DISTURBANCE?
(See how others responded to the rest of the lesson – pg. 229)

DID Eve SUBMIT TO THE LORD TRANSFORMING HER HEART AND MIND SO THE LORD COULD LIVE THROUGH HER?

PUT YOURSELF IN Eve's "SHOES" BY LISTENING TO THE AUDIO (Go to www.Feelings102.com to get or play the AUDIO)

WHAT WOULD YOUR TYPICAL HEART DISTURBANCE BE IF YOU WERE Eve IN THIS SITUATION OR ONE LIKE IT?
(You can use the list of heart disturbances on page 23)

I'd feel _____ *because* _____

_____

I'd feel _____ *because* _____

_____

I would/would not want _____

because _____

DISCUSSION QUESTIONS:
1. What is so significant about heart disturbances (feelings, emotions, and/or desires)?

2. What did Eve believe in her heart?

3. How do we know when what we believe in our hearts is actually godly?

DISCERN/OBSERVE:
Discern Fleshly Tendencies (refer to Special Consideration on pg. 33)

Discern Lying Belief (refer to Special Consideration on pg. 24)

_____.

Discern and Feel the Truth of Your Identity in Christ (Discern one of the four starting pg. 14. Feel it! Use the feeling words on pg. 27.Write how it feels using "I feel ___ because ___. An example is on pg. 58.)

Discern What The Lord Would Seek to Change in You to Transform Your Heart Disturbances So You Experience the Peace of God. [For example in your behaviors (internal too, not just external), attitude, preferences, opinions, thinking, point of view, or sensitivity (i.e., more Christ-like sensitivity to others/self or less fleshly sensitivity to others/self, etc.).]

Discern Possible Steps of Faith (refer to pg. 60); Observe Things About Your Life, Spiritual Battles, and What to Expect in Trials.

EVENTS AFTER THIS LESSON AND BEFORE THE NEXT:
None.

LESSON 2: GENESIS 2:15-3:7 CHOOSING BETWEEN GOD AND MY WIFE… THIS IS GONNA HURT (ADAM)

This lesson examines the same passage as in Lesson 1, but from Adam's perspective. While the Bible does not specifically record any heart disturbances for Adam, putting ourselves in Adam's shoes can reveal some of the challenges of cooperating with God's transformation processes. We know that in the end Adam sinned. But, what would Adam have to allow God to do with his heart in order to not sin? What would Adam have needed to be willing to face in order to NOT eat of the fruit? These hard questions can help us see what God sometimes may challenge us to be willing to embrace in our own lives and trials! They can also help us see how difficult it is to deal with Satan's attacks, as well as with the sacrifices we may have to make to let the Lord live through us, so we don't act independently of God.

SCRIPTURE SUMMARY: Genesis 2:15-3:7 – God puts Adam in the Garden of Eden to work and take care of it; instructions are given concerning not eating of the tree of knowledge of good and evil; God has Adam name the birds and beasts; God creates Eve; the serpent (great deceiver Satan) tempts (attacks) Eve in the first recorded human trial in the Bible; Eve eats of the tree of knowledge of good and evil, then Adam also eats.

CONTEXT: See CONTEXT from Lesson 1 (Eve's perspective).

WHO IS INVOLVED IN Adam's TRIAL (Main Players Only)?
God, Satan, Adam, Eve

WHAT DECISION(S) MUST Adam MAKE?
Adam has to decide whether to eat the fruit of the tree of knowledge of good and evil in the Garden of Eden. His decision is likely complicated by the fact that Eve has already eaten of the fruit.

WHAT KNOWLEDGE OF GOD COULD Adam HAVE HAD TO ASSIST HIM TO ACT AS GOD WANTS?
1. V. 2:16 – Adam knew the fruit God made was good for food.
2. V. 2:16-17 – God indicated they could eat of the tree of life, although apparently Adam and Eve had not done so.
3. V. 2:18 – God said Eve was to be Adam's helper.
4. V. 3:3 – Adam knew that God said not to eat of the tree of knowledge of good and evil.
5. V. 3:3 – Adam knew that God said that if they did eat of the tree of knowledge of good and evil, they would die.

WHAT WAS Adam's HEART DISTURBANCE?
(See how others responded to the rest of the lesson – pg. 233)

DID Adam SUBMIT TO THE LORD TRANSFORMING HIS HEART AND MIND SO THE LORD COULD LIVE THROUGH HIM?

PUT YOURSELF IN Adam's "SHOES" – LISTEN TO THE AUDIO (Go to www.Feelings102.com to get or play the AUDIO)

WHAT WOULD YOUR TYPICAL HEART DISTURBANCE BE IF YOU WERE Adam IN THIS SITUATION OR ONE LIKE IT?
(You can use the list of heart disturbances on page 23)

I'd feel _____ *because* _____

_____

I'd feel _____ *because* _____

_____

I would/would not want _____

because _____

DISCERN/OBSERVE:
Discern Fleshly Tendencies (refer to Special Consideration on pg. 33)

Discern Lying Belief (refer to Special Consideration on pg. 24)

_____.

Discern and Feel the Truth of Your Identity in Christ (Discern one of the four starting pg. 14. Feel it! Use the feeling words on pg. 27. Write how it feels using "I feel ___ because ___. An example is on pg. 58.)

Discern What The Lord Would Seek to Change in You to Transform Your Heart Disturbances So You Experience the Peace of God. [For example in your behaviors (internal too, not just external), attitude, preferences, opinions, thinking, point of view, or sensitivity (i.e., more Christ-like sensitivity to others/self or less fleshly sensitivity to others/self, etc.).]

Discern Possible Steps of Faith (refer to pg. 60); Observe Things About Your Life, Spiritual Battles, and What to Expect in Trials.

EVENTS AFTER THIS LESSON AND BEFORE THE NEXT:
1. Genesis 3:8-13 – God has Adam and Eve explain being afraid of being naked.
2. Genesis 3:14-15 – God speaks to the serpent (Satan) and foretells the offspring (Christ) of a woman, who will crush Satan's head.
3. Genesis 3:16 – God speaks to Eve mentioning the difficulty of childbirth and the relationship between wives and husbands.
4. Genesis 3:17-19 – God speaks to Adam mentioning the challenges of work and the introduction of death.
5. Genesis 3:20-24 – Adam names his wife Eve (up to this point she has simply been called woman); God makes garments for the couple and banishes them from the Garden of Eden; God puts a cherubim and flaming sword to guard the way to the tree of life.

LESSON 3: GENESIS 4:1-8A TEMPTATION AND MASTERING SIN (CAIN)

Cain's trial can sometimes be a hard one with which to identify, particularly if we approach the trial strictly focused on the external aspects of Cain's anger at Abel or the act of murder. The underlying spiritual dynamics involve Satan deceiving Cain in such a way that Cain minimizes, or at least overlooks, the issue that is between him and God concerning his unaccepted sacrifice. As a result, Cain himself gets caught up in his dispute with Abel and then acts independently of God. That is how Satan's deception gets us sidetracked with our external circumstances. The fleshly thinking is so powerful that, even when we know what God might be trying to do through us, we don't take the time to go inward and accept how God is trying to change us and transform our hearts and minds.

While you might not commit murder in similar circumstances, most of us would probably do or say something were we upset and in the same situation as Cain; we all have before! If you can identify a recent trial in which you knew what God wanted you to do, but you just couldn't manage it, then you know how tough it can be to "master sin." We can't do that without full dependence on the Lord. Focus on the part of your flesh that resists being changed in a trial. Study that dynamic, so that you will be better prepared to do your part in accepting God changing your heart and mind in your trials.

SCRIPTURE SUMMARY: Genesis 4:1-8a – Cain is tempted to reject God's rejection of his offering. Then Cain is tempted to project his heart disturbance on Abel. Cain goes to talk with Abel before he submitted to the Lord and let Him transform his heart and mind.

CONTEXT:
Other Relevant Information: There is a Hebrew Key Word **master** (as in to master sin) in V. 7. The word is לִמְשָׁל and it means "rule, govern,

control, be in charge."[37] God tells Cain he must rule and exercise authority over sin. Clearly this can't be accomplished apart from submission to the Lord with the heart. Our part of being dependent on the Lord involves submitting to the changes He works to make in us so as to transform the heart disturbance to peace during the trial. This is the aspect of "mastering sin" that we, like Cain, often find challenging to surrender to. That challenge centers literally on the temptation to act independently of God.

WHO IS INVOLVED IN Cain's TRIAL (Main Players Only)?
God, Satan, Cain, Abel

WHAT DECISION(S) MUST Cain MAKE?
Cain has to decide how he will deal with his feelings (heart disturbance) about God rejecting his sacrifice and accepting Abel's sacrifice. Cain also has to decide whether God says he is ready to talk with Abel, meaning without anger in his heart.

WHAT KNOWLEDGE OF GOD COULD Cain HAVE HAD TO ASSIST HIM TO ACT AS GOD WANTS?
1. V. 3 – Cain knew about God and about the importance of making offerings to Him.
2. V. 5 – Cain knew (or was learning) that the physical act of making an offering to the Lord wasn't enough. The heart and mind had to reflect the spirit and purpose of the offering.
3. V. 5 – Cain knew God saw that his heart and mind were not right.
4. V .6-7 – Cain knew that a trial involved making a choice and it involved submitting to God transforming him and then living through him.
5. V. 7 – Cain was told that being right with God in a trial hinges on mastery of sin in that trial.

---

[37] Swanson, James: *Dictionary of Biblical Languages With Semantic Domains: Hebrew* (Old Testament). electronic ed. Oak Harbor: Logos Research Systems, Inc., 1997, G5440.

6. Cain may have learned from his parents (Adam and Eve) about Satan's temptation in the Garden of Eden:

WHAT WAS Cain's HEART DISTURBANCE?
(See how others responded to the rest of the lesson – pg. 237)

DID Cain SUBMIT TO THE LORD TRANSFORMING HIS HEART AND MIND SO THE LORD COULD LIVE THROUGH HIM?

Special Consideration:

Before listening to the AUDIO, let's address an important aspect of this trial. God seeks to communicate to unbelievers and ungodly people. Each trial they experience gives them the opportunity to discern the path God would have them on. By seeking God's will and letting Him transform them in the trial at hand, God will use that godly choice to lead them in the direction which brings them to Him. This is part of what is implied when God tells Cain that he must "master sin," a task that cannot be done without dependence on God. So by making the choice God would have of them, even "ungodly" people have the opportunity to surrender to God and *continue* making choices that submit to His lead. In time, this can lead them to embrace the relationship with God that He hopes they will want. This is actually part of what makes everyone accountable to God. Even unbelievers have made *some* choices out of a dependence on God. If they learn from those choices, they have proof by their own actions of the importance of a relationship with God in which they are dependent on Him!

With that in mind, it is profitable to study Cain's trial in terms of putting yourself in his situation and seeking the perspective from which he has the opportunity to let God live through him so that the flesh is overcome. We know that God's will is for Cain's heart to change. But, for that to happen, Cain would have to deny his own fleshly tendency. Cain would have to be open to how God seeks to change him. Cain has to actively accept God's correction and let God live through him so that sin is mastered in this trial! If we were in Cain's situation, the question is, "Would we be willing to discern when God is telling us we are not letting Him live through us?!" Even though Cain later becomes a murderer, the profitable lesson comes from *focusing on the fact that the challenge to master sin during our trials* is a challenge we share in common with Cain! As you listen to the AUDIO, put yourself in the moments of Cain's choice between accepting that he is messing up or seeing himself as being put to shame in comparison with Abel! Remember, as believers, we are to seek out God's discipline and loving correction!

PUT YOURSELF IN Cain's "SHOES" – LISTEN TO THE AUDIO (Go to www.Feelings102.com to get or play the AUDIO)

WHAT WOULD YOUR TYPICAL HEART DISTURBANCE BE IF YOU WERE Cain IN THIS SITUATION OR ONE LIKE IT?
(You can use the list of heart disturbances on page 23)

I'd feel _____ *because* _____

_____

I'd feel _____ *because* _____

_____

I would/would not want _____

because _____

DISCERN/OBSERVE:
Discern Fleshly Tendencies (refer to Special Consideration on pg. 33)

Discern Lying Belief (refer to Special Consideration on pg. 24)

_____.

Discern and Feel the Truth of Your Identity in Christ (Discern one of the four starting pg. 14. Feel it! Use the feeling words on pg. 27. Write how it feels using "I feel ___ because ___. An example is on pg. 58.)

Discern What The Lord Would Seek to Change in You to Transform Your Heart Disturbances So You Experience the Peace of God. [For example in your behaviors (internal too, not just external), attitude, preferences, opinions, thinking, point of view, or sensitivity (i.e., more Christ-like sensitivity to others/self or less fleshly sensitivity to others/self, etc.).]

Discern Possible Steps of Faith (refer to pg. 60); Observe Things About Your Life, Spiritual Battles, and What to Expect in Trials.

DISCUSSION QUESTIONS:

1. What does it mean "to master sin?"

2. How do we "master sin?"

EVENTS AFTER THIS LESSON AND BEFORE THE NEXT:

1. Genesis 4:8b-16 – Cain kills Abel. God talking with Cain in the aftermath of Abel's murder.
2. Genesis 4:17-26 – Cain's family line; Adam and Eve's perspective on why God allows them to have Seth.
3. Genesis 5 – Adam's family line through Seth to Noah; Noah is 500 years old.
4. Genesis 6:1-2 – Number of people on the earth increases.

LESSON 4: GENESIS 6:3-21 WHAT WILL MY FAMILY THINK? (NOAH)

One of the challenges in listening to God is that there are times when He doesn't give us physical evidence that we can show to someone else to prove that we aren't just making up what we believe God wants to do through us! However, the Holy Spirit can help us double-check ourselves when trying to determine God's will for us in a specific trial. God's Spirit works to comfort us so that we let God transform our hearts and minds whenever Satan (the flesh) tries to make us fearful or doubt God's direction. This lesson focuses on how hearing God sometimes means we can't have physical evidence. This is a common aspect of trials. In many ways this is spiritually "normal!"

In this lesson's trial, we know specifically what God's will was: Noah must build the ark. God's will for Noah is going to seriously affect his family's standing in the neighborhood. It will totally change their livelihood, how they spend their time, what their priorities are... in short, it will change everything! We don't know exactly how Noah's wife reacted at first. Regardless, if I had to tell my family that we were called upon to do something that went against their expectations of what life was going to be like, they'd probably freak out! They'd want proof it is God's will. Therein is the trial.

Unfortunately, others may not always share what we've discerned God is trying to do through us. Look at Noah's trial from that perspective. Noah and his wife had lived together a long time when all of a sudden God revealed a pretty big plan. It can happen at any point in life. Remember, Satan's deceptions work to get us comfortable living with some sense of normalcy. So, when God communicates that something significant must change, we and our families are challenged to fight any follow-on spiritual battles in complete dependence on the Lord. We must be prepared to fight them in Christ quickly, as His humble and obedient servants!

SCRIPTURE SUMMARY: Genesis 6:3-21 – Noah has to contend with doing what God has told him to do for at least 85-120 years before there is "tangible proof" (that his family and others can see) to show that Noah's "hearing" of God's will was correct.

CONTEXT:
Other Relevant Information:

1. When we believe God wants to do some work through us, it is because we let God convict us in our hearts. Often there is no physical "sign;" we often have only the "knowledge of our hearts." Satan's temptations and attacks can challenge us to lose faith and waiver when there is no tangible evidence to corroborate that what is happening is actually God's will, especially if the work is not financially rewarding or comes at some other great cost! Most worldly people are not comfortable with working toward a goal that is based on anticipating some distant future event, especially if there is no physical proof or no other practical use for the work. (What practical use would the ark have been without a flood?)

2. Noah had to be steadfast in the steps of faith God expected of him during the preparation time required before God would bring His plan (the flood) to fruition. If Noah waivered, perhaps the ark would not have been built. Noah's faith had to be dependent on God for at least 85-120 years without any tangible evidence of the coming flood, other than the wickedness which he might have seen in others' hearts.

3. There are different views of the time it actually took Noah to build the ark. Some see V. 3 as implying the time was 120 years. Perhaps it was, but regardless, the time was at least 85-120 years. The reference to 85 years is a very conservative time estimate. It is based on the idea that Noah might not have gone far in building the ark until he got help from his boys once they became teenagers.

4. Genesis 5:32 – Noah was 500 years old when he has his sons (who God provided to help build the ark).

5. Genesis 7:11 – Noah was 600 years old when the flood came.

6. Genesis 6:9 – The beginning of Noah's account tells us that Noah had three sons. The account continues with how it came to be that God informed Noah of the flood and ark.

7. With that in mind, let's relate the roughly 100 years of Noah's work into what that would be like for us today. Noah's lifespan was 950 years. Let's assume a person today lives to be 80 years old. This would be the equivalent of us having to work and wait for 8½ years for God to bring his plan to fulfillment. That's a long time to be faithful without any physical evidence that God will honor the work He might ask us to do! Discerning the Spirit's guidance on how to let God work through us is important! Not something we want to mess up!

WHO IS INVOLVED IN Noah's TRIAL (Main Players Only)?
God, Satan, Noah, Noah's family, "Men of Renown," "sons of God," "Evil Men"

WHAT DECISION(S) MUST Noah MAKE?
Noah had to decide whether God really wanted him to build an ark knowing that the decision would dramatically affect the social pressure on him and his family for the years it would take to build it.

WHAT KNOWLEDGE OF GOD COULD Noah HAVE HAD TO ASSIST HIM TO ACT AS GOD WANTS?
1. V. 9 – Noah knew he had a relationship with God.
2. V. 9 – Noah knew he was different from other people and that his lifestyle reflected his relationship with God.
3. V. 13 – Noah knew what God wanted to do through him.
4. V. 13 – Noah knew the world would be destroyed.
5. V. 9:8-17 – Noah knew God promised to establish a covenant with him, although he would not know what that entire covenant would involve until later, after the flood was over.

WHAT WAS Noah's HEART DISTURBANCE?
(See how others responded to the rest of the lesson – pg. 241)

DID Noah SUBMIT TO THE LORD TRANSFORMING HIS HEART AND MIND SO THE LORD COULD LIVE THROUGH HIM?

PUT YOURSELF IN Noah's "SHOES" – LISTEN TO THE AUDIO (Go to www.Feelings102.com to get or play the AUDIO)

WHAT WOULD YOUR TYPICAL HEART DISTURBANCE BE IF YOU WERE Noah IN THIS SITUATION OR ONE LIKE IT?
(You can use the list of heart disturbances on page 23)

I'd feel _____ *because* _____

_____

I'd feel _____ *because* _____

_____

I would/would not want _____

because _____

DISCERN/OBSERVE:
Discern Fleshly Tendencies (refer to Special Consideration on pg. 33)

Discern Lying Belief (refer to Special Consideration on pg. 24)

_____.

Discern and Feel the Truth of Your Identity in Christ (Discern one of the four starting pg. 14. Feel it! Use the feeling words on pg. 27. Write how it feels using "I feel ___ because ___. An example is on pg. 58.)

Discern What The Lord Would Seek to Change in You to Transform Your Heart Disturbances So You Experience the Peace of God. [For example in your behaviors (internal too, not just external), attitude, preferences, opinions, thinking, point of view, or sensitivity (i.e., more Christ-like sensitivity to others/self or less fleshly sensitivity to others/self, etc.).]

Discern Possible Steps of Faith (refer to pg. 60); Observe Things About Your Life, Spiritual Battles, and What to Expect in Trials.

EVENTS AFTER THIS LESSON AND BEFORE THE NEXT:
1. Genesis 6:22 – Noah did everything God told him to do.
2. Genesis 7 – Noah and family go into the ark and the earth is flooded.
3. Genesis 8 – Flood recedes and Noah emerges from the ark.
4. Genesis 9 – This is a record of what happens from God's covenant with Noah up through Noah's death.
5. Genesis 10 – Family lines of Noah's sons; "nations" that emerge from Noah's sons.
6. Genesis 11 – Tower of Babel; multiple languages scatter peoples of the world; Noah's family line through Shem to Terah (Abram's father); introduction of Abram and Sarai; Terah moves the family from Ur to Haran.

LESSON 5: GENESIS 12:1-4 TIME TO MOVE! (ABRAM)

This lesson is the first of several trials related to Abram (later called Abraham) and Sarai (later called Sarah). Hebrews 11 says that both Abram and Sarai were persons of faith. What we see in their lives is that they experienced lots of trials. As they took steps of faith with God, He transformed their hearts and minds in many of their trials. In other trials, they did not discern Satan's deception against them, and they failed to master sin through dependence on God. With this lesson, try to start looking for Satan's likely attack/temptation/deception as you study their stories. We'll look more at patterns in Satan's attacks in Lesson 7.

SCRIPTURE SUMMARY: Genesis 12:1-4 – Abram lets God live through him. Abram's steps of faith involved moving his family again, but without knowing where they are going. Abram has no tangible proof to show his family that everything is going to work out.

CONTEXT:
Other Relevant Information: Abram's family already moved once... from Ur to Haran (about 675 miles). That was prior to God giving Abram the Promises.

WHO IS INVOLVED IN Abram's TRIAL (Main Players Only)?
God, Satan, Abram, Sarai

WHAT DECISION(S) MUST Abram MAKE?
Abram has to decide whether to move his family, and it is complicated by the fact that they would move away from most of their family, in addition to not knowing exactly where they are going!

WHAT KNOWLEDGE OF GOD COULD Abram HAVE HAD TO ASSIST HIM TO ACT AS GOD WANTS?
1. Genesis 11:30 – Abram knew his wife Sarai was barren and could not have children.
2. V. 1 – Abram knew God wanted him to leave his country (Haran), his people and his father's household.
3. V. 1 – Abram knew he was to move without knowing where he was moving to, and that God would tell him where to stop.
4. V. 2-3 – Abram knew God made three Promises:
   a. Personal – God will bless him and make his name great.
   b. National – God will make him into a great nation and his descendants would have their own land.
   c. Universal – God will bless all peoples on the earth through Abram.

WHAT WAS Abram's HEART DISTURBANCE?
(See how others responded to the rest of the lesson – pg. 244)

DID Abram SUBMIT TO THE LORD TRANSFORMING HIS HEART AND MIND SO THE LORD COULD LIVE THROUGH HIM?

PUT YOURSELF IN Abram's "SHOES" – LISTEN TO THE AUDIO (Go to www.Feelings102.com to get or play the AUDIO)

WHAT WOULD YOUR TYPICAL HEART DISTURBANCE BE IF YOU WERE Abram IN THIS SITUATION OR ONE LIKE IT? *(You can use the list of heart disturbances on page 23)*

I'd feel _____ *because* _____

_____

I'd feel _____ *because* _____

_____

I would/would not want _____

because _____

DISCERN/OBSERVE:
Discern Fleshly Tendencies (refer to Special Consideration on pg. 33)

Discern Lying Belief (refer to Special Consideration on pg. 24)

_____.

Discern and Feel the Truth of Your Identity in Christ (Discern one of the four starting pg. 14. Feel it! Use the feeling words on pg. 27. Write how it feels using "I feel ___ because ___. An example is on pg. 58.)

Discern What The Lord Would Seek to Change in You to Transform Your Heart Disturbances So You Experience the Peace of God. [For example in your behaviors (internal too, not just external), attitude, preferences, opinions, thinking, point of view, or sensitivity (i.e., more Christ-like sensitivity to others/self or less fleshly sensitivity to others/self, etc.).]

Discern Possible Steps of Faith (refer to pg. 60); Observe Things About Your Life, Spiritual Battles, and What to Expect in Trials.

DISCUSSION QUESTIONS: There are some challenges we have when it comes to giving over our freewill to God in trials that are especially troubling. Trials in the Bible can help us with those because there are often similarities between our trials and the trials we can study in the Bible. However, when we study God's written Word, one of the things we must always remember is that there are sometimes differences between things God promises us today versus what God promised someone in the Bible. These differences are very important to observe. They point to differences in the challenges we sometimes face in trials versus some of the challenges a person in the Bible faced.

1. What are some things God promised Abram and what are some things God promises us?
   a. Abram.

   b. Us.

2. When it comes to real-life situations, what are some differences between Abram's life and our lives?

    a. Abram.

    b. Us.

EVENTS AFTER THIS LESSON AND BEFORE THE NEXT:
None.

LESSON 6: GENESIS 12:1-4 TIME TO MOVE? (SARAI)

This lesson focuses on the same passage as the previous lesson, but from Sarai's perspective. While Abram may be certain that God wants them to move, there is no indication that Sarai had a direct confirmation of that from God. The step of faith that God challenges Sarai to have in responding to Abram gives Satan a big opportunity to create friction in the marriage relationship. When we put ourselves in Sarai's situation, we get a great chance to study a trial that is not unreasonable to consider may have occurred for Sarai. This lesson really offers the opportunity to discern from the Spirit ways in which Satan might try to influence you.

SCRIPTURE SUMMARY: Genesis 12:1-4 – Sarai faces moving again, but this time without knowing where they are going because her husband believes it is what God is doing through him.

CONTEXT: See CONTEXT from Lesson 5 (Abram's perspective).

WHO IS INVOLVED IN Sarai's TRIAL (Main Players Only)?
God, Satan, Sarai, Abram

WHAT DECISION(S) MUST Sarai MAKE?
Sarai has to decide how she is going to respond to a potentially emotional situation in which she will have to trust that God is working through her husband, Abram, with little or no confirmation of whether God is really behind Abram's leadership or not.

WHAT KNOWLEDGE OF GOD COULD Sarai HAVE HAD TO ASSIST HER TO ACT AS GOD WANTS?
1. The Bible doesn't tell us everything Sarai knew about God.
2. Sarai knew, from God's perspective, she was Abram's wife.
3. Sarai probably knew of the Promises, but that was likely second-hand through Abram. There is no record that God interacted directly with Sarai to confirm what her husband was telling her.

WHAT WAS Sarai's HEART DISTURBANCE?
(See how others responded to the rest of the lesson – pg. 249)

DID Sarai SUBMIT TO THE LORD TRANSFORMING HER HEART AND MIND SO THE LORD COULD LIVE THROUGH HER?

PUT YOURSELF IN Sarai's "SHOES" – LISTEN TO THE AUDIO (Go to www.Feelings102.com to get or play the AUDIO)

WHAT WOULD YOUR TYPICAL HEART DISTURBANCE BE IF YOU WERE Sarai IN THIS SITUATION OR ONE LIKE IT?
(You can use the list of heart disturbances on page 23)

I'd feel _____ *because* _____

_____

I'd feel _____ *because* _____

_____

I would/would not want _____

because _____

DISCERN/OBSERVE:
Discern Fleshly Tendencies (refer to Special Consideration on pg. 33)

Discern Lying Belief (refer to Special Consideration on pg. 24)

_____.

Discern and Feel the Truth of Your Identity in Christ (Discern one of the four starting pg. 14. Feel it! Use the feeling words on pg. 27.Write how it feels using "I feel ___ because ___. An example is on pg. 58.)

Discern What The Lord Would Seek to Change in You to Transform Your Heart Disturbances So You Experience the Peace of God. [For example in your behaviors (internal too, not just external), attitude, preferences, opinions, thinking, point of view, or sensitivity (i.e., more Christ-like sensitivity to others/self or less fleshly sensitivity to others/self, etc.).]

Discern Possible Steps of Faith (refer to pg. 60); Observe Things About Your Life, Spiritual Battles, and What to Expect in Trials.

EVENTS AFTER THIS LESSON AND BEFORE THE NEXT:
1. Genesis 12:5 – Sarai, Abram's nephew Lot, and all the possessions and people they had accumulated (servants, etc.) go with Abram from Haran. They arrive in Canaan.
2. Genesis 12:6-9 – Abram and family arrive near Shechem and the Canaanites are living in the land. The Lord tells Abram this land will be given to his offspring. Abram travels into the land a bit farther and sets up an altar to the Lord.

LESSON 7: GENESIS 12:10-20 HORRIBLE HUSBAND! (SARAI)

Perhaps you've faced a trial when you felt betrayed by a loved one. Satan really does a job on us in getting us riled up as well as in keeping us so preoccupied that we sometimes forget to seek out how God is trying to transform us. Nobody likes being mistreated or victimized. Still, sometimes we must face mistreatment and exercise restraint, just like Jesus did. The key is to embrace God's sanctifying and transforming process and to discern from Him if He's asking us to have faith and remain in a position that exposes us to such awful things. This can make it tough to have the faith to remain dependent on Him. Regardless of what God wants to do through you in the face of being betrayed or mistreated, such experiences are part of the spiritual war from time to time, and it is vital to let the Lord transform your heart and mind quickly!

We would likely have tough issues to deal with were we in this situation, though the Bible doesn't specifically say it was a trial for Sarai. As you listen to the AUDIO and put yourselves in Sarai's shoes, don't hold back in recognizing whatever disturbances arise in your heart. And, don't stop there! Put great effort into seeking to discern what God would want to change in you were you to experience this trial.

SCRIPTURE SUMMARY: Genesis 12:10-20 – Sarai likely faces a trial when Abram decides he will lie about her being his wife, in order to save himself from the potential threat of Pharaoh; Abram profits from the arrangement; Sarai is placed in a position for Pharaoh to court her as a "single woman."

CONTEXT:
Special Consideration About Identifying Patterns:

We know that Satan is involved in trials trying to trip us up. With some people described in Scripture we are given more information about a particular person's life and trials than we are for others. We have quite a bit of information regarding Abram's trials, and some of Sarai's. As we look at Abram's and Sarai's situation, one of the goals of the study is to try to discover patterns in Satan's attacks on them. The idea is to see the value of looking for patterns across many of their trials so that we might see that there are patterns in Satan's attacks against Christ in us. The Holy Spirit can reveal these to us concerning our own life trials.

This volume of *Feelings 102* looks at four trials specifically from Sarai's perspective (Lessons 6, 7, 12, 21). We can see patterns in Satan's attacks in those trials. However, there are six other lessons that focus on Abram's or Hagar's perspective, but which actually do, or could, involve trials for Sarai too (Lessons 8, 10, 11, 13, 16, 17). The point is that as we go along, the CONTEXT portion of lessons focusing on Sarai (later Sarah) will offer **possible** patterns in Satan's attacks against Sarai so that you can see them. Try to focus on identifying patterns Satan's attacks against you as you work the DISCERN/OBSERVE later in the lesson!

NOTE: the idea isn't about getting good at seeing patterns in other people's lives; rather it is about using God's written Word to help us be open to discerning (from the Spirit) the fleshly patterns in our lives! Let's take a look at the first pattern we can possibly recognize with Sarai. It comes from the last lesson (Lesson 6) and the potential trial she may have experienced when Abram and Sarai had to move without knowing where they were going. Just like it is with our patterns and trials, the pattern of Satan's attacks from Sarai's previous trials often become part of the CONTEXT in her next trial!

Patterns in Satan's past attacks (temptations) on Sarai, i.e., when they moved – Lesson 6 – NOTE that you will see additions to this list in **bold** as you go along through the lessons:

1. **Likely attack by Satan on Sarai in Genesis 12:1-4** – don't support moving without knowing where you are going – unknown whether she overcame Satan's attack.*

---

* The reason we (the authors) say it is unknown whether she overcame this likely

Other Relevant Information:

1. Genesis 20:12 tells us that Sarai is, in fact, Abram's half-sister.
2. Abram and Sarai had already moved once from Ur to Haran (about 675 miles). Haran was located roughly near the northern end of the Euphrates River on the border of modern day Turkey and Syria. Walking from Ur to Haran is like walking from New York to Indianapolis.
3. They moved from Haran, but without knowing where they were going, because Abram believed that's what God directed him to do.
4. When Abram and Sarai arrived in Canaan (400 miles from Haran), Abram was told it was the Promised Land. However, they had to turn right around and move to Egypt (another 300 miles) due to a famine in the region. Walking from Haran to Canaan (400 miles) is like walking from Chicago to Minneapolis. Walking from Canaan to Egypt (300 miles) is like walking from Miami to Tampa.
5. Genesis 12:5-9 – Abram and family begin traveling; God tells Abram that Canaan is the land He will give him.
6. Abram is 75 years old.

WHO IS INVOLVED IN Sarai's TRIAL (Main Players Only)?
God, Satan, Sarai, Abram, Pharaoh

WHAT DECISION(S) MUST Sarai MAKE?
Sarai has to decide whether or not to act as if she is Abram's sister, a "single woman." She will have to be convincing if Pharaoh is to believe she is a single woman! What does God want to do through her?!

WHAT KNOWLEDGE OF GOD COULD Sarai HAVE HAD TO ASSIST HER TO ACT AS GOD WANTS? (Additions to the list of Sarai's knowledge are shown in **bold**)

---

attack by Satan is because, while she went along with Abram, we don't know whether she was grumbling and complaining about the decision after it was made, or whether she accepted a godly supportive attitude.

1. The Bible doesn't tell us everything Sarai knew about God.
2. Sarai knew, from God's perspective, she was Abram's wife.
3. Sarai probably knew of the Promises, but that was likely second-hand through Abram. There is no record that God interacted directly with Sarai to confirm what her husband was telling her.
4. **Genesis 12:8 – Sarai probably knew when they arrived in the Promised Land because Abram worshipped the Lord there.**
5. **V. 11-13 – If Abram told Sarai of the Promises from God, Sarai could have figured out that God would have to protect Abram's life, if God is going to give Abram a son. From this, Sarai may have been able to conclude that Abram wouldn't have to lie because God would protect Abram.**

WHAT WAS Sarai's HEART DISTURBANCE?
(See how others responded to the rest of the lesson – pg. 251)

DID Sarai SUBMIT TO THE LORD TRANSFORMING HER HEART AND MIND SO THE LORD COULD LIVE THROUGH HER?

PUT YOURSELF IN Sarai's "SHOES" – LISTEN TO THE AUDIO (Go to www.Feelings102.com to get or play the AUDIO)

WHAT WOULD YOUR TYPICAL HEART DISTURBANCE BE IF YOU WERE Sarai IN THIS SITUATION OR ONE LIKE IT?
(You can use the list of heart disturbances on page 23)

I'd feel _____ *because* _____

_____

I'd feel _____ *because* _____

_____

I would/would not want _____

because _____

DISCUSSION QUESTIONS:

    1. Why is God watching over Sarai while she is with Pharaoh?

    2. What are Sarai's roles?

3. Is Pharaoh's action (to take Sarai into his home to marry) appropriate or inappropriate?

4. How are Abram, Sarai, and Pharaoh each responsible before God?

5. Is Sarai a victim of Abram's decision to lie to Pharaoh saying she is his sister?

DISCERN/OBSERVE:
Discern Fleshly Tendencies (refer to Special Consideration on pg. 33)

Discern Lying Belief (refer to Special Consideration on pg. 24)

_____.

Discern and Feel the Truth of Your Identity in Christ (Discern one of the four starting pg. 14. Feel it! Use the feeling words on pg. 27. Write how it feels using "I feel ___ because ___. An example is on pg. 58.)

Discern What The Lord Would Seek to Change in You to Transform Your Heart Disturbances So You Experience the Peace of God. [For example in your behaviors (internal too, not just external), attitude, preferences, opinions, thinking, point of view, or sensitivity (i.e., more Christ-like sensitivity to others/self or less fleshly sensitivity to others/self, etc.).]

Discern Possible Steps of Faith (refer to pg. 60); Observe Things About Your Life, Spiritual Battles, and What to Expect in Trials.

EVENTS AFTER THIS LESSON AND BEFORE THE NEXT: None.

LESSON 8: GENESIS 13:1-11 YOU DECIDE (ABRAM)

A husband will often consider any potential worries, concerns or issues (heart disturbances) his wife may experience when a big decision needs to be made. He may experience his own heart disturbances, especially if he realizes he must make that decision without her input! This is triply true when he realizes he made a decision independently of God before (like Abram saying Sarai was his sister), and it was a fleshly decision!

Abram is in a similar situation, which could be a trial for us were we in his shoes. Abram realizes he and Lot need to split up due to the size of their herds. Prior to this, Abram let Sarai down when he made the decision that she should lie about being his sister, and she suffered the humiliation of being courted by Pharaoh. The Bible doesn't indicate that Abram talked with Sarai about letting Lot choose the land he wanted, and, of course, Lot will probably take the choice land.

So, the potential trial we want to look at in this lesson is what concerns and issues Satan may have used to cause Abram to want to hold on to the choice land, instead of offering it to Lot. If you were Abram, what do you think your wife might feel if you basically gave the choice land away, without talking to her? To recognize these concerns, it is important to "walk the miles" that Abram and Sarai have experienced up to this point.

SCRIPTURE SUMMARY: Genesis 13:1-11 –After an epic journey to get to this place in the Promised Land, Lot's and Abram's families and herds cannot be sustained by the same piece of land; quarrelling arises between Abram's and Lot's people; Abram is going to let Lot pick either the choice land or the not-so-desirable land.

CONTEXT:
Patterns: By the time this situation comes up, it hasn't been long since Abram "failed to look out for Sarai's interests" in his trials (moving

without knowing the destination, lying to Pharaoh such that Pharaoh courts Sarai). One of the things we observe about Sarai is that she is not getting first hand input or confirmation from God on important issues affecting her life (let's assume that since the Bible doesn't indicate God is revealing His plans to her like He does with Abram). Sarai's perspective of Abram could be that he has self-defeatist behaviors; that would be a likely goal of Satan, right? The situation in this lesson exposes another potential trial dealing with their husband/wife relationship, as well as their relationships with God.

Special Consideration:
Before you glance at the patterns the authors' small group observed in Satan's attacks on Abram (below), you may want to review the **Special Consideration About Identifying Patterns** (on page 101 in the previous lesson). These possible patterns can be observed from Lessons 5 and 7. We will add to this list in future lessons involving Abram, and we will put those additions in **bold**.

Patterns in Satan's past attacks (temptations) on Abram:
1. **Likely attack by Satan on Abram in Genesis 12:1-4 – don't stand up and say you are moving without knowing where you are going – overcame Satan's attack.**
2. **An actual attack by Satan on Abram in Genesis 12:10-20 – don't stand up and say Sarai is your wife or you might be killed – fell to Satan's attack.**

Other Relevant Information:
1. Abram has moved his family about 1500+ miles by the time the issue of space between him and Lot comes up (this includes their return trip from Egypt back to the Bethel area).
2. As a result of the separation, Lot moves from Bethel to the Jordan Valley (15-20 miles), and Abram with Sarai move about 25-30 miles to the south to the area around Hebron.

WHO IS INVOLVED IN Abram's TRIAL (Main Players Only)?
God, Satan, Abram, Lot

WHAT DECISION(S) MUST Abram MAKE?
1. Abram has to make a decision on how to stop the infighting between Abram's and Lot's herdsman.
2. If they are each to have their own bit of land, Abram has to decide who gets the favorable land and who gets the less choice land.
3. If they split up, they must still remain on good terms to be able to support one another in this hostile land of "pagans." Abram has to figure out how to make that happen, if at all possible.

WHAT KNOWLEDGE OF GOD COULD Abram HAVE HAD TO ASSIST HIM TO ACT AS GOD WANTS? (Additions to the list of Abram's knowledge are shown in **bold**)
1. Genesis 11:30 – Abram knew his wife Sarai was barren and could not have children.
2. Genesis 12:1 – Abram knew God wanted him to leave his country (Haran), his people and his father's household.
3. Genesis 12:1 – Abram knew he was to move without knowing where he was moving to, and that God would show him where the Promised land was later.
4. Genesis 12:2-3 – Abram knew God made three Promises:
    a. Personal – God will bless Abram and make his name great.
    b. National – God will make Abram into a great nation and his descendants would have their own land.
    c. Universal – God will bless all peoples on the earth through Abram.
5. **Genesis 12:6-7 – Abram knew God was true to His word when He told Abram the land of Canaan was the Promised Land.**
6. **Genesis 12:10-20 – Abram knew God protected him, even when Pharaoh found out he lied. He knew God helped him to prosper during his time in Egypt. Abram knew God was true to His word.**

WHAT WAS Abram's HEART DISTURBANCE?
(See how others responded to the rest of the lesson – pg. 256)

DID Abram SUBMIT TO THE LORD TRANSFORMING HIS HEART AND MIND SO THE LORD COULD LIVE THROUGH HIM?

DISCUSSION QUESTION: Let's pause for a moment to consider what Abram might have thought Sarai might think if he let Lot pick the choice land without talking with her about that. See what heart disturbances you'd have in Abram's position. Ask, "What would my typical heart disturbance be if I were *Sarai* and I found out Abram gave away the good land without consulting me?"

PUT YOURSELF IN Abram's "SHOES" – LISTEN TO THE AUDIO (Go to www.Feelings102.com to get or play the AUDIO)

Having considered what Sarai might think about you (as Abram) giving away the choice land, then... **WHAT WOULD YOUR TYPICAL HEART DISTURBANCE BE IF YOU WERE Abram IN THIS SITUATION OR ONE LIKE IT?**
    (You can use the list of heart disturbances on page 23)

I'd feel _____ *because* _____

_____

I'd feel _____ *because* _____

_____

I would/would not want _____

because _____

DISCERN/OBSERVE:
Discern Fleshly Tendencies (refer to Special Consideration on pg. 33)

Discern Lying Belief (refer to Special Consideration on pg. 24)

_____.

Discern and Feel the Truth of Your Identity in Christ (Discern one of the four starting pg. 14. Feel it! Use the feeling words on pg. 27. Write how it feels using "I feel ___ because ___. An example is on pg. 58.)

Discern What The Lord Would Seek to Change in You to Transform Your Heart Disturbances So You Experience the Peace of God. [For example in your behaviors (internal too, not just external), attitude, preferences, opinions, thinking, point of view, or sensitivity (i.e., more Christ-like sensitivity to others/self or less fleshly sensitivity to others/self, etc.).]

Discern Possible Steps of Faith (refer to pg. 60); Observe Things About Your Life, Spiritual Battles, and What to Expect in Trials.

EVENTS AFTER THIS LESSON AND BEFORE THE NEXT:
1. Genesis 13:12-18 – Lot lives near Sodom; God reaffirms promise of land to Abram.
2. Genesis 14 – Conflict breaks out near Lot; Lot and family are taken captive; Abram raises a small army of 318 men and rescues Lot.

LESSON 9: GENESIS 15:1-16:3 WHO WILL GET MY ESTATE? (ABRAM)

A bram has been challenged to continue taking steps of faith concerning the Promises God made years prior to this passage. This lesson looks at the next TWO of Abram's trials, which are very closely related.

In the *first trial* Satan tries to attack Abram's faith using some normal worldly concerns. Abram is getting older and needs an heir. Clearly Satan would like Abram to take matters into his own hands. But, Abram remains dependent on God by taking the issue to the Lord. He refrains from acting out of fleshly thinking. The Lord reiterates His Promises and tells Abram that part of His plan is waiting to unfold basically because more time must pass. There are other pieces involved in God's plan that are still coming into place. So, Abram has his answer from the Lord.

Then, in the *second trial*, Satan uses Sarai's fleshly thinking, as well as Abram's desire to get a son, like soon! In this second trial, Satan ultimately accomplishes the very thing that the Lord helped Abram to avoid earlier concerning his estate. Satan's deception fools Abram such that he and Sarai act independently of God in an attempt to get what they want and what God said He would eventually give them – a child.

While Satan couldn't prevent Abram from seeking out and successfully hearing God's counsel in the first trial, Satan attacks again later in a second trial. This is a common strategy Satan uses against each of us, making this lesson a very profitable one to study.

SCRIPTURE SUMMARY: Genesis 15:1-16:3 –Abram has waited about 10 years for God to fulfill the promise of a son and nothing has happened; now he's trying to figure out how to handle his estate.

CONTEXT:
Patterns in Satan's past attacks (temptations) on Abram:

1. Likely attack by Satan on Abram in Genesis 12:1-4 – don't stand up and say you are moving without knowing where you are going – overcame Satan's attack.
2. An actual attack by Satan on Abram in Genesis 12:10-20 – don't stand up and say Sarai is your wife or you might be killed – fell to Satan's attack.
3. **Likely attack by Satan on Abram in Genesis 13:1-11 – stand up and say you want the choice land – overcame Satan's attack.**

Other Relevant Information:
1. Abram was about 75 years old when he received the Promises and initially moved from Haran; he's now in his 80s.
2. Abram has been in Canaan for less than a decade (based on the time-frame of his trial with Lot from the previous lesson).
3. Abram is still without a son; Sarai is still barren.
4. Abram's tentative plan is that Eliezer of Damascus (a servant of his) might be his heir. This is the first recorded "solution" that Abram comes up with since God first promised Abram an heir, and Abram embraces that this isn't what God wants.
5. It was an accepted custom, by the peoples living in Canaan, that a man could have a son through a maidservant, if his wife was barren. If a man did this, it was the man's responsibility not to abandon the maidservant or the offspring through her.

WHO IS INVOLVED IN Abram's TRIAL (Main Players Only)?
God, Satan, Abram, Sarai

WHAT DECISION(S) MUST Abram MAKE?
Abram has to decide whether to take his questions to the Lord to get His input on the trials he is facing, or to decide on his own.
1. In the *first trial* Abram must decide whether or not he needs to ask the Lord how he is to handle matters of his estate.
2. In the *second trial* Abram already has God's first answer, but Abram again has to decide whether or not he needs to ask for God's input again, even though technically Sarai's plan involves him having a son and the heir won't be Eliezer of Damascus.

WHAT KNOWLEDGE OF GOD COULD Abram HAVE HAD TO ASSIST HIM TO ACT AS GOD WANTS?

1. Genesis 11:30 – Abram knew his wife Sarai was barren and could not have children.
2. Genesis 12:1 – Abram knew God wanted him to leave his country (Haran), his people and his father's household.
3. Genesis 12:1 – Abram knew he was to move without knowing where he was moving to, and that God would show him where later.
4. Genesis 12:2-3 – Abram knew God made three Promises:
   a. Personal – God will bless Abram and make his name great.
   b. National – God will make Abram into a great nation and his descendants would have their own land.
   c. Universal – God will bless all peoples on the earth through Abram.
5. Genesis 12:6-7 – Abram knew God was true to His word when He told Abram the land of Canaan was the Promised Land.
6. Genesis 12:10-20 – Abram knew God protected him, even when Pharaoh found out he lied. He knew God helped him to prosper during his time in Egypt. Abram knew God was true to His word.
7. **Genesis 13:14-17 – Abram knew God reiterated His Promises.**
8. **Genesis 14:22-23 – Abram knew God enabled him to prevail and defeat the enemies that captured Lot.**
9. **Genesis 15 – Abram knew that God confirmed he would have a son, and God reiterated the Promises a second time and made a covenant with Abram. Abram knew that God provided a timeline of some key events in the future and that God assured his personal safety into old age.**

WHAT WAS Abram's HEART DISTURBANCE?

(See how others responded to the rest of the lesson – pg. 260)

DID Abram SUBMIT TO THE LORD TRANSFORMING HIS HEART AND MIND SO THE LORD COULD LIVE THROUGH HIM? (hint: there are 2 trials in this lesson, look at an answer for each)

DISCUSSION QUESTION: It is not unreasonable to think that Abram would probably be concerned (a heart disturbance) about what his wife would be feeling as she discusses having a baby through Hagar. How would Sarai feel if Abram said, "No?" Let's take a few minutes to do what Abram may have done and put yourself in Sarai's shoes concerning the second trial. What would your heart disturbance be if you were **Sarai** and Abram refused your plan?

PUT YOURSELF IN Abram's "SHOES" – LISTEN TO THE AUDIO (Go to www.Feelings102.com to get or play the AUDIO)

Having considered what Sarai might think about you (as Abram) if you refused to give her a baby through Hagar, then… **WHAT WOULD YOUR TYPICAL HEART DISTURBANCE BE IF YOU WERE Abram IN THIS SITUATION OR ONE LIKE IT?**
(You can use the list of heart disturbances on page 23)

I'd feel _____ *because* _____

_____

I'd feel _____ *because* _____

_____

I would/would not want _____

because _____

DISCERN/OBSERVE:
Discern Fleshly Tendencies (refer to Special Consideration on pg. 33)

Discern Lying Belief (refer to Special Consideration on pg. 24)

_____.

Discern and Feel the Truth of Your Identity in Christ (Discern one of the four starting pg. 14. Feel it! Use the feeling words on pg. 27. Write how it feels using "I feel ___ because ___. An example is on pg. 58.)

Discern What The Lord Would Seek to Change in You to Transform Your Heart Disturbances So You Experience the Peace of God. [For example in your behaviors (internal too, not just external), attitude, preferences, opinions, thinking, point of view, or sensitivity (i.e., more Christ-like sensitivity to others/self or less fleshly sensitivity to others/self, etc.).]

Discern Possible Steps of Faith (refer to pg. 60); Observe Things About Your Life, Spiritual Battles, and What to Expect in Trials.

EVENTS AFTER THIS LESSON AND BEFORE THE NEXT: None.

LESSON 10: GENESIS 16:1-6 WHY WOULD YOU WANT ME IN THIS UNHEALTHY ENVIRONMENT, LORD? (HAGAR)

Imagine you are in a really unhealthy environment... and you are pregnant! You didn't have a choice either – you are a slave! Imagine, Abram, who fathered your child, isn't protecting you. In fact, he's married. Wouldn't you be upset?! And, his wife, Sarai, is now upset because you despise her so. Sarai takes it up a notch and uses her power over you – now she is mistreating you, a pregnant woman. What's worse is that Abram isn't making it stop. Well, Hagar is upset, and she's upset with Sarai, Abram's woman!

If you were Hagar, when you think about leaving that kind of situation, what do you typically think God would want to do through you? Don't you think that God would want you to get out so you could be in a healthier environment? Wouldn't your first thought be that God's counsel would be for you to use whatever power you have to get out, and to do so quickly? Wouldn't you think that Satan's influence would to be to get you to act in a self-destructive way and to stay in the unhealthy environment? Wouldn't it be normal to think that only Satan would want you to deliberately expose you and your future child to mean attitudes and slavery?

Well, this lesson turns all that upside down. To be fair, there are times when God does want us out of an unhealthy environment, but this isn't always the case. The key is to let Him make the determination!

The passage describing this trial stops after verse 6 when Hagar makes the decision to leave the environment she is in. This lesson focuses on looking at what we would have to face in order to discern God's guidance correctly *before* we act in the flesh! This lesson gives us a great opportunity to see the kinds of heart disturbances that require us to really trust God and embrace the steps of faith He gives us whenever His counsel to us is not in accordance with *our* hopes and dreams.

SCRIPTURE SUMMARY: Genesis 16:1-6 – Sarai gives Hagar to Abram so he can sleep with her; Hagar despises Sarai, then Sarai begins to mistreat Hagar; Hagar runs away.

Special Consideration:

OPTIONAL LESSON you can study later (if you want). You could look at the text from Sarai's perspective and discover what deception tactic Satan must have used to drive her to feel so strongly about *wanting* her husband to sleep with the handmaid. Is it because she feels incomplete as a person? This optional lesson can be helpful in examining the parts of us that tend to sometimes move toward acting independently of God. It can be enlightening in terms of seeing how much our desires can compete with a full, heart-filled trust in God.

CONTEXT:

Other Relevant Information:

1. It has been more than 10 years since the Lord initially promised Abram a son.
2. Since Abram goes along with Sarai's suggestion to sleep with Hagar, this is the Bible's second recorded solution where Abram wants to fix the issue of lacking an heir.

WHO IS INVOLVED IN Hagar's TRIAL (Main Players Only)?

God, Satan, Abram, Sarai, Hagar

WHAT DECISION(S) MUST Hagar MAKE?

Hagar has to decide whether to stay in Abram's household and submit to Sarai, or whether to take matters into her own hands and flee that unhealthy environment.

WHAT KNOWLEDGE OF GOD COULD Hagar HAVE HAD TO ASSIST HER TO ACT AS GOD WANTS?

1. The Bible doesn't say exactly what Hagar knew about God.
2. Hagar probably knew that Abram and Sarai believed God wanted them to have a son.

WHAT WAS Hagar's HEART DISTURBANCE?
(See how others responded to the rest of the lesson – pg. 264)

DID Hagar SUBMIT TO THE LORD TRANSFORMING HER HEART AND MIND SO THE LORD COULD LIVE THROUGH HER?

Special Consideration:

Before listening to the AUDIO, let's address an important aspect of this trial. God seeks to communicate to unbelievers and ungodly people. Each trial they experience gives them the opportunity to discern the path God would have them on. By seeking God's will and letting Him transform them in the trial at hand, God will use that godly choice to lead them in the direction which brings them to Him. This is part of what is implied when God tells Cain that he must "master sin," a task that cannot be done without dependence on God. So by making the choice God would have of them, even "ungodly" people have the opportunity to surrender to God and *continue* making choices that submit to His lead. In time, this can lead them to embrace the relationship with God that He hopes they will want. This is actually part of what makes everyone accountable to God. Even unbelievers have made *some* choices out of a dependence on God. If they learn from those choices, they have proof by their own actions of the importance of a relationship with God in which they are dependent on Him!

With that in mind, it is profitable to study Hagar's trial in terms of putting yourself in her situation and seeking the perspective from which one has the opportunity to let God live through them. Hagar could choose God's guidance for her over Satan's influence. We know that God's will is for her to stay (V. 9). But, for her to have discerned the Lord's will for her prior to fleeing (V. 6), Hagar would have to submit to God to deny fleshly desires to escape mistreatment. (Escaping mistreatment isn't always a fleshly desire, but we know it is here because of V. 9. If we were in Hagar's situation, the question is, "Would we be faithful enough to be open to God's will for us *before* acting to fulfill that desire and flee?!") So even if Hagar isn't in a relationship with God, the challenge to deny fleshly desires during our trials is one we share in common with Hagar! As you listen to the AUDIO, put yourself in the moments of Hagar's choice between fleeing Sarai's mistreatment or seeking out what God would seek to change in you to live His will that you stay! Remember, as believers, we are to seek out God's guidance to us *before* taking things into our own hands according to our initial desires!

PUT YOURSELF IN Hagar's "SHOES" – LISTEN TO THE AUDIO (Go to www.Feelings102.com to get or play the AUDIO)

WHAT WOULD YOUR TYPICAL HEART DISTURBANCE BE IF YOU WERE Hagar IN THIS SITUATION OR ONE LIKE IT?
(You can use the list of heart disturbances on page 23)

I'd feel _____ *because* _____

_____

I'd feel _____ *because* _____

_____

I would/would not want _____

because _____

DISCERN/OBSERVE:
Discern Fleshly Tendencies (refer to Special Consideration on pg. 33)

Discern Lying Belief (refer to Special Consideration on pg. 24)

_____.

Discern and Feel the Truth of Your Identity in Christ (Discern one of the four starting pg. 14. Feel it! Use the feeling words on pg. 27. Write how it feels using "I feel ___ because ___. An example is on pg. 58.)

Discern What The Lord Would Seek to Change in You to Transform Your Heart Disturbances So You Experience the Peace of God. [For example in your behaviors (internal too, not just external), attitude, preferences, opinions, thinking, point of view, or sensitivity (i.e., more Christ-like sensitivity to others/self or less fleshly sensitivity to others/self, etc.).]

Discern Possible Steps of Faith (refer to pg. 60); Observe Things About Your Life, Spiritual Battles, and What to Expect in Trials.

EVENTS AFTER THIS LESSON AND BEFORE THE NEXT:
1. Genesis 16:7-10 – An angel of the Lord goes to Hagar, asks her where she's going, and tells Hagar she is to go back to Sarai and to submit to her as a servant; the angel also tells Hagar her descendants will be great in number.
2. Genesis 16:11-16 – The angel of the Lord tells Hagar what will happen to her son; the angel tells her to name her son Ishmael; Hagar bears Abram the son when Abram is 86 years old.

LESSON 11: GENESIS 17:1-18 GOD REMINDS US, AND OFTEN HE CHALLENGES US TO *MORE* FAITH (ABRAM)

This passage brings together two things that are often challenging: letting God change us from fleshly patterns and demonstrating our complete dependence on God through steps of faith.

At the time of this trial, it has been 24 years since God first told Abram to leave his father's household and go wherever God would lead (Genesis 12:1). Since that initial calling, Abram has had to embrace many changes God sought to make in him in the course of being transformed by the Lord. It's the same for us.

In this lesson's passage, God is instructing Abram to do some things to show his faith in God. Why is that a trial? Because while the focus is on God talking to Abram, Satan (who is not specifically mentioned) is going to work to try to find ways to make Abram stumble, to fail to act in a timely manner, or to take matters into his own hands. These are the kinds of fleshly things that we fall to when Satan's attacks are successful within us, even though God is seeking to change us.

In this trial God has some serious steps of faith for Abram as He works to live through Abram. God tells Abram to embrace changing his and Sarai's names. God also tells Abram to circumcise all the males within his household. Those steps of faith are to accompany and reflect the changes God is making in Abram.

Perhaps, at first glance, those steps of faith don't seem like such a big deal. But, when we put ourselves in Abram's shoes, those "minor" steps of faith get bigger.

SCRIPTURE SUMMARY: Genesis 17:1-18 – God is reaffirming the Promises to Abram as well as saying Abram will have a child with Sarai. God changes their names. God says He wants Abram to circumcise the male members of his family and servants. That will be a sign of Abram's part of the covenant with God... and God still hasn't given him a son; Abram asks that Ishmael be acceptable to God.

Special Consideration:

OPTIONAL LESSON you can study later (if you want). You could look at the trial from the perspective of Sarai. Abram comes home one day and announces that God spoke to him again, "Our names have been changed!" Moreover, all the males in the household are going to be incapacitated for about a week (no sterile facilities available) because they're all going to get circumcised! That's one thing when you are a boy baby, but as a male teen or adult?!! That's painfully different! What steps of faith would God have for you? Oh, and Sarai, God still hasn't given you and Abram a son, so are there grounds for questioning whether God is really giving Abram all this info? How would you respond if your husband took steps of faith like this in your household without even opening it up for discussion? You get the picture. Oh and fellas, this optional lesson isn't just for the women, you can try this lesson too!

CONTEXT:

Patterns: Overall we see that the trial this lesson presents is the third recorded time Abram comes up with a way to "help" God resolve his lack of a son (Abram asks if Ishmael is under God's blessing – V. 18).

Patterns in Satan's past attacks (temptations) on Abram:
1. Likely attack by Satan on Abram in Genesis 12:1-4 – don't stand up and say you are moving without knowing where you are going – overcame Satan's attack.
2. An actual attack by Satan on Abram in Genesis 12:10-20 – don't stand up and say Sarai is your wife or you might be killed – fell to Satan's attack.
3. Likely attack by Satan on Abram in Genesis 13:1-11 – stand up and say you want the choice land – overcame Satan's attack.
4. **An actual attack by Satan on Abram in Genesis 15:1-16:3 – stand up and say that Eliezer of Damascus will be your heir – overcame Satan's attack.**
5. **An actual attack by Satan on Abram in Genesis 16:1-6 – don't stand up and refuse to sleep with Hagar or you might not get an heir – fell to Satan's attack.**

Other Relevant Information:
1. Abram is now 99 years old; it has been 24 years since God first promised him a son.
2. God renames Abram to Abraham and Sarai to Sarah.

WHO IS INVOLVED IN Abram's TRIAL (Main Players Only)?
God, Satan, Abram

WHAT DECISION(S) MUST Abram MAKE?
1. The "decision" Abram faces is whether he will have faith that God has promised a son to Sarai and him, and that it will actually come to be. In this trial, Abram immediately laughs at the idea (V. 17). The lack of intentional reflection on Abram's part can make it seem like there really isn't any kind of decision being made. Like Abram, some of our trials happen so quickly that we really don't take any time to think about what we are doing. This is one of those knee-jerk reaction type trials for Abram. It is a trial that comes up fast and is reacted to inappropriately without taking a pause for discerning. It shows that Satan was probably successful in maintaining some bastion of disbelief in Abram's heart prior to God approaching Abram in this lesson's situation.
2. Abram also has to decide:
   a. Whether to embrace his new name, which may involve enforcing that decision such that everyone uses his new name, as well as Sarai's new name.
   b. Whether to embrace and enforce the circumcision of all males in his household, as well as teaching his children to carry that directive on through the generations.

WHAT KNOWLEDGE OF GOD COULD Abram HAVE HAD TO ASSIST HIM TO ACT AS GOD WANTS?
1. Genesis 11:30 – Abram knew his wife Sarai was barren and could not have children.
2. Genesis 12:1 – Abram knew God wanted him to leave his country (Haran), his people and his father's household.

3. Genesis 12:1 – Abram knew he was to move without knowing where he was moving to, and that God would show him where later.
4. Genesis 12:2-3 – Abram knew God made three Promises:
   a. Personal – God will bless Abram and make his name great.
   b. National – God will make Abram into a great nation and his descendants would have their own land.
   c. Universal – God will bless all peoples on the earth through Abram.
5. Genesis 12:6-7 – Abram knew God was true to His word when He told Abram the land of Canaan was the Promised Land.
6. Genesis 12:10-20 – Abram knew God protected him, even when Pharaoh found out he lied. He knew God helped him to prosper during his time in Egypt. Abram knew God was true to His word.
7. Genesis 13:14-17 – Abram knew God reiterated His Promises.
8. Genesis 14:22-23 – Abram knew God enabled him to prevail and defeat the enemies that captured Lot.
9. Genesis 15 – Abram knew that God confirmed he would have a son, and God reiterated the Promises a second time and made a covenant with Abram. Abram knew that God provided a timeline of some key events in the future and that God assured his personal safety into old age.
10. **Genesis 17 – Abram knew he was to be "blameless." This is not possible when one lives independently of God. Abram knew God reiterated the Promises a third time and established His covenant as an everlasting one. Abram knew God gave him some directives and assured Abram that Sarai would bear a son through whom God's covenant would be fulfilled.**

WHAT WAS Abram's HEART DISTURBANCE? (i.e., as shown by his laughter)
(See how others responded to the rest of the lesson – pg. 267)

DID Abram SUBMIT TO THE LORD TRANSFORMING HIS HEART AND MIND SO THE LORD COULD LIVE THROUGH HIM?

PUT YOURSELF IN Abram's "SHOES" – LISTEN TO AUDIO (Go to www.Feelings102.com to get or play the AUDIO)

WHAT WOULD YOUR TYPICAL HEART DISTURBANCE BE IF YOU WERE Abram IN THIS SITUATION OR ONE LIKE IT? *(You can use the list of heart disturbances on page 23)*

I'd feel _____ *because* _____

_____

I'd feel _____ *because* _____

_____

I would/would not want _____

because _____

DISCERN/OBSERVE:
Discern Fleshly Tendencies (refer to Special Consideration on pg. 33)

Discern Lying Belief (refer to Special Consideration on pg. 24)

_____.

Discern and Feel the Truth of Your Identity in Christ (Discern one of the four starting pg. 14. Feel it! Use the feeling words on pg. 27. Write how it feels using "I feel ___ because ___. An example is on pg. 58.)

Discern What The Lord Would Seek to Change in You to Transform Your Heart Disturbances So You Experience the Peace of God. [For example in your behaviors (internal too, not just external), attitude, preferences, opinions, thinking, point of view, or sensitivity (i.e., more Christ-like sensitivity to others/self or less fleshly sensitivity to others/self, etc.).]

Discern Possible Steps of Faith (refer to pg. 60); Observe Things About Your Life, Spiritual Battles, and What to Expect in Trials.

EVENTS AFTER THIS LESSON AND BEFORE THE NEXT:
1. Genesis 17:19-22 – God tells Abraham that Sarah will bear him a son and that God's covenant will be established with the son as it was with Abraham; God says that Ishmael will be blessed and will have numerous descendants; God reiterates that His covenant will be established with the future son, Isaac.
2. Genesis 17:23-27 – Abraham takes Ishmael and all in his household and circumcises them as God said to do; Abraham is 99 years old and Ishmael is 13 years old.

LESSON 12: GENESIS 18:1-15 IT'S BEEN SO LONG, I DOUBT GOD REALLY SAID THAT (SARAH)

One of Satan's favorite tactics is to drive us to continually struggle with cooperating with God as He works to transform our doubts and concerns. Satan works this angle when God's guidance requires that we wait on His timing. Satan's goals are simple. Satan tries to get us to hurry to do something on our own to create the outcome we seek, so we can stop worrying. Satan tries to get us to reason that it's OK to do so when it is within our power to try to influence a situation. Or, Satan causes us to think it's OK to have a downcast spirit with skepticism in our minds and attitudes while we wait on God. Either way, Satan seeks to lead us into fleshly behaviors called sin.

But, Satan's attacks can be even more complex. The kinds of trials that come with God's "wait" guidance can be even harder to handle when our role, before God, is one that requires us to follow someone else's lead. In other words, our role may be that of a spouse, an employee at work, a church congregation member, or a child or young adult, etc. When our role isn't the lead role before God in a given situation, we like to think that being equal in God's sight means we can share roles as believers. However, being equal in God's sight doesn't mean we have carte blanche to step out of our God-given roles in order to "make the right thing happen" or to avoid feeling down.

Hopefully, whoever God has us follow is discerning God's counsel. Hopefully they avoid taking things into their own hands, and they are being the person God wants them to be through them. Still, Satan's attacks make for hard trials, even with good, solid leaders and even within a strong spiritual family. This is often true whenever Satan takes advantage of the fact that God doesn't always directly give us (as followers) the same info He gives to our leaders. This is one reason why leaders are doubly or triply accountable before God.

This is Sarah's situation in this lesson. Satan's attacks cause her to doubt. Perhaps it is because God's Promises were made to Abraham and were not directly confirmed to her personally. Regardless, this lesson helps us experience Sarah's challenges, so that we might reflect on times when we have faced or might face such spiritual battles.

SCRIPTURE SUMMARY: Genesis 18:1-15 – Sarah is challenged to believe in God's Promise of a son for Abraham through her.

CONTEXT:
Patterns in Satan's past attacks (temptations) on Sarah:[*]
1. Likely attack by Satan on Sarai in Genesis 12:1-4 – don't support moving without knowing where you are going – unknown whether she overcame Satan's attack.[**]
2. **Likely attack by Satan on Sarai in Genesis 12:10-20** – don't support Abram's lie that you are his sister – overcame Satan's attack.
3. **Likely attack by Satan on Sarai in Genesis 13:1-11** – don't support the hardship that comes with getting the less choice land – unknown whether she overcame Satan's attack.[**]
4. **An actual attack by Satan on Sarai in Genesis 16:1-6** – support the idea of doing what it takes to have a son (through Hagar) – fell to Satan's attack.
5. **Likely attack by Satan on Sarai in Genesis 17:1-18** – don't support name change, circumcision or believe that you will have a son – unknown whether she overcame Satan's attack.[**]

Other Relevant Information:
1. Remember, God changed Abram's name to Abraham and Sarai's name to Sarah (recorded in Genesis 17).
2. In this Biblical record, what Abraham and Sarah physically saw were three men. V. 17 and 19:1 indicate that the three men were the LORD and two angels.
3. God's promise of a son is about 24 years old at this point.

WHO IS INVOLVED IN Sarah's TRIAL (Main Players Only)?
Abraham, Sarah, 3 men (one was the LORD, 2 were angels and it is not clear whether Sarah recognized the men as the LORD and two angels), Satan.

---

[*] See Special Consideration About Identifying Patterns from Lesson 7.
[**] The reason we (the authors) say it is unknown whether she overcame this likely attack by Satan is because, while she went along with Abram, we don't know whether she was grumbling and complaining about the decision after it was made, or whether she let God live a supportive attitude through her.

WHAT DECISION(S) MUST Sarah MAKE?

Sarah's trial is like part of Abraham's trial in the previous lesson (Lesson 11). In this trial, Sarah immediately laughs. The lack of intentional reflection on Sarah's part can make it seem like there really isn't any kind of decision being made. Still, the "decision" she faces is whether she will believe that God has promised a son to her and Abraham, and that it will actually come to be. Some trials happen so quickly that we really don't take any time to think about what we are doing. This is one of those knee-jerk reaction type trials for Sarah. It involves a reaction that is a reflection of fleshly thinking. It comes up fast and is inappropriately responded to without discernment. It shows that Satan was probably successful in maintaining some bastion of disbelief in Sarah's heart prior to God approaching Sarah in this lesson's situation.

WHAT KNOWLEDGE OF GOD COULD Sarah HAVE HAD TO ASSIST HER TO ACT AS GOD WANTS? (Additions to the list of Sarai's knowledge are shown in **bold**)

1. The Bible doesn't tell us everything Sarai knew about God.
2. Sarai knew, from God's perspective, she was Abram's wife.
3. Sarai probably knew of the Promises, but that was likely second-hand through Abram. There is no record that God interacted directly with Sarai to confirm what her husband was telling her.
4. Genesis 12:8 – Sarai probably knew when they arrived in the Promised Land because Abram worshiped the Lord there.
5. Genesis 12:11-13 – If Abram told Sarai of the Promises from God, Sarai could have figured out that God would have to protect Abram's life, if God is going to give Abram a son. From this, Sarai may have been able to conclude that Abram wouldn't have to lie because God would protect Abram.
6. **Genesis 14 – Sarai probably knew that Abram gave God the credit for his victory in saving Lot and family from captivity.**
7. **Genesis 15:4-6 – Sarai probably knew that Abram believed that God did not consider Eliezer of Damascus to be the one through whom God would fulfill His promise of descendants.**

8. **Genesis 17:15-16, 19 – Although Sarai had given Hagar to Abram to get a son, Sarai probably knew that Abram believed God was still going to give him the "right" son through Sarai herself.**

WHAT WAS Sarah's HEART DISTURBANCE?
(See how others responded to the rest of the lesson – pg. 270)

DID Sarah SUBMIT TO THE LORD TRANSFORMING HER HEART AND MIND SO THE LORD COULD LIVE THROUGH HER?

PUT YOURSELF IN Sarah's "SHOES" – LISTEN TO THE AUDIO (Go to www.Feelings102.com to get or play the AUDIO)

WHAT WOULD YOUR TYPICAL HEART DISTURBANCE BE IF YOU WERE Sarah IN THIS SITUATION OR ONE LIKE IT?
(You can use the list of heart disturbances on page 23)

I'd feel _____ *because* _____

_____

I'd feel _____ *because* _____

_____

I would/would not want _____

because _____

DISCERN/OBSERVE:
Discern Fleshly Tendencies (refer to Special Consideration on pg. 33)

Discern Lying Belief (refer to Special Consideration on pg. 24)

_____.

Discern and Feel the Truth of Your Identity in Christ (Discern one of the four starting pg. 14. Feel it! Use the feeling words on pg. 27. Write how it feels using "I feel ___ because ___. An example is on pg. 58.)

Discern What The Lord Would Seek to Change in You to Transform Your Heart Disturbances So You Experience the Peace of God. [For example in your behaviors (internal too, not just external), attitude, preferences, opinions, thinking, point of view, or sensitivity (i.e., more Christ-like sensitivity to others/self or less fleshly sensitivity to others/self, etc.).]

Discern Possible Steps of Faith (refer to pg. 60); Observe Things About Your Life, Spiritual Battles, and What to Expect in Trials.

EVENTS AFTER THIS LESSON AND BEFORE THE NEXT:
None.

LESSON 13: GENESIS 18:16-33 YOUR WILL IS FOR ME *NOT* TO HELP MY FAMILY? (ABRAHAM)

"Family is everything! God always wants us to take care of family!" These sentiments are common and often true. But, the passage in this lesson demonstrates there are times when it is not our place to try to warn or directly aid someone else in their trials, even if they are family! Oh boy, now that takes some serious discernment!

Typically our perspective of demonstrating godly love and support to one another means getting involved in a family member's trial. If we see a family member in a dangerous trial, don't we think that "letting the trial unfold without our loving assistance" is of Satan? Why would God want us to risk letting others "go astray" when we have the ability to help? If God were to want us to risk that, then what if others left us on our own when we were in one of our trials? What right does a loved one have to withhold or deny us aid or help?

Those can be some very challenging and uncomfortable issues requiring lots of discernment. They demonstrate the importance of knowing for certain what God wants to do or not do through us when we see others in a trial. When we struggle to figure out what God wants of us in those situations, we enter into a trial of our own. This is because Satan influences us such that we *must* discern between God's will for us and Satan's.

Sometimes Satan gets us to fear that those we love might think we are acting superior if we see they are in trouble and yet we do nothing. On the other hand, others may actually think we are acting superior if we try to help. Satan works to influence our thinking so that we'll fail to let the Lord live through us in whatever way He thinks that should look like.

In this lesson, Abraham sees that Lot and his family are going to face a trial. The Bible tells us that Abraham looked out upon the city where Lot lived, and he asked the Lord what it would take to spare it. But, somehow Abraham discerned it was not his place to walk down into the city and personally advise or assist Lot. Abraham knew that though Lot's trial involved life or death, the spiritual battle was Lot's to face with God. This lesson focuses on what heart disturbances we might experience were we in Abraham's situation. It focuses on what we would have to be willing for God to transform in us, whenever His will is that we "just stand by."

SCRIPTURE SUMMARY: Genesis 18:16-33 – In this easy-to-overlook trial, Abraham learns that God is going to destroy Sodom and Gomorrah, and he is concerned about the well-being of his nephew Lot and his extended family.

Special Consideration:

OPTIONAL LESSON you can study later (if you want). You could look at the text from Sarah's perspective. Ask yourself how you would feel if your spouse knew members of your family were in trouble, but your spouse didn't believe it was God's will to provide them aid! Would you be asking why? Why would a loving God not want us to help? Why would God want a husband to make this decision without talking to his wife? Why wouldn't God share this important information with the wife too (so she could be assured)? Wouldn't your family *want* to be distant from you after such an act? In the end, we know that what Abraham did was of God. So being in Sarah's shoes, what would God seek to change in us in such a situation?

CONTEXT:

Patterns in Satan's past attacks (temptations) on Abraham:
1. Likely attack by Satan on Abram in Genesis 12:1-4 – don't stand up and say you are moving without knowing where you are going – overcame Satan's attack.
2. An actual attack by Satan on Abram in Genesis 12:10-20 – don't stand up and say Sarai is your wife or you might be killed – fell to Satan's attack.
3. Likely attack by Satan on Abram in Genesis 13:1-11 – stand up and say you want the choice land – overcame Satan's attack.
4. An actual attack by Satan on Abram in Genesis 15:1-16:3 – stand up and say that Eliezer of Damascus will be your heir – overcame Satan's attack.

5. An actual attack by Satan on Abram in Genesis 16:1-6 – don't stand up and refuse to sleep with Hagar or you might not get an heir – fell to Satan's attack.

6. **Likely attack by Satan on Abram in Genesis 17:1-18 – don't stand up and make changes in the household that others may not like – overcame Satan's attack.**

Other Relevant Information: Abraham rescued Lot from harm before. This happened when Lot chose to move close to the influences of the ungodly city of Sodom (Genesis 14).

WHO IS INVOLVED IN Abraham's TRIAL (Main Players Only)?
God, Satan, Angels, Abraham, inhabitants of Sodom (including Abraham's relatives)

WHAT DECISION(S) MUST Abraham MAKE?
Abraham has to decide whether or not to go down into the town to intervene and personally warn Lot and his family.

WHAT KNOWLEDGE OF GOD COULD Abraham HAVE HAD TO ASSIST HIM TO ACT AS GOD WANTS?
1. Genesis 11:30 – Abram knew his wife Sarai was barren and could not have children.
2. Genesis 12:1 – Abram knew God wanted him to leave his country (Haran), his people and his father's household.
3. Genesis 12:1 – Abram knew he was to move without knowing where he was moving to, and that God would show him where later.
4. Genesis 12:2-3 – Abram knew God made three Promises:
   a. Personal – God will bless Abram and make his name great.
   b. National – God will make Abram into a great nation and his descendants would have their own land.
   c. Universal – God will bless all peoples on the earth through Abram.
5. Genesis 12:6-7 – Abram knew God was true to His word when He told Abram the land of Canaan was the Promised Land.

6. Genesis 12:10-20 – Abram knew God protected him, even when Pharaoh found out he lied. He knew God helped him to prosper during his time in Egypt. Abram knew God was true to His word.
7. Genesis 13:14-17 – Abram knew God reiterated His Promises.
8. Genesis 14:22-23 – Abram knew God enabled him to prevail and defeat the enemies that captured Lot.
9. Genesis 15 – Abram knew that God confirmed he would have a son, and God reiterated the Promises a second time and made a covenant with Abram. Abram knew that God provided a timeline of some key events in the future and that God assured his personal safety into old age.
10. Genesis 17 – Abram knew he was to be blameless. He knew God reiterated the Promises a third time and established His covenant as an everlasting one. Abram knew God gave him some directives and assured Abram that Sarai would bear a son through whom God's covenant would be fulfilled.
11. **Genesis 18:20-21 – Abraham knew about sin and that God holds people accountable for sin. Abraham knew God was going to hold Sodom and Gomorrah accountable.**

WHAT WAS Abraham's HEART DISTURBANCE?
(See how others responded to the rest of the lesson – pg. 274)

DID Abraham SUBMIT TO THE LORD TRANSFORMING HIS HEART AND MIND SO THE LORD COULD LIVE THROUGH HIM?

PUT YOURSELF IN Abraham's "SHOES" – LISTEN TO AUDIO (Go to www.Feelings102.com to get or play the AUDIO)

WHAT WOULD YOUR TYPICAL HEART DISTURBANCE BE IF YOU WERE Abraham IN THIS SITUATION OR ONE LIKE IT?

(You can use the list of heart disturbances on page 23)

I'd feel _____ *because* _____

_____

I'd feel _____ *because* _____

_____

I would/would not want _____

because _____

DISCERN/OBSERVE:

Discern Fleshly Tendencies (refer to Special Consideration on pg. 33)

Discern Lying Belief (refer to Special Consideration on pg. 24)

_____.

Discern and Feel the Truth of Your Identity in Christ (Discern one of the four starting pg. 14. Feel it! Use the feeling words on pg. 27. Write how it feels using "I feel ___ because ___. An example is on pg. 58.)

Discern What The Lord Would Seek to Change in You to Transform Your Heart Disturbances So You Experience the Peace of God. [For example in your behaviors (internal too, not just external), attitude, preferences, opinions, thinking, point of view, or sensitivity (i.e., more Christ-like sensitivity to others/self or less fleshly sensitivity to others/self, etc.).]

Discern Possible Steps of Faith (refer to pg. 60); Observe Things About Your Life, Spiritual Battles, and What to Expect in Trials.

EVENTS AFTER THIS LESSON AND BEFORE THE NEXT:
None.

LESSON 14: GENESIS 19:1-8 TAKING THINGS INTO OUR OWN HANDS "TO PROTECT GOD'S INTERESTS" (LOT)

This lesson looks at Lot's willingness to give up his daughters to, well basically, be raped by the men of Sodom. He does this because of his desire to protect the two men (angels of the Lord), who are visiting in his home. Several questions arise. Is it God's will that Lot give up his daughters as a sacrifice in the same way God later wanted Abraham to be willing to sacrifice Isaac? Is Lot taking matters into his own hands? In other words, if Lot asked God for guidance, would God have had different steps of faith for him to take, other than offering his daughters to the men of Sodom? What is Satan trying to get Lot to do or not do in his trial? Is the fact that Lot wants to do the right thing enough to make whatever he does to *be* the right thing, i.e., the thing God wanted to do through him?

The Bible does not specifically tell us the answers which Lot would need in order to serve God without sinning. So, the purpose of this lesson's poieological study is to put ourselves in Lot's position in order to better appreciate challenges we sometimes face when we have to discern need-to-know answers to hard questions in short-fused, complex, real-life trials. When we don't discern God's guidance from His Spirit during a trial, then we usually act on our "own (fleshly) understanding" without actually meaning to do so. When we don't make time to be dependent on God because we think there is no time, then the same thing may be true. This is the effect that Satan's attacks and influences can have on us during trials.

SCRIPTURE SUMMARY: Genesis 19:1-8 – Two men (who are actually angels) arrive in Sodom; Lot wants them to come to his house, and they go with Lot; men of Sodom go to Lot's house and want to have sex with the two new men in town (the angels); Lot doesn't want that to happen, so he offers to the men of Sodom his two engaged daughters.

Special Consideration:
Read also Genesis 19:14, which tells us that Lot's two daughters were already engaged to marry at the time Lot's trial started.

Special Consideration:
OPTIONAL LESSON you can study later (if you want). You could look at the text from Lot's wife's perspective. You could also do it from the perspective of Lot's two unmarried daughters. Follow the template for the study being sure to identify your heart disturbances, as well as identifying what God would seek to change in you, so you could to be at peace with the kind of actions Lot takes, from the women's perspectives!

CONTEXT:
Other Relevant Information:
1. Remember, Lot has spent much time with Abraham and Sarah. When they moved from Haran (Genesis 12:4-5), Lot was with them. Lot was with them when they went into Egypt as well.
2. The Bible is not clear whether Lot realized the two men were angels, although he did recognize that they were worth special attention. He strongly insisted they stay at his house. Even while Lot may have known who they were, it is not clear whether his family or the men of Sodom recognized who they were. If Lot recognized the two men as angels and Lot's family did not, then that could have made it easier for Satan to attack his family. It could have made it more difficult for Lot's family to understand and support the extent to which Lot was going to fulfill his strong desire to protect his guests.
3. It was part of the Middle Eastern culture that if someone entered one's home, that person was to come under the protection of the homeowner. How far that obligation was carried probably varied.

WHO IS INVOLVED IN Lot's TRIAL (Main Players Only)?
God, Satan, Lot, two angels of the Lord in physical form (looked like men), Lot's two daughters, men of Sodom

WHAT DECISION(S) MUST Lot MAKE?

Lot has to decide what to do when the men of Sodom continue to aggressively seek to obtain the two angels in Lot's house. Lot's actions included:

1. Lot talked with "the perpetrators-to-be" and sought to reason with them.
2. Lot offered his daughters to the men of Sodom.

Is Lot going to the Lord for guidance in his heart while the trial is rapidly unfolding? Is Lot rationalizing that sex with women (his daughters) is more "right" since they are technically single? Are the daughters being treated like commodities in a financial-like negotiation? Is Lot pimping his daughters?!

WHAT KNOWLEDGE OF GOD COULD Lot HAVE HAD TO ASSIST HIM TO ACT AS GOD WANTS?

1. The Bible doesn't make it clear exactly what knowledge Lot personally had about God. Most of Lot's knowledge of God might have been second-hand through Abram, although Lot could have recognized God's favor upon Abram.
2. Genesis 12:4-5 – Lot probably knew that Abram believed God had given him the 3 promises and that God's direction was the reason he moved from Haran.
3. Genesis 12:8 – Lot probably knew that Abram worshipped the Lord.
4. Genesis 12:17-20 to 13:2 – Lot could have recognized that God delivered Abram and Sarai (and himself) from Pharaoh in Egypt, and that Abram's wealth increased as a result.
5. Genesis 14 – Lot could have recognized God delivered him through Abram when he was captured at Sodom. Lot probably knew Abram gave God the glory for the victory.

WHAT WAS Lot's HEART DISTURBANCE?

(See how others responded to the rest of the lesson – pg. 277)

DID Lot SUBMIT TO THE LORD TRANSFORMING HIS HEART AND MIND SO THE LORD COULD LIVE THROUGH HIM?

DISCUSSION QUESTION 1: The two men (angels) were under the protection of Lot because they were in his home. Some view Lot's obligation as implying that he had the responsibility to protect them "*at any cost.*" Was that cultural obligation absolutely right (godly) meaning that Lot didn't need to seek God's counsel on how to fulfill it, or did Lot have the responsibility to seek God's counsel regardless?

PUT YOURSELF IN Lot's "SHOES" – LISTEN TO THE AUDIO
(Go to www.Feelings102.com to get or play the AUDIO)

WHAT WOULD YOUR TYPICAL HEART DISTURBANCE BE IF YOU WERE Lot IN THIS SITUATION OR ONE LIKE IT?
(You can use the list of heart disturbances on page 23)

I'd feel _____ *because* _____

_____

I'd feel _____ *because* _____

_____

I would/would not want _____

because _____

DISCUSSION QUESTION 2: Let's imagine for a moment that God *did* want Lot to give up his daughters. That probably would have been hard for Lot's wife to handle, let alone for the daughters. *If* it were God's will (in the sense of a test as with Abraham), then God would be working to transform Lot's wife so He could live through her. That wouldn't mean she'd necessarily happy, but rather she'd have to take steps of faith that enabled her to avoid being driven by Satan to act in a fleshly way. Obviously God can transform us to that extent, but would we cooperate with God's love?

In this DISCUSSION QUESTION, look at how your heart feels and how your actions look when you experience the peace of God about a course of action. This way we can see the state of mind and level of conduct that a solid heart transformation produces. This exercise can assist us in doing a better job of examining our willingness to be transformed by the Lord in a trial. Whenever we discern that God wants us to embrace a desire other than one that is of the flesh, our responses to this DISCUSSION QUESTION show us what to look for in ourselves to see if we are experiencing the peace of God.

When we are at peace with God about a course of action, how do we act and how do our hearts feel?

DISCERN/OBSERVE
Discern Fleshly Tendencies (refer to Special Consideration on pg. 33)

Discern Lying Belief (refer to Special Consideration on pg. 24)

_____.

Discern and Feel the Truth of Your Identity in Christ (Discern one of the four starting pg. 14. Feel it! Use the feeling words on pg. 27.Write how it feels using "I feel ___ because ___. An example is on pg. 58.)

Discern What The Lord Would Seek to Change in You to Transform Your Heart Disturbances So You Experience the Peace of God. [For example in your behaviors (internal too, not just external), attitude, preferences, opinions, thinking, point of view, or sensitivity (i.e., more Christ-like sensitivity to others/self or less fleshly sensitivity to others/self, etc.).]

Discern Possible Steps of Faith (refer to pg. 60); Observe Things About Your Life, Spiritual Battles, and What to Expect in Trials.

EVENTS AFTER THIS LESSON AND BEFORE THE NEXT:
1. Genesis 19:9-17 – The men (2 angels) tell Lot, who in turn tells his wife, daughters and sons-in-law, that God is going to destroy Sodom. They are to flee, but not look back.
2. Genesis 19:18-29 – Lot, his wife and daughters escape the catastrophe on Sodom and Gomorrah; Lot's wife looks back and dies; Abraham sees the aftermath.

LESSON 15: GENESIS 19:30-38 THERE'S NO WAY I'M *NOT* HAVING KIDS (LOT'S DAUGHTERS)

This lesson could have been titled, "Some Desires Are Normal And Always Seem OK To Have!" Sometimes we may think it's OK to have certain desires when we face a trial, especially when our situation is contrary to "the normal way of things." When we think this way, Satan can get us to justify doing and wanting what the flesh wants. Satan can cause us to overlook important spiritual goings-on in certain real-life situations! In such trials, Satan tries to get us to justify our desires, feelings, and actions by inappropriately applying Scripture. Satan tries to get us to "make rules" out of some things in the Bible when it is quite inappropriate to do so.

Had Lot's daughters had the Bible available to them, they may have cited God's directive to "Be fruitful and increase in number...," (Genesis 1:28) as part of justifying their desires for children. Lot's daughters' desire for children wasn't evil or fleshly in and of itself. However, the way they went about it was sinful. While the way Lot's daughters approach their trial may be outrageously different than the way we might behave, there is something important to observe. Satan's influences often give us fleshly thoughts that justify our actions. So, while our desires may not always be fleshly in and of themselves, Satan's tactics often include getting us to act in fleshly ways and according to fleshly timing. Satan is often behind our drive to try to get what we want when we want it.

SCRIPTURE SUMMARY: Genesis 19:30-38 – Lot's daughters are tempted to take matters into their own hands in order to ensure they have children soon, but to do so they will have to sleep with their own father.

CONTEXT:
Other Relevant Information:
1. Sarah was Abraham's half-sister, so perhaps part of Satan's deception with Lot's daughters involved rationalizing that sleeping with their father wasn't *that* unnatural. The Bible does not speak to everything the daughters might have thought.
2. Abraham and Lot had to separate due to the size of their herds. Lot was permitted to choose the good land in the valley of Sodom and Gomorrah. As a result, Lot and his family became intertwined with the ungodly thinking and lifestyles of the peoples there.

WHO IS INVOLVED IN Lot's Daughters' TRIALS (Main Players Only)?
God, Satan, Lot, Lot's two daughters

WHAT DECISION(S) MUST Lot's Daughters MAKE?
Lot's daughters must decide what they will do with their desire to have kids, like right now! They also must decide how to handle the apparent lack of prospects for gaining husbands with whom to have children. After all, their dad "kinda blew their man prospects!"

WHAT KNOWLEDGE OF GOD COULD Lot's Daughters HAVE HAD TO ASSIST THEM TO ACT AS GOD WANTS?
1. The Bible doesn't specify exactly what knowledge Lot's daughters had about God.
2. Lot had traveled from Ur to Haran to Canaan to Egypt and back to Canaan with Abraham. So, Lot's daughters were likely exposed to Abraham and his beliefs in God to some extent. The Bible does not make this clear.
3. Lot's daughters were likely exposed to Abraham's belief in God and Abraham's belief that God was leading the family and watching over them in many situations (Pharaoh in Egypt, Lot and family being delivered from captivity).
4. Lot's daughters may have known their father believed that God was responsible for destroying Sodom and Gomorrah, and that he believed God permitted them to escape.

5. They knew their mother became a pillar of salt, and probably that Lot believed this was because she did not trust and obey God's command not to look back.

6. V. 19:8 – Lot's daughters probably didn't like the fact that their father offered them to the men of Sodom without a proper marriage relationship. Satan may have used this in his attack on the daughters to lead them to justify sleeping with their father without a proper marriage relationship!

WHAT WAS Lot's Daughters' HEART DISTURBANCE?
(See how others responded to the rest of the lesson – pg. 281)

DID Lot's Daughters SUBMIT TO THE LORD TRANSFORMING THEIR HEARTS AND MINDS SO THE LORD COULD LIVE THROUGH THEM?

Special Consideration:
Before listening to the AUDIO, let's address an important aspect of this trial. As in the lesson dealing with Cain (Lesson 3) and Hagar (Lesson 10), it can be difficult to try to identify with the challenges of Lot's daughters' heart disturbances because their actions are so clearly sinful.

God seeks to communicate to unbelievers and ungodly people. Each trial they experience gives them the opportunity to discern the path God would have them on. By seeking God's will and letting Him transform them in the trial at hand, God will use that godly choice to lead them in the direction which brings them to Him. This is part of what is implied when God tells Cain that he must "master sin," a task that cannot be done without dependence on God. So by making the choice God would have of them, even "ungodly" people have the opportunity to surrender to God and *continue* making choices that submit to His lead. In time, this can lead them to embrace the relationship with God that He hopes they will want. This is actually part of what makes everyone accountable to God. Even unbelievers have made *some* choices out of a dependence on God. If they learn from those choices, they have proof by their own actions of the importance of a relationship with God in which they are dependent on Him!

With that in mind, it is profitable to study Lot's daughters' trial in terms of putting yourself in their situation and seek out the perspective from which they have the opportunity for God to live through them. It challenges you to see, from their perspective, what it would have taken to discern and choose God's guidance for them over their fleshly thinking. We know that God brought them out of the cities He destroyed (V. 29). We know that their husbands-to-be were killed in that destruction and that had to be hard for them to handle. But, for the daughters to have discerned the Lord's will concerning having children, they would have to deny their own fleshly desires to take things into their own hands. So even though Lot's daughters sinned in this trial, we share a similar challenge to deny our own tendencies to take things in our own hands during our trials! As you listen to the AUDIO, put yourself in the moments of Lot's daughters' feelings of isolation and seek out what God would seek to change in you so that you could embrace being isolated at the time!

PUT YOURSELF IN Lot's Daughters' "SHOES" – LISTEN TO THE AUDIO (Go to www.Feelings102.com to get or play the AUDIO)

WHAT WOULD YOUR TYPICAL HEART DISTURBANCE BE IF YOU WERE Lot's Daughters IN THIS SITUATION OR ONE LIKE IT? *(You can use the list of heart disturbances on page 23)*

I'd feel _____ *because* _____

_____

I'd feel _____ *because* _____

_____

I would/would not want _____

because _____

DISCERN/OBSERVE:
Discern Fleshly Tendencies (refer to Special Consideration on pg. 33)

Discern Lying Belief (refer to Special Consideration on pg. 24)

_____.

Discern and Feel the Truth of Your Identity in Christ (Discern one of the four starting pg. 14. Feel it! Use the feeling words on pg. 27. Write how it feels using "I feel ___ because ___. An example is on pg. 58.)

Discern What The Lord Would Seek to Change in You to Transform Your Heart Disturbances So You Experience the Peace of God. [For example in your behaviors (internal too, not just external), attitude, preferences, opinions, thinking, point of view, or sensitivity (i.e., more Christ-like sensitivity to others/self or less fleshly sensitivity to others/self, etc.).]

Discern Possible Steps of Faith (refer to pg. 60); Observe Things About Your Life, Spiritual Battles, and What to Expect in Trials.

EVENTS AFTER THIS LESSON AND BEFORE THE NEXT:
None.

LESSON 16: GENESIS 20:1-13 I'M STILL RELUCTANT TO TRUST GOD (ABRAHAM)

The Bible records that Abraham faces a second trial where he lies about Sarah being his wife. And again, this puts Sarah in a compromising situation (as in Lesson 7). This happens less than a year after the Lord said, "…At the appointed time I will return to you, at this time next year, and Sarah will have a son" (Genesis 18:14). Abraham lies again even though God demonstrated His sufficiency to Abraham and his family after Abraham lied to Pharaoh. If anyone had good reasons to avoid fleshly thinking, it was Abraham. Still, Abraham is reluctant to stop taking matters into his own hands, just like we are sometimes. That reluctance stems from the pull of the power of sin, which works to bring out fleshly fears and promotes independence from God in our trials.

An important revelation comes out in this lesson's passage in Scripture. In the last verse of this lesson's reading, Abraham reveals that he put the pressure on Sarah to pretend to be his sister way back when God told first told him to leave Haran (Genesis 12:1, Lesson 5)!! That would have been about 24 years prior to the trial he faces in this lesson. This shows that from the beginning, when God first called him, Abraham had placed certain limits on how much he was willing to be transformed by God. This isn't said to disparage Abraham. We aren't better than him in some way even though he did that. It just shows God's grace and love is always available even when we're scared.

A key point to observe is that God tolerates Abraham's reluctance (to some extent), not because Abraham is worthy on his own, but because God loves him and made certain Promises that He chose to fulfill through Abraham! Another key point is that a vital part of God transforming us and sanctifying us involves taking the opportunity to look back in our own lives and discern (from the Spirit) where we, under Satan's influence, have placed *our* own limits on ways in which we trust God. This lesson's study of Abraham challenges us to look for areas where we might be holding back, so we can take those to God and seek His help.

SCRIPTURE SUMMARY: Genesis 20:1-13 –Abraham and family are in the Negev region and again he passes Sarah off as his sister; Abimelech takes her; God speaks to Abimelech in a dream and reveals Sarah is married; Abimelech pleads innocence to God, Who tells him to return Sarah to Abraham; Abimelech obeys God and approaches Abraham on his offense; Abraham confesses to being challenged to "save his own skin" by lying about his relationship with Sarah, and telling her that "if you love me you'll lie for me."

Special Consideration:

OPTIONAL LESSON you can study later (if you want). You could look at the text from Sarah's perspective. As Sarah, what would God be trying to transform in you so you could trust Him and experience His peace despite Abraham's decision to lie about his relationship to you for a second time?! Do you, Sarah, have to agree with the decision? What steps of faith might God seek to have you take, even though Abraham takes things into his own hands in an ungodly way. Note that Sarah, again, fulfills her role as "sister" well and God intervenes to deliver her and Abraham from the situation. Sarah does not display a disgruntled, negative attitude, which would have hinted to Abimelech that Abraham was lying about Sarah's relationship to him.

CONTEXT:

Patterns in Satan's past attacks (temptations) on Abraham:
1. Likely attack by Satan on Abram in Genesis 12:1-4 – don't stand up and say you are moving without knowing where you are going – overcame Satan's attack.
2. An actual attack by Satan on Abram in Genesis 12:10-20 – don't stand up and say Sarai is your wife or you might be killed – fell to Satan's attack.
3. Likely attack by Satan on Abram in Genesis 13:1-11 – stand up and say you want the choice land – overcame Satan's attack.
4. An actual attack by Satan on Abram in Genesis 15:1-16:3 – stand up and say that Eliezer of Damascus will be your heir – overcame Satan's attack.
5. An actual attack by Satan on Abram in Genesis 16:1-6 – don't stand up and refuse to sleep with Hagar or you might not get an heir – fell to Satan's attack.

6. Likely attack by Satan on Abram in Genesis 17:1-18 – don't stand up and make changes in the household that others may not like – overcame Satan's attack.

7. **Likely attack by Satan on Abraham in Genesis 18:16-33 – stand up and get involved to assist Lot and his family or they may die – overcame Satan's attack.**

Other Relevant Information: After the destruction of Sodom and Gomorrah, Abraham and family move again about 20 miles from the Hebron area to Gerar, where they run into Abimelech.

WHO IS INVOLVED IN Abraham's TRIAL (Main Players Only)?
God, Satan, Abraham, Sarah, Abimelech

WHAT DECISION(S) MUST Abraham MAKE?
Abraham has to make a decision on how to deal with the possible threat from Abimelech: tell the truth about Sarah, or lie.

WHAT KNOWLEDGE OF GOD COULD Abraham HAVE HAD TO ASSIST HIM TO ACT AS GOD WANTS?
1. Genesis 11:30 – Abram knew his wife Sarai was barren and could not have children.
2. Genesis 12:1 – Abram knew God wanted him to leave his country (Haran), his people and his father's household.
3. Genesis 12:1 – Abram knew he was to move without knowing where he was moving to, and that God would show him where later.
4. Genesis 12:2-3 – Abram knew God made three Promises:
    a. Personal – God will bless Abram and make his name great.
    b. National – God will make Abram into a great nation and his descendants would have their own land.
    c. Universal – God will bless all peoples on the earth through Abram.
5. Genesis 12:6-7 – Abram knew God was true to His word when He told Abram the land of Canaan was the Promised Land.

6. Genesis 12:10-20 – Abram knew God protected him, even when Pharaoh found out he lied. He knew God helped him to prosper during his time in Egypt. Abram knew God was true to His word.
7. Genesis 13:14-17 – Abram knew God reiterated His Promises.
8. Genesis 14:22-23 – Abram knew God enabled him to prevail and defeat the enemies that captured Lot.
9. Genesis 15 – Abram knew that God confirmed he would have a son, and God reiterated the Promises a second time and made a covenant with Abram. Abram knew that God provided a timeline of some key events in the future and that God assured his personal safety into old age.
10. Genesis 17 – Abram knew he was to be blameless. He knew God reiterated the Promises a third time and established His covenant as an everlasting one. Abram knew God gave him some directives and assured Abram that Sarai would bear a son through whom God's covenant would be fulfilled.
11. Genesis 18:20-21 – Abraham knew about sin and that God holds people accountable for sin. Abraham knew God was looking to hold Sodom and Gomorrah accountable.
12. **Genesis 20:11-13 – Abraham knew that saying Sarah was his sister was a half-truth and that he was lying to protect himself.**
13. **Genesis 20:17-18 – Abraham knew that his lie placed Abimelech and his household in the position of sinning without realizing it. (Abraham knew that, before God, he had dealt falsely with Abimelech; see their conversation in Genesis 21:23-24.) Abraham knew that even Sarah had been exposed to the consequences of his fleshly ways. Abraham knew he had to go before God to intervene on behalf of those he had influenced to go against God's will.**

WHAT WAS Abraham's HEART DISTURBANCE?
(See how others responded to the rest of the lesson – pg. 283)

DID Abraham SUBMIT TO THE LORD TRANSFORMING HIS HEART AND MIND SO THE LORD COULD LIVE THROUGH HIM?

PUT YOURSELF IN Abraham's "SHOES" – LISTEN TO AUDIO (Go to www.Feelings102.com to get or play the AUDIO) **WHAT WOULD YOUR TYPICAL HEART DISTURBANCE BE IF YOU WERE Abraham IN THIS SITUATION OR ONE LIKE IT?** *(You can use the list of heart disturbances on page 23)*

I'd feel _____ *because* _____

_____

I'd feel _____ *because* _____

_____

I would/would not want _____

because _____

DISCERN/OBSERVE:
Discern Fleshly Tendencies (refer to Special Consideration on pg. 33)

Discern Lying Belief (refer to Special Consideration on pg. 24)

_____.

Discern and Feel the Truth of Your Identity in Christ (Discern one of the four starting pg. 14. Feel it! Use the feeling words on pg. 27. Write how it feels using "I feel ___ because ___. An example is on pg. 58.)

Discern What The Lord Would Seek to Change in You to Transform Your Heart Disturbances So You Experience the Peace of God. [For example in your behaviors (internal too, not just external), attitude, preferences, opinions, thinking, point of view, or sensitivity (i.e., more Christ-like sensitivity to others/self or less fleshly sensitivity to others/self, etc.).]

Discern Possible Steps of Faith (refer to pg. 60); Observe Things About Your Life, Spiritual Battles, and What to Expect in Trials.

DISCUSSION QUESTIONS:
1. What are some *similarities* between our trials and Abraham's?

2. What are some *differences* between our trials and Abraham's?

EVENTS AFTER THIS LESSON AND BEFORE THE NEXT:
1. Genesis 20:14-15 – Abimelech gives Abraham livestock and the opportunity to live anywhere on his land.
2. Genesis 20:16-17 – Abimelech gives Sarah silver to make restitution for his unintentional offense toward her; Abraham prays to God for Abimelech; God heals Abimelech and his family and allows the women to have children again.

LESSON 17: GENESIS 21:1-11 HOW DO YOU WANT TO DEAL WITH MY WIFE'S DISSATISFACTION, LORD? (ABRAHAM)

While Hagar is not Abraham's wife, he had a son by her. Hagar and Ishmael live with Abraham and Sarah. Talk about a touchy situation! Imagine Abraham spending time with his son, young Ishmael, doing whatever kinds of things fathers did with their sons back then, and at the same time both Sarah and Hagar are there!

While Abraham may not have been super close to Hagar (she was a servant), the relationship with Ishmael as his son was likely somewhat different. Ishmael and Abraham have been together for about 14 years. They had a father-son relationship. But, when *Isaac* was born, Sarah's heart disturbances against Hagar became stronger. As time passed, things became more stressful in the house of Abraham. It all stemmed from Abraham trying to gain a son by sleeping with "the help," an action taken independently of God.

Eventually things came to a head. Sarah, who was blessed by God with her own child Isaac, has her reasons to want Hagar gone. As a result, Sarah put pressure on Abraham to kick Hagar and Ishmael out. Sarah's thinking was convinced it was OK for her to want her husband to abandon his son Ishmael! In turn, Satan attacked Abraham and his heart became troubled about losing his son. The Lord provided guidance to Abraham, and this time Abraham listened closely.

Keep in mind, the cultural customs of the day were that it was wrong to abandon a servant woman or her child fathered by the householder (in this case, Abraham). Still, Abraham decides to do exactly that, not just because it is what his wife wants, but because, interestingly enough, it is a step of faith he must take for God!

SCRIPTURE SUMMARY: Genesis 21:1-11 – Sarah wants (desires) Abraham to kick Hagar and Ishmael out on their own.

Special Consideration:
OPTIONAL LESSON you can study later (if you want). You could look at the text from Sarah's perspective. In the previous lesson, Sarah had great faith to endure being "given" to Abimelech. God delivered her (and Abraham). God also made good on His promise, and Sarah had a son! Still, Sarah's heart was not automatically softened. Satan attacked Sarah and focused her attention against Hagar. As Sarah, would Hagar and Ishmael be constant reminders of your past failures in following the Lord? How would you feel if you were in Sarah's situation? How strong would those feelings have to be to want Abraham to kick Hagar and Ishmael out? Of course, what would God seek to change in you to be at peace with embracing Hagar and Ishmael?

CONTEXT:
Patterns in Satan's past attacks (temptations) on Abraham:
1. Likely attack by Satan on Abram in Genesis 12:1-4 – don't stand up and say you are moving without knowing where you are going – overcame Satan's attack.
2. An actual attack by Satan on Abram in Genesis 12:10-20 – don't stand up and say Sarai is your wife or you might be killed – fell to Satan's attack.
3. Likely attack by Satan on Abram in Genesis 13:1-11 – stand up and say you want the choice land – overcame Satan's attack.
4. An actual attack by Satan on Abram in Genesis 15:1-16:3 – stand up and say that Eliezer of Damascus will be your heir – overcame Satan's attack.
5. An actual attack by Satan on Abram in Genesis 16:1-6 – don't stand up and refuse to sleep with Hagar or you might not get an heir – fell to Satan's attack.
6. Likely attack by Satan on Abram in Genesis 17:1-18 – don't stand up and make changes in the household that others may not like – overcame Satan's attack.
7. Likely attack by Satan on Abraham in Genesis 18:16-33 – stand up and get involved to assist Lot and his family or they may die – overcame Satan's attack.
8. **An actual attack by Satan on Abraham in Genesis 20:1-13 – don't stand up and say Sarah is your wife or you might be killed – fell to Satan's attack.**

Other Relevant Information:
1. Sarah is concerned (heart disturbance) about Ishmael having access to the inheritance.
2. Abraham was 100 years old when Isaac was born. He was 86 years old when Ishmael was born. At the time of this lesson's trial, Isaac is eight days old, and Ishmael is about 14 years old.
3. God told Hagar to stay with the family about 14 years prior (Genesis 16:9).
4. We mentioned (in the CONTEXT of Lesson 9) that it was an accepted custom, by the peoples living in Canaan, that a man could have a son through a maidservant, if his wife was barren. If a man did this, it was the man's responsibility not to abandon the maidservant or the offspring through her.

WHO IS INVOLVED IN Abraham's TRIAL (Main Players Only)?
God, Satan, Abraham, Hagar, Ishmael, Sarah, Isaac

WHAT DECISION(S) MUST Abraham MAKE?
Abraham has to decide whether to reject Hagar and Ishmael by making them leave, or whether to reject Sarah's wishes by allowing them to stay.

WHAT KNOWLEDGE OF GOD COULD Abraham HAVE HAD TO ASSIST HIM TO ACT AS GOD WANTS?
1. Genesis 11:30 – Abram knew his wife Sarai was barren and could not have children.
2. Genesis 12:1 – Abram knew God wanted him to leave his country (Haran), his people and his father's household.
3. Genesis 12:1 – Abram knew he was to move without knowing where he was moving to, and that God would show him where later.
4. Genesis 12:2-3 – Abram knew God made three Promises:
   a. Personal – God will bless Abram and make his name great.
   b. National – God will make Abram into a great nation and his descendants would have their own land.
   c. Universal – God will bless all peoples on the earth through Abram.

5. Genesis 12:6-7 – Abram knew God was true to His word when He told Abram the land of Canaan was the Promised Land.

6. Genesis 12:10-20 – Abram knew God protected him, even when Pharaoh found out he lied. He knew God helped him to prosper during his time in Egypt. Abram knew God was true to His word.

7. Genesis 13:14-17 – Abram knew God reiterated His Promises.

8. Genesis 14:22-23 – Abram knew God enabled him to prevail and defeat the enemies that captured Lot.

9. Genesis 15 – Abram knew that God confirmed he would have a son, and God reiterated the Promises a second time and made a covenant with Abram. Abram knew that God provided a timeline of some key events in the future and that God assured his personal safety into old age.

10. Genesis 17 – Abram knew he was to be blameless. He knew God reiterated the Promises a third time and established His covenant as an everlasting one. Abram knew God gave him some directives and assured Abram that Sarai would bear a son through whom God's covenant would be fulfilled.

11. Genesis 18:20-21 – Abraham knew about sin and that God holds people accountable for sin. Abraham knew God was looking to hold Sodom and Gomorrah accountable.

12. Genesis 20:11-13 – Abraham knew that saying Sarah was his sister was a half-truth and that he was lying to protect himself.

13. Genesis 20:17-18 – Abraham knew that his lie placed Abimelech and his household in the position of sinning without realizing it. (Abraham knew that, before God, he had dealt falsely with Abimelech; see their conversation in Genesis 21:23-24.) Abraham knew that even Sarah had been exposed to the consequences of his sin. Abraham knew he had to go before God to intervene on behalf of those he had influenced to go against God's will.

14. **Genesis 21:2 – Abraham knew God again made good on His promise of Sarah having a son, and it happened in the time God said it would happen (Genesis 17:21 and 18:10).**

15. **Genesis 21:9-10 – Abraham knew Sarah was fearful of Ishmael, even though God told Abraham that His promise and covenant would be fulfilled through Isaac (Genesis 17:19-21).**

WHAT WAS Abraham's HEART DISTURBANCE?
(See how others responded to the rest of the lesson – pg. 287)

DID Abraham SUBMIT TO THE LORD TRANSFORMING HIS HEART AND MIND SO THE LORD COULD LIVE THROUGH HIM?

PUT YOURSELF IN Abraham's "SHOES" – LISTEN TO AUDIO (Go to www.Feelings102.com to get or play the AUDIO)

WHAT WOULD YOUR TYPICAL HEART DISTURBANCE BE IF YOU WERE Abraham IN THIS SITUATION OR ONE LIKE IT?
(You can use the list of heart disturbances on page 23)

I'd feel _____ *because* _____

_____

I'd feel _____ *because* _____

_____

I would/would not want _____

because _____

DISCERN/OBSERVE:
Discern Fleshly Tendencies (refer to Special Consideration on pg. 33)

Discern Lying Belief (refer to Special Consideration on pg. 24)

_____.

Discern and Feel the Truth of Your Identity in Christ (Discern one of the four starting pg. 14. Feel it! Use the feeling words on pg. 27. Write how it feels using "I feel ___ because ___. An example is on pg. 58.)

Discern What The Lord Would Seek to Change in You to Transform Your Heart Disturbances So You Experience the Peace of God. [For example in your behaviors (internal too, not just external), attitude, preferences, opinions, thinking, point of view, or sensitivity (i.e., more Christ-like sensitivity to others/self or less fleshly sensitivity to others/self, etc.).]

Discern Possible Steps of Faith (refer to pg. 60); Observe Things About Your Life, Spiritual Battles, and What to Expect in Trials.

EVENTS AFTER THIS LESSON AND BEFORE THE NEXT:
1. Genesis 21:12-13 – God tells Abraham to make Hagar and Ishmael leave. God says He will increase Abraham's descendants through Isaac, as well as increasing the descendants of Ishmael.
2. Genesis 21:14-21 – Abraham makes Hagar and Ishmael leave. They run into trouble trying to survive. God provides for them. In time God provides a wife for Ishmael from Egypt, Hagar's home country.

LESSON 18: GENESIS 21:1-16 UNLOVED, USED, AND DUMPED (HAGAR)

This lesson examines the same passage as the last lesson, but this time we'll look at it from Hagar's perspective.

As in Lesson 10, Abraham hasn't always stuck up for Hagar. When someone treats us similarly and the leader doesn't bring that mistreatment to an end, we have heart disturbances. Those situations turn into trials marked by powerful and unwanted feelings, as well as fleshly desires.

Typically we tend to believe God doesn't want us in such environments. But as we saw in Lesson 10, that isn't always true (God told Hagar to stay and not run away from Sarah). Hagar heard God's counsel 14 years prior to this lesson's trial, and she took steps of faith.

However, in this trial the stakes are higher for Hagar. She has a 14 year old son! We can all probably agree that isn't the best time for Hagar, a servant woman, to have to venture out on her own, especially back then. God has a different view. God's wants Abraham, contrary to the social and legal customs of the day, to release Hagar and Ishmael into His care. To anyone other than Abraham it could look as if the reason is because it's what his wife, Sarah, wants. Imagine how that must have looked to Hagar. What painful heart disturbances she must have felt! Satan attacked everyone involved! In this lesson, the attack we want to focus on is in V. 15-16. Hagar is finally tempted to leave her son because she thinks they are going to die and it pains her too much to watch her son die.

This lesson is another in which we (the authors) have left out the verses describing the outcome of the trial. The selected passage stops with Hagar wandering in the desert of Beersheba. This challenges us to focus on discerning what God's Spirit would reveal about transforming us and taking steps of faith, so the Lord responds through us in the trial. Put yourself in Hagar's shoes. Identify the heart disturbances that you would have. Discern what God would want to transform in you. Remember to approach Hagar's situation as if you don't know the outcome. What would God want to change in you so you are fulfilled in Him during such a trial full of external lack and insecurity?

SCRIPTURE SUMMARY: Genesis 21:1-16 – Abraham kicks Hagar and Ishmael out of the household; Hagar has to deal with it; externally the reason appears to be because Sarah wants Hagar and Ishmael gone; it looks as if Hagar and Ishmael will die of thirst and that is too much for Hagar; she walks off by herself and is debating on whether to leave Ishmael so she doesn't have to watch him die.

CONTEXT:
Other Relevant Information:
1. God told Hagar to stay with Abraham and Sarah about 14 years earlier (Genesis 16:9). In other words, God's steps of faith for Hagar were for her to stay. At that time, God told Hagar (Genesis 16:11-12) that Ishmael would live to be a man and would have many descendants (Genesis 16:10).
2. In this lesson, Ishmael is about 14 years old.

WHO IS INVOLVED IN Hagar's TRIAL (Main Players Only)?
God, Satan, Abraham, Hagar, Sarah, Ishmael

WHAT DECISION(S) MUST Hagar MAKE?
Hagar must decide whether to let God transform her, so she believes what God has revealed to her 14 years before, or to run away from her son in anticipation that he will die.

WHAT KNOWLEDGE OF GOD COULD Hagar HAVE HAD TO ASSIST HER TO ACT AS GOD WANTS?
1. In Genesis 16:9, Hagar knew God told her to return to Sarah and to submit to her.
2. In Genesis 16:10, Hagar knew God told her He would increase her descendants until they are too numerous to count.

WHAT WAS Hagar's HEART DISTURBANCE?
(See how others responded to the rest of the lesson – pg. 289)

DID Hagar SUBMIT TO THE LORD TRANSFORMING HER HEART AND MIND SO THE LORD COULD LIVE THROUGH HER?

PUT YOURSELF IN Hagar's "SHOES" – LISTEN TO THE AUDIO (Go to www.Feelings102.com to get or play the AUDIO)

WHAT WOULD YOUR TYPICAL HEART DISTURBANCE BE IF YOU WERE Hagar IN THIS SITUATION OR ONE LIKE IT?
(You can use the list of heart disturbances on page 23)

I'd feel _____ *because* _____

_____

I'd feel _____ *because* _____

_____

I would/would not want _____

because _____

DISCERN/OBSERVE:
Discern Fleshly Tendencies (refer to Special Consideration on pg. 33)

Lesson 18: Genesis 21:1-16 (Hagar)

Discern Lying Belief (refer to Special Consideration on pg. 24)

_____.

Discern and Feel the Truth of Your Identity in Christ (Discern one of the four starting pg. 14. Feel it! Use the feeling words on pg. 27.Write how it feels using "I feel ___ because ___. An example is on pg. 58.)

Discern What The Lord Would Seek to Change in You to Transform Your Heart Disturbances So You Experience the Peace of God. [For example in your behaviors (internal too, not just external), attitude, preferences, opinions, thinking, point of view, or sensitivity (i.e., more Christ-like sensitivity to others/self or less fleshly sensitivity to others/self, etc.).]

Discern Possible Steps of Faith (refer to pg. 60); Observe Things About Your Life, Spiritual Battles, and What to Expect in Trials.

EVENTS AFTER THIS LESSON AND BEFORE THE NEXT:
1. Genesis 21:17-19 – God's angel speaks to Hagar and calls on her to trust God. God opens Hagar's eyes to a well of water, and He reiterates His Promise to her that He will make a great nation through her son.
2. Genesis 21:20-21 – God is with Ishmael as he grows up; Ishmael becomes an archer and he marries.

LESSON 19: GENESIS 21:22-32 SOMETIMES THE UNBELIEVER CHALLENGES US TO OWN OUR STUFF (ABRAHAM)

In this lesson we again look at ourselves through another of Abraham's experiences with Abimelech. While Abimelech recognizes that God is with Abraham, he also recognizes that Abraham hasn't always demonstrated God living through him. In other words, Abimelech remembers that Abraham lied about Sarah in an attempt to protect himself, even though God clearly is with Abraham and the lie wasn't necessary. The "unbeliever" (Abimelech) recognized God's will concerning Abraham when the "believer" (Abraham) failed to have faith in God's will.

We all act in the flesh sometimes. When we examine ourselves before the Lord, He can reveal to us patterns of fleshly behaviors and beliefs using our past trials. When we fall to the power of sin, there are times when our action or inaction impacts others in the process. It sometimes takes a lot to submit to God's plan to transform us so He can grow us out of the patterns Satan seeks to reinforce within us. In this lesson, Abraham demonstrates one way God sometimes uses to discipline us and get our attention.

As you put yourself in Abraham's trial, remember that in real-life we often have a hard time hearing the criticisms of others, no matter how kindly they are communicated. Satan is behind any resistance and difficulty we have in hearing the truth of how others perceive us. This is why it is so important to be open to what the Holy Spirit, through others, can reveal to us about our temptation to act in the flesh.

SCRIPTURE SUMMARY: Genesis 21:22-32 – When Abraham claims Abimelech's servants have taken over his well, Abraham faces the fact that his past dishonesty toward Abimelech has made it hard for Abimelech to trust him.

CONTEXT:

Patterns in Satan's past attacks (temptations) on Abraham:

1. Likely attack by Satan on Abram in Genesis 12:1-4 – don't stand up and say you are moving without knowing where you are going – overcame Satan's attack.
2. An actual attack by Satan on Abram in Genesis 12:10-20 – don't stand up and say Sarai is your wife or you might be killed – fell to Satan's attack.
3. Likely attack by Satan on Abram in Genesis 13:1-11 – stand up and say you want the choice land – overcame Satan's attack.
4. An actual attack by Satan on Abram in Genesis 15:1-16:3 – stand up and say that Eliezer of Damascus will be your heir – overcame Satan's attack.
5. An actual attack by Satan on Abram in Genesis 16:1-6 – don't stand up and refuse to sleep with Hagar or you might not get an heir – fell to Satan's attack.
6. Likely attack by Satan on Abram in Genesis 17:1-18 – don't stand up and make changes in the household that others may not like – overcame Satan's attack.
7. Likely attack by Satan on Abraham in Genesis 18:16-33 – stand up and get involved to assist Lot and his family or they may die – overcame Satan's attack.
8. An actual attack by Satan on Abraham in Genesis 20:1-13 – don't stand up and say Sarah is your wife or you might be killed – fell to Satan's attack.
9. **An actual attack by Satan on Abraham in Genesis 21:1-11 – stand up and refuse to support Sarah's ungodly attitude – overcame Satan's attack.**

Other Relevant Information:

1. Abimelech acted honorably even though Abraham lied about Sarah (Genesis 20:1-10).
2. Abraham prayed for Abimelech to be healed (Genesis 20:17-18).

WHO IS INVOLVED IN Abraham's TRIAL (Main Players Only)?

God, Satan, Abimelech, Abraham

WHAT DECISION(S) MUST Abraham MAKE?

Abraham has to decide whether to hear and embrace Abimelech's criticisms of him, and to determine how to relate to Abimelech, in view of lying to Abimelech in the past. Actions:

1. Abimelech asks Abraham to swear to be honest, and to treat him and his people with kindness.
2. Abraham raises a complaint to Abimelech about a well.
3. Abimelech states he has only just heard of the dispute over the well.

WHAT KNOWLEDGE OF GOD COULD Abraham HAVE HAD TO ASSIST HIM TO ACT AS GOD WANTS?

1. Genesis 11:30 – Abram knew his wife Sarai was barren and could not have children.
2. Genesis 12:1 – Abram knew God wanted him to leave his country (Haran), his people and his father's household.
3. Genesis 12:1 – Abram knew he was to move without knowing where he was moving to, and that God would show him where later.
4. Genesis 12:2-3 – Abram knew God made three Promises:
    a. Personal – God will bless Abram and make his name great.
    b. National – God will make Abram into a great nation and his descendants would have their own land.
    c. Universal – God will bless all peoples on the earth through Abram.
5. Genesis 12:6-7 – Abram knew God was true to His word when He told Abram the land of Canaan was the Promised Land.
6. Genesis 12:10-20 – Abram knew God protected him, even when Pharaoh found out he lied. He knew God helped him to prosper during his time in Egypt. Abram knew God was true to His word.
7. Genesis 13:14-17 – Abram knew God reiterated His Promises.
8. Genesis 14:22-23 – Abram knew God enabled him to prevail and defeat the enemies that captured Lot.
9. Genesis 15 – Abram knew that God confirmed he would have a son, and God reiterated the Promises a second time and made a covenant with Abram. Abram knew that God provided a timeline of some key events in the future and that God assured his personal safety into old age.

10. Genesis 17 – Abram knew he was to be blameless. He knew God reiterated the Promises a third time and established His covenant as an everlasting one. Abram knew God gave him some directives and assured Abram that Sarai would bear a son through whom God's covenant would be fulfilled.

11. Genesis 18:20-21 – Abraham knew about sin and that God holds people accountable for sin. Abraham knew God was looking to hold Sodom and Gomorrah accountable.

12. Genesis 20:11-13 – Abraham knew that saying Sarah was his sister was a half-truth and that he was lying to protect himself.

13. Genesis 20:17-18 – Abraham knew that his lie placed Abimelech and his household in the position of sinning without realizing it. (Abraham knew that, before God, he had dealt falsely with Abimelech; see their conversation in Genesis 21:23-24.) Abraham knew that even Sarah had been exposed to the consequences of his sin. Abraham knew he had to go before God to intervene on behalf of those he had influenced to go against God's will.

14. Genesis 21:2 – Abraham knew God again made good on His promise of Sarah having a son, and it happened in the time God said it would happen (Genesis 17:21 and 18:10).

15. Genesis 21:9-10 – Abraham knew Sarah was fearful of Ishmael, even though God told Abraham that His promise and covenant would be fulfilled through Isaac (Genesis 17:19-21).

16. **Genesis 21:11-13 – Abraham knew God wanted him to go against the customs of the culture of the day and kick Hagar out of the household. Abraham knew God would watch over her.**

17. **Genesis 21:23-24 – Abraham knew that, before God, he had dealt falsely with Abimelech (back in Genesis 20:11-13).**

WHAT WAS Abraham's HEART DISTURBANCE?

(See how others responded to the rest of the lesson – pg. 292)

DID Abraham SUBMIT TO THE LORD TRANSFORMING HIS HEART AND MIND SO THE LORD COULD LIVE THROUGH HIM?

PUT YOURSELF IN Abraham's "SHOES" – LISTEN TO AUDIO (Go to www.Feelings102.com to get or play the AUDIO)

WHAT WOULD YOUR TYPICAL HEART DISTURBANCE BE IF YOU WERE Abraham IN THIS SITUATION OR ONE LIKE IT?
(You can use the list of heart disturbances on page 23)

I'd feel _____ *because* _____

_____

I'd feel _____ *because* _____

_____

I would/would not want _____

because _____

DISCERN/OBSERVE:
Discern Fleshly Tendencies (refer to Special Consideration on pg. 33)

Discern Lying Belief (refer to Special Consideration on pg. 24)

_____.

Discern and Feel the Truth of Your Identity in Christ (Discern one of the four starting pg. 14. Feel it! Use the feeling words on pg. 27. Write how it feels using "I feel ___ because ___. An example is on pg. 58.)

Discern What The Lord Would Seek to Change in You to Transform Your Heart Disturbances So You Experience the Peace of God. [For example in your behaviors (internal too, not just external), attitude, preferences, opinions, thinking, point of view, or sensitivity (i.e., more Christ-like sensitivity to others/self or less fleshly sensitivity to others/self, etc.).]

Discern Possible Steps of Faith (refer to pg. 60); Observe Things About Your Life, Spiritual Battles, and What to Expect in Trials.

EVENTS AFTER THIS LESSON AND BEFORE THE NEXT:
Genesis 21:33-34 – Abraham plants a tree at Beersheba and calls upon the name of the Lord; Abraham remains in the land of the Philistines for a long time.

LESSON 20: GENESIS 22:1-10 DON'T TAKE AWAY WHAT I HAVE EARNED THROUGH MY PATIENCE (ABRAHAM)

In this lesson's trial, pay special attention to the following attitudes, perspectives and points of view God has been working to transform in both Abraham and Sarah. God reveals these when communicating the steps of faith Abraham must take in sacrificing Isaac:

1. God makes it clear that Abraham and Sarah have Isaac, not simply because they wanted a child, but because *God* wanted Isaac.

2. God makes it clear that Abraham and Sarah do not have final say or "possession" of Isaac. God seeks to transform their perspective of Isaac in the sense that Isaac is His, not theirs.

3. God makes it clear that, among the steps of faith Abraham must take, he has to be willing to face any potential distain or uncomfortable disagreement that Sarah might have with him whenever God tells him to do something Sarah might not like.

4. God makes it clear that there are times when love for family members must bow before for a greater love of God. The question is, can we be at peace with that sacrifice? Do we desire to let the Lord live through us whether others in our family are willing to or not?

5. God makes it clear that "bad" things aren't always "bad" things from His perspective. The key is to discern what God wants with us versus what Satan wants from us. When seeking the Lord in a trial, it is important to discern those two things, even though the Spirit may not reveal how the trial itself will turn out! God makes it clear that we can't always discern His will simply by trying to figure how to make the trial turn out "good" from our perspective!

As you study this passage and put yourself in Abraham's trial, think about how you would feel and what you would want if it were your family in the trial. Use this lesson as a tool to discern what God would reveal to you about how the power of sin works to bait you whenever God wants you to do something that is not "normal."

SCRIPTURE SUMMARY: Genesis 22:1-10 – Abraham waited 25 years for God's Promise of a son to be fulfilled, and now Abraham knows God wants him to sacrifice Isaac. Isaac is old enough to understand how offerings work (V. 7).

CONTEXT:

Patterns in Satan's past attacks (temptations) on Abraham:

1. Likely attack by Satan on Abram in Genesis 12:1-4 – don't stand up and say you are moving without knowing where you are going – overcame Satan's attack.
2. An actual attack by Satan on Abram in Genesis 12:10-20 – don't stand up and say Sarai is your wife or you might be killed – fell to Satan's attack.
3. Likely attack by Satan on Abram in Genesis 13:1-11 – stand up and say you want the choice land – overcame Satan's attack.
4. An actual attack by Satan on Abram in Genesis 15:1-16:3 – stand up and say that Eliezer of Damascus will be your heir – overcame Satan's attack.
5. An actual attack by Satan on Abram in Genesis 16:1-6 – don't stand up and refuse to sleep with Hagar or you might not get an heir – fell to Satan's attack.
6. Likely attack by Satan on Abram in Genesis 17:1-18 – don't stand up and make changes in the household that others may not like – overcame Satan's attack.
7. Likely attack by Satan on Abraham in Genesis 18:16-33 – stand up and get involved to assist Lot and his family or they may die – overcame Satan's attack.
8. An actual attack by Satan on Abraham in Genesis 20:1-13 – don't stand up and say Sarah is your wife or you might be killed – fell to Satan's attack.
9. An actual attack by Satan on Abraham in Genesis 21:1-11 – stand up and refuse to support Sarah's ungodly attitude – overcame Satan's attack.
10. **Likely attack by Satan on Abraham in Genesis 21:22-32 – stand up and don't let Abimelech make you feel guilty for trying to protect yourself (lying about Sarah); don't stand up and make an issue about the well or it could push Abimelech to far and lead to conflict with him – overcame Satan's attack.**

Other Relevant Information: A Hebrew Key Word from this passage is הָסַּנ and it is found in V. 1. It is translated as **test**, and it means "test, try, i.e., attempt to learn the true nature of something; to cause or allow hardship or trouble in a circumstance, often with choices within the situation."[38] There is a difference between **test**, in V. 1 and the Greek word for **tempt** used in the book of James, as well as the Greek word for **temptation** used in the Lord's prayer (aside from the language differences). James says God doesn't **tempt** us. Often we may loosely translate **tempt** as **test**, but there actually is a big difference depending on the passage being examined. Satan, and our fleshly tendencies **tempt**, which involves luring us or baiting us as part of his deception and manipulation effort to drive us to act independently of God. God tests us, not for the purpose of manipulating, deceiving, or driving us. God tests us to allow us to demonstrate to Him *and* ourselves that we need Him – are we willing to be dependent on Him? The key difference between God and Satan lies in their purposes and motives.*

WHO IS INVOLVED IN Abraham's TRIAL (Main Players Only)?

God, Satan, Abraham, Isaac, Sarah

WHAT DECISION(S) MUST Abraham MAKE?

Abraham has to decide whether to sacrifice Isaac or not. Here are some possible concerns (stuff that comes out of heart disturbances):

1. At some point Abraham is going to actually have to get Isaac on the altar. What will he say (without lying) to Isaac to make that happen? Is he going to have to man-handle his son to get him in position to sacrifice him? How will this affect Isaac mentally, emotionally, etc.?

2. What will Abraham tell his servants when he returns alone? How will they take it and how will their perceptions of

---

[38] Swanson, James: *Dictionary of Biblical Languages With Semantic Domains: Hebrew* (Old Testament). electronic ed. Oak Harbor: Logos Research Systems, Inc., 1997, G5814.

* For more about **test** versus **tempt** you can download the July 2011 "Hearts Up" edition from the authors' website. Read the *Keys Words* featured article. "Hearts Up" is a free *Keys To Understanding Life Series* ePublication.

Abraham's actions affect the overall atmosphere within his household?

3. If God allows him to go through with the sacrifice, Abraham is going to have to tell Sarah something. She isn't going to be happy. What will he say? What will their relationship be like after that?

WHAT KNOWLEDGE OF GOD COULD Abraham HAVE HAD TO ASSIST HIM TO ACT AS GOD WANTS?

1. Genesis 11:30 – Abram knew his wife Sarai was barren and could not have children.
2. Genesis 12:1 – Abram knew God wanted him to leave his country (Haran), his people and his father's household.
3. Genesis 12:1 – Abram knew he was to move without knowing where he was moving to, and that God would show him where later.
4. Genesis 12:2-3 – Abram knew God made three Promises:
   a. Personal – God will bless Abram and make his name great.
   b. National – God will make Abram into a great nation and his descendants would have their own land.
   c. Universal – God will bless all peoples on the earth through Abram.
5. Genesis 12:6-7 – Abram knew God was true to His word when He told Abram the land of Canaan was the Promised Land.
6. Genesis 12:10-20 – Abram knew God protected him, even when Pharaoh found out he lied. He knew God helped him to prosper during his time in Egypt. Abram knew God was true to His word.
7. Genesis 13:14-17 – Abram knew God reiterated His Promises.
8. Genesis 14:22-23 – Abram knew God enabled him to prevail and defeat the enemies that captured Lot.
9. Genesis 15 – Abram knew that God confirmed he would have a son, and God reiterated the Promises a second time and made a covenant with Abram. Abram knew that God provided a timeline of some key events in the future and that God assured his personal safety into old age.
10. Genesis 17 – Abram knew he was to be blameless. He knew God reiterated the Promises a third time and established His covenant as an everlasting one. Abram knew God gave him

some directives and assured Abram that Sarai would bear a son through whom God's covenant would be fulfilled.

11. Genesis 18:20-21 – Abraham knew about sin and that God holds people accountable for sin. Abraham knew God was looking to hold Sodom and Gomorrah accountable.

12. Genesis 20:11-13 – Abraham knew that saying Sarah was his sister was a half-truth and that he was lying to protect himself.

13. Genesis 20:17-18 – Abraham knew that his lie placed Abimelech and his household in the position of sinning without realizing it. (Abraham knew that, before God, he had dealt falsely with Abimelech; see their conversation in Genesis 21:23-24.) Abraham knew that even Sarah had been exposed to the consequences of his sin. Abraham knew he had to go before God to intervene on behalf of those he had influenced to go against God's will.

14. Genesis 21:2 – Abraham knew God again made good on His promise of Sarah having a son, and it happened in the time God said it would happen (Genesis 17:21 and 18:10).

15. Genesis 21:9-10 – Abraham knew Sarah was fearful of Ishmael, even though God told Abraham that His promise and covenant would be fulfilled through Isaac (Genesis 17:19-21).

16. Genesis 21:11-13 – Abraham knew God wanted him to go against the customs of the culture of the day and send Hagar away. Abraham knew God would watch over her.

17. Genesis 21:23-24 – Abraham knew that, before God, he had dealt falsely with Abimelech (back in Genesis 20:11-13).

18. **Genesis 22:2 – Abraham knew God wanted him to sacrifice Isaac.**

WHAT WAS Abraham's HEART DISTURBANCE?
(See how others responded to the rest of the lesson – pg. 295)

DID Abraham SUBMIT TO THE LORD TRANSFORMING HIS HEART AND MIND SO THE LORD COULD LIVE THROUGH HIM?

PUT YOURSELF IN Abraham's "SHOES" – LISTEN TO AUDIO (Go to www.Feelings102.com to get or play the AUDIO)

WHAT WOULD YOUR TYPICAL HEART DISTURBANCE BE IF YOU WERE Abraham IN THIS SITUATION OR ONE LIKE IT?
(You can use the list of heart disturbances on page 23)

I'd feel _____ *because* _____

_____

I'd feel _____ *because* _____

_____

I would/would not want _____

because _____

DISCUSSION QUESTIONS:
1. How does taking steps of faith involve being willing to be detached?

2. What would we need to be willing to embrace in order to be detached, wherever God is challenging us to do that in a trial?

DISCERN/OBSERVE:
Discern Fleshly Tendencies (refer to Special Consideration on pg. 33)

Discern Lying Belief (refer to Special Consideration on pg. 24)

_____.

Discern and Feel the Truth of Your Identity in Christ (Discern one of the four starting pg. 14. Feel it! Use the feeling words on pg. 27. Write how it feels using "I feel ___ because ___. An example is on pg. 58.)

Discern What The Lord Would Seek to Change in You to Transform Your Heart Disturbances So You Experience the Peace of God. [For example in your behaviors (internal too, not just external), attitude, preferences, opinions, thinking, point of view, or sensitivity (i.e., more Christ-like sensitivity to others/self or less fleshly sensitivity to others/self, etc.).]

Discern Possible Steps of Faith (refer to pg. 60); Observe Things About Your Life, Spiritual Battles, and What to Expect in Trials.

EVENTS AFTER THIS LESSON AND BEFORE THE NEXT: None.

LESSON 21: GENESIS 22:1-10 WHAT ARE YOU DOING? YOU DIDN'T CONSULT ME! (SARAH)

This lesson looks at the same Scripture text as the last lesson. In this lesson we are going to look at Abraham's steps of faith – to sacrifice Isaac – but from Sarah's point of view. Sarah's perspective is not specifically recorded in the Bible. However, it is not unreasonable to study this potential trial. In this lesson, let's assume we are in Sarah's situation **and we found out beforehand what Abraham was going to do**! This is a profitable study because whether Sarah found out or not does not change the steps of faith God asked of Abraham.

Looking at this perspective is a good exercise for examining what God would work to transform in us in a similar situation. Though it is a hypothetical situation, we do know that God definitely told Abraham to sacrifice his son. God did indeed want Abraham to go through everything that was needed to sacrifice their son! Though God knew He would stop Abraham, Abraham did not; therefore, Sarah also would not have known.

This lesson's study points to the importance of roles and how discerning God's will for us often involves discerning (from the Spirit) which roles are the key ones for us (from God's perspective) in a trial. Knowing God's will, from the Bible, makes this exercise safe and very useful. The Holy Spirit can use this lesson to help you discern how Satan may attack you in trials when you feel strongly about an issue, when you have a particular strong desire, or when you have a strong sense of "rightness" about what should or should not happen in life.

SCRIPTURE SUMMARY: Genesis 22:1-10 – Read the same passage as in the previous lesson. **IMPORTANT NOTE: This time approach it as if you somehow became aware that Abraham was intending to sacrifice Isaac, your son, in the name of God!**

Special Consideration:

OPTIONAL LESSON you can study later (if you want). You could look at Isaac's perspective. If you do this optional lesson, think about the psychological effect it would have upon a young person being tied up and placed on an altar with a knife poised overhead, waiting to fall! Today, social services would take the child away, Abraham would be arrested and charged with attempted murder, and some people might be suggesting Sarah divorce her husband. They'd want to give Isaac counseling for the rest of his life. We've heard stories of how traumatic situations can affect a person's thinking and heart. If the person does bad things later in life, it is often blamed, to some degree, on the abuse received from a parent at a tender age! What would your heart disturbances be, and what would the Lord have to change in you so you could be at peace with what was indeed God's will, if such a thing happened to you?

CONTEXT:

Patterns in Satan's past attacks (temptations) on Sarah:*

1. Likely attack by Satan on Sarai in Genesis 12:1-4 – don't support moving without knowing where you are going – unknown whether she overcame Satan's attack.**

2. Likely attack by Satan on Sarai in Genesis 12:10-20 – don't support Abram's lie that you are his sister – overcame Satan's attack.

3. Likely attack by Satan on Sarai in Genesis 13:1-11 – don't support the hardship that comes with getting the less choice land – unknown whether she overcame Satan's attack.**

4. An actual attack by Satan on Sarai in Genesis 16:1-6 – support the idea of doing what it takes to have a son (through Hagar) – fell to Satan's attack.

5. Likely attack by Satan on Sarai in Genesis 17:1-18 – don't support name change, circumcision or believe that you will have a son – unknown whether she overcame Satan's attack.

---

* See Special Consideration About Identifying Patterns from Lesson 7.

** The reason we (the authors) say it is unknown whether she overcame this likely attack by Satan is because, while she went along with Abram, we don't know whether she was grumbling and complaining about the decision after it was made, or whether she let God live a supportive attitude through her.

6. **An actual attack by Satan on Sarah in Genesis 18:1-15** – don't believe you will have a son – fell to Satan's attack.

7. **Likely attack by Satan on Sarah in Genesis 18:16-33** – don't support the idea of not helping rescue your extended family – unknown whether she overcame Satan's attack.

8. **Likely attack by Satan on Sarah in Genesis 20:1-13** – don't support Abraham's lie that you are his sister – overcame Satan's attack.

9. **An actual attack by Satan on Sarah in Genesis 21:1-11** – don't support Hagar; support idea of kicking her out – fell to Satan's attack.

WHO IS INVOLVED IN Sarah's TRIAL (Main Players Only)?

God, Satan, Sarah, Abraham, Isaac

WHAT DECISION(S) MUST Sarah MAKE?

Sarah would have had to decide whether to believe that God told Abraham to sacrifice Isaac, and to decide how to respond to God's steps of faith for Abraham.

WHAT KNOWLEDGE OF GOD COULD Sarah HAVE HAD TO ASSIST HER TO ACT AS GOD WANTS? (…in the event she had discovered Abraham's intention to sacrifice Isaac "for God?") (Additions to the list of Sarai's knowledge are shown in **bold**)

1. The Bible doesn't tell us everything Sarai knew about God.
2. Sarai knew, from God's perspective, she was Abram's wife.
3. Sarai probably knew of the Promises, but that was likely second-hand through Abram. There is no record that God interacted directly with Sarai to confirm what her husband was telling her.
4. Genesis 12:8 – Sarai probably knew when they arrived in the Promised Land because Abram worshipped the Lord there.
5. Genesis 12:11-13 – If Abram told Sarai of the Promises from God, Sarai could have figured out that God would have to protect Abram's life, if God is going to give Abram a son. From this, Sarai may have been able to conclude that Abram wouldn't have to lie because God would protect Abram.

6. Genesis 14 – Sarai probably knew that Abram gave God the credit for his victory in saving Lot and family from captivity.

7. Genesis 15:4-6 – Sarai probably knew that Abram believed that God did not consider Eliezer of Damascus to be the one through whom God would fulfill His promise of descendants.

8. Genesis 17:15-16, 19 – Although Sarai had given Hagar to Abram to get a son, Sarai probably knew that Abram believed God was still going to give him the "right" son through Sarai herself.

9. **Genesis 18:13-33 – Sarah probably learned from Abraham that the three men that visited them (before the destruction of Sodom and Gomorrah) were the Lord and two angels. She knew that it was again foretold that she would have a son herself, which was in line with what Abraham had likely been saying about the three promises. Abraham also probably told her about the Lord's judgment on Sodom and Gomorrah.**

10. Genesis 20 – Sarah could have seen the Lord's provision when Abraham lied again about her being his sister (with Abimelech). Again, at the end, Sarah likely recognized that when Abraham prayed to the Lord, the Lord honored his prayer and healed the house of Abimelech.

11. Genesis 21:1-2 – Sarah saw that the Lord's promise of a son through her was fulfilled.

WHAT WAS Sarah's HEART DISTURBANCE?
(See how others responded to the rest of the lesson – pg. 299)

DID Sarah SUBMIT TO THE LORD TRANSFORMING HER HEART AND MIND SO THE LORD COULD LIVE THROUGH HER?

Special Consideration:
As you work to really put yourself in Sarah's position in this trial, make sure you stay focused on what *you* would want or feel! Remember, being in Sarah's shoes you do not know the outcome of the trial. This trial can really bring up a lot, so stay focused on clearly stating your heart's desires and your heart's feelings.

PUT YOURSELF IN Sarah's "SHOES" – LISTEN TO THE AUDIO (Go to www.Feelings102.com to get or play the AUDIO)

WHAT WOULD YOUR TYPICAL HEART DISTURBANCE BE IF YOU WERE Sarah IN THIS SITUATION OR ONE LIKE IT?
(You can use the list of heart disturbances on page 23)

I'd feel _____ *because* _____

_____

I'd feel _____ *because* _____

_____

I would/would not want _____

because _____

DISCERN/OBSERVE:
Discern Fleshly Tendencies (refer to Special Consideration on pg. 33)

Discern Lying Belief (refer to Special Consideration on pg. 24)

_____.

Discern and Feel the Truth of Your Identity in Christ (Discern one of the four starting pg. 14. Feel it! Use the feeling words on pg. 27. Write how it feels using "I feel ___ because ___. An example is on pg. 58.)

Discern What The Lord Would Seek to Change in You to Transform Your Heart Disturbances So You Experience the Peace of God. [For example in your behaviors (internal too, not just external), attitude, preferences, opinions, thinking, point of view, or sensitivity (i.e., more Christ-like sensitivity to others/self or less fleshly sensitivity to others/self, etc.).]

Discern Possible Steps of Faith (refer to pg. 60); Observe Things About Your Life, Spiritual Battles, and What to Expect in Trials.

DISCUSSION QUESTIONS:

1. Think about the heart disturbance(s) you felt when you put yourself in this potential trial. Now, short of Abraham saying, "You're right, Sarah, God probably doesn't want me to sacrifice Isaac, so I'm not going to do it," is there really

anything that Abraham can say to you to cause your heart to transform to peace? Why?

2. If you are not at peace about sacrificing Isaac, is your issue really with Abraham, or is it more of an issue with God?

EVENTS AFTER THIS LESSON AND BEFORE THE NEXT:
1. Genesis 22:11-19 – An angel of the Lord stays Abraham's hand from sacrificing Isaac; the angel relates God's intention to fulfill His promise for making a nation of Abraham's descendants.
2. Genesis 22:20-24 – Abraham learns that his brother, Nahor, also has a number of descendants.

LESSON 22: GENESIS 23 BEING KICKED WHEN YOU'RE DOWN (ABRAHAM)

If you've ever felt as though someone were taking advantage of you when you were down and out, then you'll have no problem identifying with Abraham in this trial. The spiritual challenge we face in such trials is in discerning when God wants to speak up through us versus when God wants to say nothing through us!

Sometimes the power of sin tempts us to lash out when God would seek to make us calm as part of demonstrating our dependence on Him. At other times, the power of sin tempts us to be passive when God seeks to be more demonstrative and to speak out through us. We must discern which steps of faith He wants, one trial at a time.

Open your heart to let the Holy Spirit help you discern how this passage's particular trial would affect you. Try to open yourself as the Spirit reveals to you the fleshly thinking that would come up for you.

SCRIPTURE SUMMARY: Genesis 23 – Abraham has to deal with Ephron, who is pretending he cares about Abraham's loss of Sarah. Ephron's outward expression of concern is actually a mask that hides his intention to set a high price for the burial site Abraham needs. The external circumstances of Abraham's trial center on being taken advantage of during his time of grief and mourning over Sarah's death.

CONTEXT:
Patterns in Satan's past attacks (temptations) on Abraham:
1. Likely attack by Satan on Abram in Genesis 12:1-4 – don't stand up and say you are moving without knowing where you are going – overcame Satan's attack.
2. An actual attack by Satan on Abram in Genesis 12:10-20 – don't stand up and say Sarai is your wife or you might be killed – fell to Satan's attack.

3. Likely attack by Satan on Abram in Genesis 13:1-11 – stand up and say you want the choice land – overcame Satan's attack.

4. An actual attack by Satan on Abram in Genesis 15:1-16:3 – stand up and say that Eliezer of Damascus will be your heir – overcame Satan's attack.

5. An actual attack by Satan on Abram in Genesis 16:1-6 – don't stand up and refuse to sleep with Hagar or you might not get an heir – fell to Satan's attack.

6. Likely attack by Satan on Abram in Genesis 17:1-18 – don't stand up and make changes in the household that others may not like – overcame Satan's attack.

7. Likely attack by Satan on Abraham in Genesis 18:16-33 – stand up and get involved to assist Lot and his family or they may die – overcame Satan's attack.

8. An actual attack by Satan on Abraham in Genesis 20:1-13 – don't stand up and say Sarah is your wife or you might be killed – fell to Satan's attack.

9. An actual attack by Satan on Abraham in Genesis 21:1-11 – stand up and refuse to support Sarah's ungodly attitude – overcame Satan's attack.

10. Likely attack by Satan on Abraham in Genesis 21:22-32 –stand up and don't let Abimelech make you feel guilty for trying to protect yourself before (lying about Sarah); don't stand up and make an issue about the well or it could push Abimelech to far and lead to conflict with him – overcame Satan's attack.

11. **Likely attack by Satan on Abraham in Genesis 22:1-10 – don't stand up in this ridiculous way thinking God would want you to sacrifice Isaac – overcame Satan's attack.**

Other Relevant Information:
1. Sarah's burial site was part of the land that God promised would be in Abraham's descendants' possession.
2. "In this legal transaction Abraham wanted to purchase only the cave owned by Ephron (23:9), but Ephron wanted to sell the whole field. When Ephron said he would give the field and the cave (V. 11), he did not mean it was free. This was Bedouin bargaining – giving for giving. Though Abraham did not want the whole field, he was willing to take it (V.12-13) at a high price (400 shekels of silver) to get the cave (V.15-16). The transaction was then finalized in the presence of all the Hittites

at the city gate, the place of legal and business dealings (cf. 19:1).

"The point of this event was to ensure that the cave and field would be Abraham's possession. He was not presumptuous. In faith he bought the land, taking nothing from these people (cf. 14:21-24). It was important then where people buried their dead; burial was to be done in their native land. Thus there was no going back."[39]

3. "Hittite laws stipulated that when a landowner sold only part of his property to someone else, the original and principal landowner had to continue paying all dues on the land. But if the landowner disposed of an entire tract, the new owner had to pay the dues."[40]

WHO IS INVOLVED IN Abraham's TRIAL (Main Players Only)?
God, Satan, Abraham, Ephron, Hittites

WHAT DECISION(S) MUST Abraham MAKE?
Abraham has to decide whether to accept the way Ephron was treating him, get all wound up about it, or whether to reject the high price altogether.

WHAT KNOWLEDGE OF GOD COULD Abraham HAVE HAD TO ASSIST HIM TO ACT AS GOD WANTS?
1. Genesis 11:30 – Abram knew his wife Sarai was barren and could not have children.

---

[39] Walvoord, John F.; Zuck, Roy B.; Dallas Theological Seminary: *The Bible Knowledge Commentary: An Exposition of the Scriptures*. Wheaton, IL: Victor Books, 1983-c1985, S. 1:66

[40] Kenneth Barker, ed., *The NIV Study Bible New International Version* (Grand Rapids, MI.: Zondervan Corporation, 1985), 39

2. Genesis 12:1 – Abram knew God wanted him to leave his country (Haran), his people and his father's household.

3. Genesis 12:1 – Abram knew he was to move without knowing where he was moving to, and that God would show him where later.

4. Genesis 12:2-3 – Abram knew God made three Promises:
   a. Personal – God will bless Abram and make his name great.
   b. National – God will make Abram into a great nation and his descendants would have their own land.
   c. Universal – God will bless all peoples on the earth through Abram.

5. Genesis 12:6-7 – Abram knew God was true to His word when He told Abram the land of Canaan was the Promised Land.

6. Genesis 12:10-20 – Abram knew God protected him, even when Pharaoh found out he lied. He knew God helped him to prosper during his time in Egypt. Abram knew God was true to His word.

7. Genesis 13:14-17 – Abram knew God reiterated His Promises.

8. Genesis 14:22-23 – Abram knew God enabled him to prevail and defeat the enemies that captured Lot.

9. Genesis 15 – Abram knew that God confirmed he would have a son, and God reiterated the Promises a second time and made a covenant with Abram. Abram knew that God provided a timeline of some key events in the future and that God assured his personal safety into old age.

10. Genesis 17 – Abram knew he was to be blameless. He knew God reiterated the Promises a third time and established His covenant as an everlasting one. Abram knew God gave him some directives and assured Abram that Sarai would bear a son through whom God's covenant would be fulfilled.

11. Genesis 18:20-21 – Abraham knew about sin and that God holds people accountable for sin. Abraham knew God was looking to hold Sodom and Gomorrah accountable.

12. Genesis 20:11-13 – Abraham knew that saying Sarah was his sister was a half-truth and that he was lying to protect himself.

13. Genesis 20:17-18 – Abraham knew that his lie placed Abimelech and his household in the position of sinning without realizing it. (Abraham knew that, before God, he had dealt falsely with Abimelech; see their conversation in Genesis 21:23-24.) Abraham knew that even Sarah had been exposed to

the consequences of his sin. Abraham knew he had to go before God to intervene on behalf of those he had influenced to go against God's will.

14. Genesis 21:2 – Abraham knew God again made good on His promise of Sarah having a son, and it happened in the time God said it would happen (Genesis 17:21 and 18:10).

15. Genesis 21:9-10 – Abraham knew Sarah was fearful of Ishmael, even though God told Abraham that His promise and covenant would be fulfilled through Isaac (Genesis 17:19-21).

16. Genesis 21:11-13 – Abraham knew God wanted him to go against the customs of the culture of the day and send Hagar away. Abraham knew God would watch over her.

17. Genesis 21:23-24 – Abraham knew that, before God, he had dealt falsely with Abimelech (back in Genesis 20:11-13).

18. Genesis 22:2 – Abraham knew God wanted him to sacrifice Isaac.

19. **Genesis 22:11-12 – Abraham knew God had delivered Isaac and that he had been tested by God.**

20. **Genesis 22:15-18 – Abraham knew that God reiterated His Promises a fourth time, and that God promised Abraham's descendants would take possession of the cities of their enemies.**

WHAT WAS Abraham's HEART DISTURBANCE?
(See how others responded to the rest of the lesson – pg. 304)

DID Abraham SUBMIT TO THE LORD TRANSFORMING HIS HEART AND MIND SO THE LORD COULD LIVE THROUGH HIM?

PUT YOURSELF IN Abraham's "SHOES" – LISTEN TO AUDIO (Go to <u>www.Feelings102.com</u> to get or play the AUDIO)

WHAT WOULD YOUR TYPICAL HEART DISTURBANCE BE IF YOU WERE Abraham IN THIS SITUATION OR ONE LIKE IT?
(You can use the list of heart disturbances on page 23)

I'd feel _____ *because* _____

_____

I'd feel _____ *because* _____

_____

I would/would not want _____

because _____

DISCERN/OBSERVE:
Discern Fleshly Tendencies (refer to Special Consideration on pg. 33)

Discern Lying Belief (refer to Special Consideration on pg. 24)

_____.

Discern and Feel the Truth of Your Identity in Christ (Discern one of the four starting pg. 14. Feel it! Use the feeling words on pg. 27.Write how it feels using "I feel ___ because ___. An example is on pg. 58.)

Discern What The Lord Would Seek to Change in You to Transform Your Heart Disturbances So You Experience the Peace of God. [For example in your behaviors (internal too, not just external), attitude, preferences, opinions, thinking, point of view, or sensitivity (i.e., more Christ-like sensitivity to others/self or less fleshly sensitivity to others/self, etc.).]

Discern Possible Steps of Faith (refer to pg. 60); Observe Things About Your Life, Spiritual Battles, and What to Expect in Trials.

EVENTS AFTER THIS LESSON AND BEFORE THE NEXT:
None.

LESSON 23: GENESIS 24:1-16 A BIG, PERSONAL TASK TO TAKE ON FOR THE BOSS (CHIEF SERVANT OF ABRAHAM)

Sometimes it seems that the more we take our jobs and responsibilities as if everything is all on us, the harder life can become. But, does that mean God wants us to work on *not* taking some things seriously, just so we can avoid the weight of responsibility?

While we usually don't mind working for or assisting someone else, sometimes our feelings and desires can get stirred up (our hearts can become disturbed). This can be true when certain tasks are given to us with lots of constraints and specifics. Sometimes, we may even feel like others are treating us unfairly, or taking advantage of us.

Abraham's Chief Servant took his job seriously. He had a sense of discipline and pride that comes from wanting to serve others well. In this lesson's trial, it seems he did so out of respect for Abraham and God.

When we see that serving God will require steps of faith that are uncomfortable to us, the Holy Spirit can reveal to us when we harbor subtle feelings of resentment toward the way God works to transform us. Abraham's Chief Servant demonstrates a great godly example for us. The challenge of letting God live a godly attitude through us toward our own life's circumstances and commitments will become clear the more you imagine trying to meet the heart's standards of Abraham's Chief Servant.

SCRIPTURE SUMMARY: Genesis 24:1-16 – Abraham's Chief Servant faces the difficult task of finding a wife for Isaac. The woman must not be of the Canaanites (in whose land Abraham is living). She must be of Abraham's relatives. Additionally, the wife-to-be must agree to leave her home and to be wed without meeting her future husband, Isaac.

CONTEXT:
Other Relevant Information: The Chief Servant had to go back to the area of Haran where Abraham's people were. Haran was 400+ miles away, the distance of walking from Washington, DC to Columbus, Ohio!

WHO IS INVOLVED IN Abraham's Chief Servant's TRIAL (Main Players Only)?
God, Satan, Chief Servant, Abraham

WHAT DECISION(S) MUST Abraham's Chief Servant MAKE?
1. The Chief Servant has to decide which woman should be the wife for Isaac.
2. He has to decide what criteria God wants him to use in identifying her, or whether to use his own judgment.

WHAT KNOWLEDGE OF GOD COULD the Chief Servant HAVE HAD TO ASSIST HIM TO ACT AS GOD WANTS?
1. Even if we assume the Chief Servant didn't have lots of knowledge about God, what we do know is that he knew some significant things about what Abraham believed about God.
   a. V. 7 - He knew Abraham believed God made promises to him.
   b. V. 7 – He knew Abraham believed God would provide an angel to guide him to the woman who was to be Isaac's wife.
   c. The Chief Servant probably knew Abraham was expecting him to follow the angel's lead and not his own judgment.
2. V. 12 shows us that the Chief Servant knew he could ask for God's help, and that trust was a factor in receiving whatever help God choose to offer.

WHAT WAS the Chief Servant's HEART DISTURBANCE?
(See how others responded to the rest of the lesson – pg. 307)

DID the Chief Servant SUBMIT TO THE LORD TRANSFORMING HIS HEART AND MIND SO THE LORD COULD LIVE THROUGH HIM?

PUT YOURSELF IN the Chief Servant's "SHOES" – LISTEN TO THE AUDIO (Go to www.Feelings102.com to get or play the AUDIO)

WHAT WOULD YOUR TYPICAL HEART DISTURBANCE BE IF YOU WERE the Chief Servant IN THIS SITUATION OR ONE LIKE IT?
(You can use the list of heart disturbances on page 23)

I'd feel _____ *because* _____

_____

I'd feel _____ *because* _____

_____

I would/would not want _____

because _____

DISCERN/OBSERVE:
Discern Fleshly Tendencies (refer to Special Consideration on pg. 33)

Discern Lying Belief (refer to Special Consideration on pg. 24)

_____.

Discern and Feel the Truth of Your Identity in Christ (Discern one of the four starting pg. 14. Feel it! Use the feeling words on pg. 27. Write how it feels using "I feel ___ because ___. An example is on pg. 58.)

Discern What The Lord Would Seek to Change in You to Transform Your Heart Disturbances So You Experience the Peace of God. [For example in your behaviors (internal too, not just external), attitude, preferences, opinions, thinking, point of view, or sensitivity (i.e., more Christ-like sensitivity to others/self or less fleshly sensitivity to others/self, etc.).]

Discern Possible Steps of Faith (refer to pg. 60); Observe Things About Your Life, Spiritual Battles, and What to Expect in Trials.

EVENTS AFTER THIS LESSON AND BEFORE THE NEXT:
1. Genesis 24:17-33 – Rebekah passes the Chief Servant's test, so he gives her jewelry and thanks the Lord; Rebekah invites him to her home and she tells her mother what has happened; Rebekah's brother also invites the Chief Servant to their home.
2. Genesis 24:34-48 – The Chief Servant recounts, to Laban and his family, all that has happened.

APPENDIX 1: FACILITATING A POIEOLOGICAL BIBLE STUDY

Growth Step: To highlight suggestions for small group facilitators.

Poieological Bible Studies need more of a facilitator and encourager than a leader that lectures or teaches. The *Feelings 102* lessons don't require that the facilitator do tons of research or preparation in advance. However, we (the authors) recommend that facilitators go through the week's lesson on their own, including listening to the AUDIO, before walking through it with the small group.

The most useful facilitator is going to be a person that is familiar with the "Overview of the Biblical Basics of Trials" chapter (page 11), the "How to Participate in a Poieological Bible Study" chapter (page 39), and the particulars of the template used for each lesson (page 48). A facilitator must be able to tactfully help others stick with the particulars of how this kind of Bible Study works.

There is a vital transition that must take place during the study. The transition goes from focusing on the Biblical person to focusing on how Satan might attack us personally were we in the trial being studied. This transition starts at the "LISTEN TO THE AUDIO" part of the study. Once your group gets to that part of the study, the hardest part of the Poieological Bible Study is staying with that transition. For a facilitator, it is vital to be prepared to regularly remind fellow believers to work on writing down the heart disturbances they'd have (using "I," "me," "my") were they in the trial. Again, writing down those heart disturbances should happen while listening to the AUDIO.

Due to this important transition, a facilitator assists the group by ensuring there is a smooth integration of the AUDIO. You may want to download the AUDIO to your electronic device in advance. DON'T WAIT until the last minute on this! God forbid that at the time of your lesson, bad weather rolls in and you can't get a good internet connection to play the AUDIO directly from the website!

The AUDIO moves along at a pretty good clip. You can pause the AUDIO if you want so people can write down their heart disturbances. Having said that, we (the authors) haven't found it to be necessary much at all. Remind participants to use the simple format shown in *italics* in the "WHAT WOULD YOUR TYPICAL HEART DISTURBANCE BE…" part of the lesson. Encourage them to focus on filling in the blanks while listening to the AUDIO.

Participants can write down as many heart disturbances as they want during the AUDIO. The idea is to zoom in on the "biggest" heart disturbance when they get to the DISCERN/OBSERVE section.

If you are using butcher paper or a dry erase board to write heart disturbances people elect to share with the group, just have them give you one that they are willing to share. It is also best if you lead the way by writing down a heart disturbance that you came up with, which you are willing to share with the group, before you ask them to share one.

A challenge for facilitators is that we can often be "knowledge-focused" when studying the Bible. While the Poieological Bible Study builds on Scriptural knowledge that is exciting, the point is assist participants in discerning what God's Spirit can reveal to them about discerning fleshly tendencies that come up for them, about being transformed by the Lord, and about possible steps of faith God would want them to take. This requires being "heart-focused" too. As the group transitions to the second part of the study (by listening to the AUDIO), the heart-focus is central.

Again, the heart-focus part of the study starts with the AUDIO part. But, it is easy to slip into focusing on what the *Biblical person* should have, could have or would have done, felt or thought about. Also, our minds tend to jump to other Bible verses that we feel are germane to the inner conflict we experience when we put ourselves in the Biblical person's trial. While those things aren't wrong, they are best saved until the group gets to the end of the DISCERN/OBSERVE section. If the group doesn't wait until then, it takes the focus off getting better at pin-pointing one's heart disturbances *and then* focusing on discerning what God might seek to change in them such that they return to a place of peace DURING the trial.

Again, a good facilitator helps his or her small group stick with the goals of each portion of the study template. In this way, a good facilitator helps participants to experience a number of growth steps. It helps participants increase their sensitivity to God's Spirit and what He seeks to reveal about how God is using a trial to transform and sanctify us. It helps participants increase their sensitivity to what the Holy Spirit would reveal in a trial about how God seeks to live through them in response to the trial, including discerning the steps of faith the Lord lays before us in a particular trial. It helps participants to gain fresh insights into heart disturbances, which influence us during trials. It helps participants to discern more of the Spirit's revelations about how Satan, evil and the power of sin use wants, desires, feelings, etc. to draw us away from the Lord during trials.

As a facilitator, be patient when the group gets to the AUDIO part and is writing their own heart disturbances. Don't expect everyone to "get it" right away. Let the Lord work through you to assist and encourage those who don't.

May God bless you and those He puts in your small group.

William and William Clark

Appendix 1: Facilitating a Poieological Bible Study

APPENDIX 2: INTRO TO THE AUDIO PART OF THE STUDY

Growth Step 1:

To learn more about the AUDIO and where it fits into the lessons.

Growth Step 2:

To emphasize using the AUDIO to transition from the studying the person, whose trial we read about, to studying one's self.

Growth Step 3:

To reiterate how to express heart disturbances in a concise way.

The Poieological Bible Study lessons challenge us to look at aspects of trials to which we don't typically pay attention. This involves introspecting and discerning the thoughts we have in our minds and the desires in our hearts. For this reason, this appendix touches on a few important aspects of how the AUDIO fits in to discerning one's own heart disturbances while "getting into the Biblical person's shoes."

There is an AUDIO excerpt of this appendix. It starts at the next paragraph and goes to the end of the appendix. To listen to the excerpt, go to www.Feelings102.com, look for the Tips for Facilitators link. Some facilitators may want their groups to listen to the excerpt together, rather than read through this appendix individually. That's up to you and your group. If you don't want to listen to it as a group, then the first few times you get to a given lesson's AUDIO piece, recap the goal of the AUDIO, so everyone remembers the purpose. Keep it simple.

In a given lesson, before we try to get into the shoes of a person who is facing a trial recorded in the Bible, it is important to touch on a couple things.

Obviously, there are times during trials when God sees that our thoughts or our perceptions are being influenced by Satan. When they are **and we make decisions that we act on before we let God transform us**, then those actions are not actually based on what God really wants to do through us. In these cases we are using "DECISIVE THOUGHTS" that are of the flesh.

At other times God sees that we are in a trial, but while our thoughts and perceptions may be fleshly, we haven't acted on them yet. When we are open to discerning what the Spirit would reveal to us about a trial, we pay attention to what is in our minds and our hearts. This involves discerning the revelations of the Spirit concerning thoughts and feelings that may lead to sin if we don't allow God to change and transform us. When we discern these from the Spirit recognizing they are of the flesh, then we have "DISCERNING THOUGHTS." This is a normal part of what should happen within us before acting during trials. Again, DISCERNING THOUGHTS are not sin, though they may include looking at thoughts and feelings that could lead to sin if we act on them!

We know that God can see whether we are trying to discern the godly versus ungodly parts of our thoughts before acting. The problem is that when we are upset, frustrated, worried, etc., we don't think clearly. This is because our hearts are disturbed. Unclear thinking and disturbed hearts happen because God designed us to experience this whenever a trial begins! It's kind of like an alert, which warns us that we are under attack by Satan and the power of sin AND that God is trying to communicate guidance to our hearts!

So, when heart disturbances arise, Satan is attacking, twisting things up in our minds, while using the emotions and/or desires in our hearts. Satan knows exactly what God wants to do or not do through us in a given trial. Satan's goal is to influence us to take *any* course of action that won't be in harmony with God's actual will. Satan can accomplish this when we don't first allow the Lord to transform our hearts back to peace in Christ Jesus! Remember, Colossians 3:15 says, "Let the peace of Christ rule in your hearts...."

The challenge is that while we have to be careful in our thinking, we can't always control what pops into our minds! That's the part we must be careful in minimizing or dismissing out of hand. Believe it or not, these thoughts are a very critical part of trials. Godly introspection and discernment involve being increasingly aware of what we are thinking and assuming the moment our hearts are disturbed!

We have "why" kinds of questions in our minds when trials arise. We have thoughts that reflect how our minds are interpreting the heart disturbances we experience. We also have thoughts that look at various angles of the situation as we try to discern what Satan is doing and what God is trying to do with us. Sometimes DISCERNING THOUGHTS may seem to challenge God. Satan gets us to try to pretend we don't have these, when in fact we do. God knows all this. He also knows that Satan can make us fearful of DISCERNING THOUGHTS, thus raising even more heart disturbances in an attempt to interrupt what the Holy Spirit seeks to reveal to us. The Spirit can reveal to us important information about our heart's disturbances, how God wants to transform us and about faith steps we must take, but if we aren't focusing on discerning the Spirit, because we are in a hurry to feel better, then we can miss out on this part of God's heartfelt dialogue with us.

The AUDIO part of these Bible Study lessons is designed to help you become more aware of some possible thoughts and assumptions that you might have if you were in the trials recorded in the Bible. This can help and encourage you to introspect and pay attention to the Spirit in your own real-life trials. While working with the lessons about a trial from the Bible, remain open to what the Spirit can reveal to you about how they relate to your own life's trials. Put yourself into the trial you are studying. Basically, once you reach the AUDIO part of the study, the remainder of the Bible Study lesson is all about what the Lord is trying to do with YOU!

The thoughts, sentiments and concerns you'll hear on the AUDIO are DERIVED from information available from the Bible. However, don't misconstrue the AUDIO as meaning the things you hear are exactly what the person in the Bible experienced or thought! That's not necessarily the case or the point. The goal of the AUDIO is not so much about the person in the Bible, but about you putting yourself in his or her trial! The point is to put yourself in their situation and see what the Lord does to grow you.

In many ways, the AUDIO part of the study is very fluid – each Bible Study participant will likely have different experiences in response to what they hear. The AUDIO part of the study involves experiencing how Satan and the power of sin attempts to use our thoughts and concerns about real-life trials, but by doing it in a "controlled environment," so to speak. While the trial isn't actually happening to you, by using your God-given imagination to put yourself there, God can bring to light how Satan would start to attack you. Don't be concerned though. The DISCERN/OBSERVE part of the study that come later in each lesson focuses on discerning what God might be seeking to transform in you. The great part is that this same process can be applied to your own real-life trials!

During the AUDIO part of the study, you may be able to relate with some of the perspectives that you hear; others, maybe not. Focus on the ones that you tend to connect with, or on whatever perspective you lean toward while "being in the trial yourself." As you do that, you will have your own heart disturbances concerning the trial. You will begin to be aware of wants, or of things you don't want, were you to be in the trial. You may even suddenly remember another trial from your own real-life while listening to the AUDIO! <u>When any of these things happen, realize that you're getting it</u>! You are taking a really big step in getting the most out of LIVING God's Written Word. Make notes.

Discerning Satan's deception, as well as the rationale he twists in our heads during trials, is part of the process through which God works to transform us. When we discern what the Spirit can reveal about the temptation and deception in a trial, this helps us appreciate our need to submit to God and letting Him renew our minds during a trial. Discerning the temptation and deception helps us be thankful to be dependent on God, because we can't overcome the flesh on our own! When you discern these things, you are becoming aware of what's in your heart and mind in that moment of trial. You are discerning the fleshly perspectives Satan might use to make you miss the mark. That's HUGE. God is making you aware! When this happens for you, grab a paper and pen and express what you feel or want, and why. It is part of clarifying the *spiritual* side of the battle you face. Use the format shown in the "WHAT WOULD YOUR TYPCIAL HEART DISTURBANCE BE..." section of the study (page 56). Keep it simple. Write down "I'd feel ___ because ___," or "I'd want/desire ___ because ___." Fill in the blanks provided for yourself, not what you'd think the person from the Bible would or should have written in those blanks. Just for yourself.

If you are doing this study in a small group, then when you're done with the AUDIO part, let everyone in your group finish writing down their own heart disturbances. Then, continue to the next part of the lesson by sharing the ones you feel comfortable sharing with the group. When sharing, it is very important to support and encourage one another in focusing on their heart disturbances. Remember, when you start sharing with one another, don't judge. Encourage. Listen to each other. Different people will experience different heart disturbances. That's OK. Don't go into why the heart disturbances are "off" even though you may begin to see Satan's deceptions in them. Just identify them first. Later in the study you will work to discern what the Holy Spirit can reveal about how God will transform them to peace in Christ.

Success with the AUDIO portion involves identifying your own heart disturbances as if were you in the trial yourself.

This completes the "Introduction to the AUDIO Part of the Study." You should now be prepared to listen to the AUDIO part for the particular lesson you are studying from *Feelings 102: Bible Studies for LIVING God's Written Word.*

Appendix 2: Intro to the AUDIO Part of the Study

APPENDIX 3: AUTHORS' EXAMPLES

LESSON 1: GENESIS 2:15-3:7 (EVE)

WHAT WAS Eve's HEART DISTURBANCE?
1. V. 3:6 – Eve desired wisdom.
2. V. 3:6 – Eve "longed" for the fruit because of the thought of gaining wisdom.

DID Eve SUBMIT TO THE LORD TRANSFORMING HER HEART AND MIND SO THE LORD COULD LIVE THROUGH HER?
Eve knew things about God, but she acted independently of Him, she didn't take her question about the fruit to Him.

DISCUSSION QUESTIONS:
1. What is so significant about heart disturbances (uncomfortable feelings, emotions, and/or desires)?
   a. It means there is a temptation present.
   b. Satan is trying to influence us and God is trying to reach us.
   c. We cannot think clearly. It is a biological fact that strong desires, feelings and emotions shift the way the brain functions and thinks.
   d. Our knowledge of God is somehow being twisted by the flesh. Sometimes the flesh causes us to forget certain aspects of God's character. When we don't let the Lord transform us, the flesh will cause us to fail to depend on God to act through us when a trial comes up.
2. What did Eve believe in her heart?
   a. What we can recognize for sure is that in her heart she believed she lacked or was missing out on being a whole person, which is a Lying Belief.
   b. Conclusion: Eve's sense of lack was Satan's deception. Eve didn't recognize how Satan was deceiving her about true identity as God designed her. She was perfect as God designed

her. She may have lacked some aspect of wisdom, but, based on how God made her, she had no need of the kind of wisdom she sought.

3. How do we know when what we believe in our hearts is actually godly?

   a. We know that what we believe in our hearts is godly when the inner struggle within us ends and is replaced with peace in our hearts, even for a moment during the trial. God helps us to think clearly when we receive His peace.

   b. Just because we get to peace during a trial doesn't necessarily mean the trial itself is over. It is important to be unshakably centered in the Lord. This means it is important to discern from the Holy Spirit whatever He might reveal about what God looks to change in us so we don't act in the flesh.

   c. We can have peace in our hearts and know what steps of faith God wants of us in response to a trial. But, we might still be persecuted either externally by others, or inwardly by fleshly thoughts that keep trying to come up. We have a need to keep taking those things to the Lord and letting Him transform us.

   d. We sometimes evaluate, in a general way, our level of faithfulness when we aren't in a trial. However, this doesn't mean that later we won't struggle to let God live through us in a trial. This is God working to show us our need to be changed in ways we have to embrace, changes only He can make in us. The flesh tries to make us too over-confident in a sense of our own godliness – as if that's possible on our own!

ONE PERSON'S EXPERIENCE
WHAT WOULD YOUR TYPICAL HEART DISTURBANCE BE IF YOU WERE Eve IN THIS SITUATION OR ONE LIKE IT?

While it may sound weird, I'd want to have wisdom because in some ways it might make me a better person and maybe I might be able to better recognize Satan's deceptions.

DISCERN/OBSERVE:
Discern Fleshly Tendencies

1. Fleshly thinking says that God made me with a brain because I'm supposed to figure out solutions to my own problems.

2. The flesh gets me to act on my own, as if my relationship with God isn't really real.
3. The flesh says that it is OK to do things to compensate for a sense of not being good enough, or to do things that make me feel or look as if I am a good person.

Discern Lying Belief
I am not good enough.

Discern and Feel the Truth of Your Identity in Christ
The truth of my identity is in Christ I am good enough! I feel valued because You really do love me God! I feel relaxed because I can't earn Your love, and yet You love me! I feel joyful and relieved from not having to try to be good on my own because when You live through me You live Your goodness through me! I feel free because You are always doing what can be done to change me to be like You, and I don't have to try on my own anymore!

Discern What The Lord Would Seek to Change in You to Transform Your Heart Disturbances So You Experience the Peace of God.
God would be seeking to change a fleshly point of view. God doesn't want me to see myself as lacking as to who I am in the Lord, even though according to the flesh I am lacking all the time!

Discern Possible Steps of Faith; Observe Things About Your Life, Spiritual Battles, and What to Expect in Trials.
1. One step of faith is to just stop whenever I start thinking I have to do something to be whole in Christ!
2. Another step of faith is that the Lord might want me to do certain things as part of letting Him live through me, but I really have to make sure my heart isn't focused on me, but on Him.
3. In this trial, a big step of faith would be to say, "NO!" to eating the fruit and saying "YES!" to seeking the Lord and opening my heart to Him by focusing on my true identity in Christ!
4. Some part of Eve's mind interpreted her heart disturbance. The Spirit is revealing to me that is what fleshly thinking does, but its interpretations aren't true. Fleshly thinking interprets good feelings as meaning it is "good" to fulfill them. Good feelings don't always lead to dependence on Christ; painful feelings don't mean Christ

isn't with me. What is "good" about me is not defined by how I feel, but rather how I let God live through me.

5. Eve said she believed God said not to eat. I'm like that. I sometimes say things I believe, then my actions show I really doubted in my heart of hearts.

ANOTHER PERSON'S EXPERIENCE
WHAT WOULD YOUR TYPICAL HEART DISTURBANCE BE IF YOU WERE Eve IN THIS SITUATION OR ONE LIKE IT?

I'd feel justified in seeking wisdom because wisdom itself isn't a bad thing.

Discern Fleshly Tendencies
1. Fleshly thinking makes me confident in myself.
2. Fleshly thinking says I am responsible for the good things in my life.
3. Fleshly thinking says I have good reasons to take pride in myself.

Discern Lying Belief
I am good enough the way I am.

Discern and Feel the Truth of Your Identity in Christ
The truth of my identity is that only in Christ am I good enough! I feel thankful not just because You've forgiven me for living by fleshly pride, but also because You have not given up on changing me. I feel trusting about You changing me because You know that it's the only way for You to shine through me. I feel strong because You love me so much that You want to use me despite the fleshly selfishness I have often acted upon. I actually feel joyful because You accept my surrendering to You!

Discern What The Lord Would Seek to Change in You to Transform Your Heart Disturbances So You Experience the Peace of God.
1. God would want to change fleshly thinking. I would be tempted to think it's OK to eat the fruit because of the wisdom I might get, and I usually trust my own judgment over anyone else's, even God's, unfortunately.
2. God would also want to change a fleshly opinion. That opinion is that the fleshly thinking is right and therefore is of God. The Lord

is trying to show me that He is responsible for every good thing in my life! Jesus died for me because I need Him and it is important for me to take that to heart!

Discern Possible Steps of Faith; Observe Things About Your Life, Spiritual Battles, and What to Expect in Trials.

1. One step of faith would be to be motivated to deny the fleshly thinking that God made me to handle things without Him.
2. Another step of faith is to humble myself before the Lord when something comes up that I'd usually feel confident enough to deal with in my own way. I think the Spirit is saying my prayer life needs to reflect more dependence on Him. I have to hold on to that in my heart. That way when a trial like this comes up, fleshly thinking has a harder time of causing me to fail to seek the Lord.
3. Through this lesson, the Holy Spirit is revealing to me that wisdom comes from experience, but it must lead to a sound choice which is all about depending on the Lord to live through me; otherwise it isn't wisdom. Wisdom isn't about me succeeding because of how I assess situations, but Christ living through me in all situations.
4. Experience includes not just what is happening in my thinking, but how I am feeling and what I want. In general, I can reflect on my life and see my experiences in self-confidence and independence from the Lord, but real experience involves discerning the spiritual side of a trial by God's Spirit so that I see how much I've always needed Him.

LESSON 2: GENESIS 2:15-3:7 (ADAM)

WHAT WAS Adam's HEART DISTURBANCE?
Not specifically recorded in Scripture.

DID Adam SUBMIT TO THE LORD TRANSFORMING HIS HEART AND MIND SO THE LORD COULD LIVE THROUGH HIM?
Though Adam clearly had knowledge of what God wanted, it did not help him let God transform his heart and mind so he would avoid acting independently of God.

ONE PERSON'S EXPERIENCE
WHAT WOULD YOUR TYPICAL HEART DISTURBANCE BE IF YOU WERE Adam IN THIS SITUATION OR ONE LIKE IT?

I'd feel angry and have a fear of being alone because if I don't eat of the fruit, maybe I won't die, but Eve will.

DISCERN/OBSERVE:
Discern Fleshly Tendencies
1. Fleshly thinking says it is OK to blame someone else when they are wrong and that I should not be concerned about making a hard decision that might be wrong – it's not my fault if I mess up after someone else screwed up first.
2. The flesh gets me to do whatever it takes to not be alone.
3. The flesh says it isn't good that other people make decisions that change things in life, even though I do the same thing sometimes.
4. The flesh justifies me acting in anger or fear.

Discern Lying Belief

I'm not good enough.

Discern and Feel the Truth of Your Identity in Christ

The truth of my identity is in Christ I am good enough! I feel calm because in You I am good enough. I feel relaxed because nothing is out of Your hands. I feel accepting because I need to be changed by You, on my own I'm a mess. I feel accepted because You love me. I feel hopeful because, no matter what happens, when You live through me I see how You are in control of all the possibilities in life. I feel thankful because when You live through me, life is never out of control!

Discern What The Lord Would Seek to Change in You to Transform Your Heart Disturbances So You Experience the Peace of God.

God would want to change a fleshly attitude towards Eve. God would want to change my attitude to reflect who I am in Christ. The point isn't to try to control everything, but to let Christ live through me in everything. What could be better? By letting Him change the fleshly attitude, the Lord transforms the fear and anger to peace. I think the Spirit is saying that my heart's fear and anger are really about me trying to be in control! I'd also have to let the Lord transform my desire for things to be the way they were before

Eve ate. I have to let Him be in control and trust Him, no matter what happens.

Discern Possible Steps of Faith; Observe Things About Your Life, Spiritual Battles, and What to Expect in Trials.

1. Even though Eve violated what God said we shouldn't do, and that might split us apart, a step of faith is to make time to go to the Lord first! So, if I hadn't eaten the fruit and had discerned the fleshly tendencies at work against Christ in me, then letting the Lord connect me with my identity in Christ would help me to discern how God is trying to change me. That step of faith involves a serious reality check for me. What I'm saying is that the step of faith is I'd have to have a loving attitude when I tell Eve I can't eat the fruit right now because I need to get with God!

2. The flesh also makes me want to die because it makes me afraid to be alone, even if it is for a little while! By letting the Lord connect me to my true identity in Christ, there is a sense of courage to live because I know He is trying to live through me. So I think another step of faith is to let His Spirit show me how to experience hope in Christ, and to just watch how the Lord handles the future for me.

3. My thinking usually tries to evaluate the situation and find a solution when my heart is disturbed. In evaluating the situation, the flesh makes my mind create perspectives of things, which can also include an assessment of what is going on in me spiritually. That perspective leads to a fleshly attitude when my heart is disturbed, and it leads me away from the truth of who I am in Christ, and I get mad because the flesh tells me not to accept change!

4. I am responsible for the decision to submit to the Lord or not in a trial. I must not forget that choice of mine just because of what others do or don't do!

ANOTHER PERSON'S EXPERIENCE
WHAT WOULD YOUR TYPICAL HEART DISTURBANCE BE IF YOU WERE Adam IN THIS SITUATION OR ONE LIKE IT?

I'd feel doubt about God's plan because He made Eve to be my partner, so in a way it doesn't make sense that He'd expect me to allow myself to be separated from her by not eating.

DISCERN/OBSERVE:
Discern Fleshly Tendencies
1. The flesh says that I would be smart just to go along with things whenever I feel worried about how to make things turn out the way I think they should be.
2. The flesh gets me to resist letting God change me when others might not approve of what God wants to do through me.
3. The flesh says godliness means I should avoid conflict at all costs.
4. Fleshly thinking rationalizes why it is good to do things that make others happy, even when that means doing something independently of God.

Discern Lying Belief
I am alone.

Discern and Feel the Truth of Your Identity in Christ
The truth of my identity is in Christ I am not alone! I feel encouraged because You are always with me, even when others might leave me! I feel trusting of You because You alone can give me the strength to accept the changes You know need to happen in me. I feel blessed because You love me and seek to live through me! I feel honored because You can live through me and use the life You gave me to be an example for others to follow You. I feel grateful because You love me. I feel protected because You are always trying to save me from evil, Satan and fleshly thinking that would try to separate us!

Discern What The Lord Would Seek to Change in You to Transform Your Heart Disturbances So You Experience the Peace of God.
If I had been in Adam's position, God would want to change the fleshly preference to not be alone. It is hard to accept when the flesh is all my mind focuses on. God would want me to remember that He created me and loves me, and that He will always be with me no matter what. This leads my heart to believe and trust Him.

Discern Possible Steps of Faith; Observe Things About Your Life, Spiritual Battles, and What to Expect in Trials.
1. A step of faith I think God would have wanted of me would be to not eat the fruit even though Eve did.

2. Another step of faith is to not eat the fruit and completely trust that while Eve and I might be separated, in letting the Lord live through me, I'm not separated from Him! I'm sure God would have a solution.

3. When I'm in a trial where all the choices appear to have a negative side to them, an important step of faith is to make time to seek out the Lord, even if others resist that.

4. In all trials, the big question is, "Do I rely on God or do I rely on myself or others?"

5. I cannot make another person's decision for them. I can only take my decisions to Christ, or not.

LESSON 3: GENESIS 4:1-8A (CAIN)

WHAT WAS Cain's HEART DISTURBANCE?
V. 5, 6 – Cain was angry because Abel's sacrifice was accepted and his was not.

DID Cain SUBMIT TO THE LORD TRANSFORMING HIS HEART AND MIND SO THE LORD COULD LIVE THROUGH HIM?
Even though Cain had knowledge of God and what God wanted of him, that knowledge didn't enable Cain to depend on God because Cain didn't let God change his heart and mind.

ONE PERSON'S EXPERIENCE
WHAT WOULD YOUR TYPICAL HEART DISTURBANCE BE IF YOU WERE Cain IN THIS SITUATION OR ONE LIKE IT?
I'd feel angry because I don't like being wrong.

Discern Fleshly Tendencies
1. The flesh leads me to be reluctant to accept corrections.
2. Fleshly thinking focuses my attention on comparing myself to others.
3. The flesh says it is OK to judge others when I feel I'm being judged.
4. Fleshly thinking is that and want to live for Him so God doesn't need to change me.

Discern Lying Belief
    I am good enough the way I am.

Discern and Feel the Truth of Your Identity in Christ
    The truth of my identity is that only in Christ am I good enough! I feel humbled in a good way because You continue to transform me and to live through me. I feel thankful because You don't give up on me. I feel connected to You because Your Spirit has shown me that I need to be changed, and only You can do that. I feel trusting because You have my best interests in Your heart.

Discern What The Lord Would Seek to Change in You to Transform Your Heart Disturbances So You Experience the Peace of God.
    God would want to change both a fleshly attitude. The flesh works to make me have a bad attitude toward the idea of God actively correcting me, particularly when it involves painful or undesirable consequences. The flesh then gets me to focus on judging and trying to change others in ways that aren't loving. At the same time, the truth is my spirit might be united in Christ but my heart and mind need to be transformed when the flesh works to get me to act as if I am independently sufficient without the Lord.

Discern Possible Steps of Faith; Observe Things About Your Life, Spiritual Battles, and What to Expect in Trials.
1.   One step of faith is to embrace the attitude that, while I am a grown adult, I am a child to God and I need to let His love flow through me!
2.   Another step of faith would be to apologize to Abel. Maybe Abel didn't even know that the flesh was getting me to compare myself to him. But I think God would want me to go tell Abel that my heart was upset with him. I believe God would use that experience to live more humility through me.
3.   Simply knowing the truths from the Bible is not sufficient to change my heart and mind when the flesh comes up. Just because I know truth, that does not mean I will automatically let the Lord change me and live through me in my trials. I need God. I think Cain probably "went over the edge" because he had so many issues with Abel; issues that Cain didn't let God transform on a regular

basis by depending on his relationship with God. The Lord has revealed to me that I need to let Him transform me more often!

4. God was talking to Cain, yet Cain rejected Him. That tells me Satan's deceptions can be very powerful. Those deceptions try to manipulate my opinions and my thinking. If I don't pay attention to God's warnings in my heart, then the flesh leads me to act as if the Lying Belief is actually true!

ANOTHER PERSON'S EXPERIENCE
WHAT WOULD YOUR TYPICAL HEART DISTURBANCE BE IF YOU WERE Cain IN THIS SITUATION OR ONE LIKE IT?
I'd feel anxious and "behind" because it's like Abel is doing better than me and is "ahead" of me with God. I don't like the idea of being behind, even in a spiritual sense, because we are all supposed to be equal in God's sight, and being behind makes me feel less than.

DISCERN/OBSERVE:
Discern Fleshly Tendencies
1. The flesh gets me to compare myself to others.
2. The flesh gets me to act as if my "goodness" is about me being good instead of letting the Lord's goodness come through me.

Discern Lying Belief
I am not good enough.

Discern and Feel the Truth of Your Identity in Christ
In Christ I am good enough! I feel released from the burden of trying to be good on my own because only You can live good through me. I feel safe and secure because You love me just as much as You love anyone else. I feel free and light because You can change my heart and thinking so that You can show Yourself to others through me!

Discern What The Lord Would Seek to Change in You to Transform Your Heart Disturbances So You Experience the Peace of God.
God would want to change a fleshly point of view because Abel isn't really the problem. The real problem is the flesh convincing me that the fleshly point of view of me is not the problem! I don't

know if Abel was one of those people that act like they are better than others. Even if he was like that, my true identity in Christ helps me see that the Lord living through me is the only way to keep my point of view on Him, not on fleshly desires or things I don't like about others.

Discern Possible Steps of Faith; Observe Things About Your Life, Spiritual Battles, and What to Expect in Trials.
1. One step of faith would be to acknowledge to Abel that his sacrifice was acceptable to God and to tell Abel I'm really working to allow the Lord live through me too! You know, so that we encourage each other instead of me comparing myself to him.
2. Another step of faith would be to work on acknowledging the Lord more often for giving me the strength to handle the difficulties of harvesting the land. To me this means being more detached from the results of the harvest and not evaluating myself based on whether the harvests are good one year and maybe less in another year.
3. Acting in the flesh can be avoided, but only as God transforms me during a trial. I have free will to choose whether I will rely on me or on God, Who seeks to change me into who I am in Christ.

DISCUSSION QUESTIONS:
1. What does it mean "to master sin?"
    a. It means we don't act in the flesh in a trial, but we let God live through us as we take steps of faith in Christ. We can only do this one trial at a time.
    b. It means we must be sensitive to God's Spirit so He can help us discern between Satan's influences and the influence God would have in us.
    c. We can't defeat the flesh on our own. Mastering sin involves opening our hearts to and connecting with God in a trial.
2. How do we "master sin?"
    a. We must make a choice between depending on God versus depending on the father of all evil in a trial.
    b. We must open ourselves to our true identity in Christ. We have to incline our hearts to the Lord and seek out what He is working to change in us. God's Spirit reveals this.
    c. Mastering sin can only happen in the present moment.

d. We have to actually embrace the changes God seeks to make in us! That will go against fleshly fears.

LESSON 4: GENESIS 6:3-21 (NOAH)

WHAT WAS Noah's HEART DISTURBANCE?
Not specifically recorded in Scripture.

DID Noah SUBMIT TO THE LORD TRANSFORMING HIS HEART AND MIND SO THE LORD COULD LIVE THROUGH HIM?
Noah had knowledge of God and what God wanted of him. Noah did his part to let God consistently transform his heart and mind in the face of any doubt, uncertainty and temptations that might have arisen for him. As a result, God lived Noah's knowledge of Him through Noah during the ark-building, though Noah had no physical proof of God's will.

ONE PERSON'S EXPERIENCE
WHAT WOULD YOUR TYPICAL HEART DISTURBANCE BE IF YOU WERE Noah IN THIS SITUATION OR ONE LIKE IT?
I'd feel overwhelmed because, first, God's direction involves a change of the direction in my life and that of my family, and because, second, I don't have anything tangible to keep others, including my family, from doubting me.

DISCERN/OBSERVE:
Discern Fleshly Tendencies
1. The flesh says that if my spouse or family don't approve of what I believe God wants of me then I probably don't really know what God wants of me.
2. The flesh makes me think that God will always supply me with others who are supportive.
3. The flesh makes me think that if other Christians aren't doing what I think God wants of me, then I'm wrong.
4. The flesh makes me think it is best to hold off and keep praying when doubts come up about the steps of faith God already told me to take!

Discern Lying Belief
    I am alone.

Discern and Feel the Truth of Your Identity in Christ
    In Christ I am NOT alone; You are with me always! I can feel Your presence within me because You are with me! I feel relaxed in letting go of needing others' approval because You are all I really need. I feel confident because You can live through me and others will see You if they want to do so. I feel safe because You will never leave me, and I feel secure because You are changing me and making me safe in a dependence on You!

Discern What The Lord Would Seek to Change in You to Transform Your Heart Disturbances So You Experience the Peace of God.
    God would want to change the fleshly preference that God give me tangible proof to show others I heard Him correctly because the flesh only wants that proof so others would approve of me!

Discern Possible Steps of Faith; Observe Things About Your Life, Spiritual Battles, and What to Expect in Trials.
1. One step of faith would be to simply tell my family what God is seeking to do through me. I also would need to be honest with them about wanting their support, and to tell them that I trust God and will let Him build that ark through me, whether my family likes that or not. I think that if my husband did this with me, it would be hard for him, but God would want me to support him.
2. A big step of faith would to be prepared to allow God to love my family through me, even if they struggle to approve of God's plan or not. I feel great peace about that! It's like getting everything out in the open. God would be working to transform me (as a wife) if He told my husband He was going to do something through him that would take a while. I believe the Lord would want to live through me in a way that wouldn't make me a stumbling block to my husband letting the Lord live through him.
3. Sometimes when God communicates to me what He wants to do through me, a big part of my trial is to keep focused on the steps of faith. Just because God has a plan for me doesn't mean I am guaranteed the plan will come to fruition right away. It does mean that I must be diligent in depending on Him so my actions don't

give Him cause for any delays in things coming to fruition. I don't want delays to be because of times I lack faith in Him.

ANOTHER PERSON'S EXPERIENCE
WHAT WOULD YOUR TYPICAL HEART DISTURBANCE BE IF YOU WERE Noah IN THIS SITUATION OR ONE LIKE IT?
I'd feel worry and deep concern because I'm wondering how my family will survive if everything we have has to go into doing something where there is relatively no immediate return.

DISCERN/OBSERVE:
Discern Fleshly Tendencies
1. The fleshly thinking is that if there is a long "incubation period" (like several months) before God's will is going to become visible then I probably misunderstood God.
2. The flesh says God leaves it up to me to take care of my finances, job, family, etc.
3. The flesh points out that I have failed God before.
4. The flesh says that a loving God would never put my family's survival at risk in any way in the first place. It says God wouldn't need me to have faith like that.

Discern Lying Belief
I am not good enough.

Discern and Feel the Truth of Your Identity in Christ
The truth is that ONLY in Christ am I good enough! I feel certain and confident because all You've allowed me and my family to have is so that we might be Your instruments. I feel safe and trusting because You love me enough to be willing to live through me to reach others. I feel joyful because You want me to serve You with all YOU'VE given me, including with my family!

Discern What The Lord Would Seek to Change in You to Transform Your Heart Disturbances So You Experience the Peace of God.
God would want to change a fleshly sensitivity toward the external (finances, self-empowerment) to being more sensitive about Christ living through me, however that looks.

Discern Possible Steps of Faith; Observe Things About Your Life, Spiritual Battles, and What to Expect in Trials.

1. The steps of faith I think God would want of me are about sitting my family down and telling them that I trust God to take care of us. It means I'd have to tell them that we need to allow the Lord to change our lifestyle as He lives through us. I don't know how that would go, but I know the Lord's love could flow through me to my family and others if I allow Him to keep my heart centered in Him.

2. In America it is not uncommon for us to think that God wouldn't do something through us where our reputation could be tarnished drastically. In our country, it seems that most of the time the norm is to serve God by living a fairly normal life, doing well at work, planning for family in retirement, and then having a life of retirement. If some steps of faith are hard or if it may not produce any tangible results anytime soon, then most believers I know would think that that action is not about what God is doing through me.

LESSON 5: GENESIS 12:1-4 (ABRAM)

WHAT WAS Abram's HEART DISTURBANCE?
   Not specifically recorded in Scripture.

DID Abram SUBMIT TO THE LORD TRANSFORMING HIS HEART AND MIND SO THE LORD COULD LIVE THROUGH HIM?
   Abram had knowledge of God and what God wanted of him, and because he let God transform his heart and mind, he embraced and took steps of faith to allow God to lead his decision-making.

ONE PERSON'S EXPERIENCE
WHAT WOULD YOUR TYPICAL HEART DISTURBANCE BE IF YOU WERE Abram IN THIS SITUATION OR ONE LIKE IT?
   I'd feel frustrated and upset because I have to deal with this kind of issue (not being able to prove I'm right) to Sarai in the first place.

DISCERN/OBSERVE:
Discern Fleshly Tendencies
1. The flesh tries to get me to think that God would not want my family's lifestyle to be effected in the course of serving Him.
2. The flesh reasons that God knows my family struggles with change, so God would not ask me to have to deal with that.

Discern Lying Belief
    I am not good enough.

Discern and Feel the Truth of Your Identity in Christ
    In Christ I am good enough! I feel a lot more relaxed because You have the plan and I only need to take the steps of faith You ask. I feel released from having to worry about making peace for everyone because only You can do that within others. I feel trusting because You are seeking to use me to serve You. I feel protected because You made me good enough in YOU and circumstances can't take that away!

Discern What The Lord Would Seek to Change in You to Transform Your Heart Disturbances So You Experience the Peace of God.
    God would want to change the fleshly preference that He not tell me that me or my family have to do something that might affect our lifestyle so drastically. The flesh causes me to fear big changes because my family doesn't handle them well. This leads to the Lying Belief that I'm not good enough. Allowing the Lord to change my preference, He can make the changes through me and use me to help and support my family if they stress out over changes they can't control.

Discern Possible Steps of Faith; Observe Things About Your Life, Spiritual Battles, and What to Expect in Trials.
1. A step of faith God would ask of me is to do what Abram probably did – just be honest with my family. The Lord gives me everything I need to take that step for Him.
2. Another step of faith is to be resolved that I will follow the Lord through the trial, no matter how it turns out. In letting Him change my preference, I would then prefer to let things turn out however the Lord allows with my family.

3. A step of faith would also be to let the Lord work through me by being patient and sincere in helping my family remember ways the Lord blessed us, so they can remember He is worth trusting.
4. Anyone can "feel good enough" if everything goes their way. I must let the Lord change me so He lives the truth that in HIM I'm good enough!
5. Sometimes God does have me live moment by moment without tangible assurances. God's Spirit is revealing that part of discerning what God wants to change in me involves letting that weigh in on my thinking more than I like for it to weigh in.

ANOTHER PERSON'S EXPERIENCE
WHAT WOULD YOUR TYPICAL HEART DISTURBANCE BE IF YOU WERE Abram IN THIS SITUATION OR ONE LIKE IT?
    I do not want (desire) my family to feel as though they do not have a good family leader, which I think they'd feel because I am telling them we must move again, and this time it is without knowing where we are going!

DISCERN/OBSERVE:
Discern Fleshly Tendencies
1. The fleshly thinking is that I'm supposed to have reasonable answers to reasonable questions, and when I don't then I must not be doing what God wants.
2. The flesh tries to make me think I'm supposed to measure godliness by how happy my family is with me.
3. The flesh tries to get me to think that if my family is unhappy then God is unhappy with me.

Discern Lying Belief
    I don't have enough.

Discern and Feel the Truth of Your Identity in Christ
    The truth is that in Christ I have everything I need! I feel blessed because in You I have everything I need. I feel secure because I only have to let YOU do things through me. I feel calm and peaceful because it is OK to leave the outcome of this trial to YOU! I feel humbled because You are showing me that it's not about my plan, but Yours! I feel thankful because You can do this!

Discern What The Lord Would Seek to Change in You to Transform Your Heart Disturbances So You Experience the Peace of God.

God would want to change a distorted fleshly point of view. I love my family, but this trial shows me that it is a fleshly view if it leads me to put my family in front of the Lord. Having harmony in my family often requires compromise, but not compromising what the Lord wants to do through me! This lesson shows me that letting God do what He wants to do through me and then taking steps of faith means there are certain things the flesh will fight. The flesh leaves no room for depending on the Lord. Family has to support each other in letting God transform us.

Discern Possible Steps of Faith; Observe Things About Your Life, Spiritual Battles, and What to Expect in Trials.

1. The first step of faith for me is to accept that being a good leader for my family isn't about me, but God living through me.
2. So, the next step of faith is to let Christ use me to show my family that being a leader for Christ is about being willing to take the tough steps of faith for Him whenever that is needed. To do this, I have got to make sure that I am letting the Lord center me in my identity in Christ before and during the time I break the news to my family about His guidance to me.
3. God's Spirit is revealing to me that it is really important to submit my will to the Lord before talking with others about what God is doing through me, otherwise I'll be emotional (have heart disturbances) and the flesh will use that to try to create really bad conflicts in my family. The flesh works to cause me to have expectations of being accepted by others when taking the steps of faith God asks of me! It's like I'm being rejected when it isn't really about me. By being centered in my identity in Christ, I am allowing Him to change me to the point where I actually do leave the outcome of the trial to Him.
4. This is another example that, to me, is like the one from Noah. God does put me in positions where I have no tangible proof that things are going to work out according to normal (worldly) expectations and hopes. I have to know for sure what steps of faith God wants of me, but I have to know with my heart. I can't try to figure out what He wants to do through me based on an assessment of risks versus gain. That is how the world does it. If Abram and Noah approached their trials like that, they wouldn't have taken the steps

of faith that they did. The risks were obviously very high. Today, if believers make decisions like Abram and Noah, people call it "self-destructive behavior," unless it all pans out.

DISCUSSION QUESTIONS:
1. What are some things God promised Abram and what are some things God promises us?
    a. Abram.
        i.   God made an unconditional promise to Abram about a son.
        ii. God's promise of a son was tangible and wasn't only a promise of a spiritual nature; however, God's timing was mostly unknown to Abram.
        iii. By implication, God promised Abram protection so he could have a child.
    b. Us.
        i.   God promises us everlasting life, which is not a guarantee for a certain kind of life in this world.
        ii. God promises us counsel we need in life's trials. However, we have to be open to discern it from His Holy Spirit.
        iii. God promises us that He will always be with us. We might have to take steps of faith where we are alone in human terms or don't have others' approval, but God is always with us – that can be our reality when we surrender to Christ in a trial.
        iv. God promises us that we can have His peace within. This doesn't mean we won't have trials. It does mean we have to embrace the way God seeks to change us *during* trials. And, the peace only lasts until the flesh comes up again, but then we can connect with the Lord again. We don't have to live lives full of worry and fear.

2. When it comes to real-life situations, what are some differences between Abram's life and our lives?
    a. Abram.
        i.   God's promise of a son was tangible.
        ii. Abram's plans would not prevent God from doing as He said, i.e., Abram would receive a son regardless of what he did. God would show Abram the land his descendants would have regardless of what he did. Abram had limited

ability to affect certain things in his future.
   iii. Abram and his descendants would receive certain results regardless of what Abram did.
   iv. Abram's occasional disbelief would not affect the fulfillment of the Promises God made.
b. Us.
   i. God's promises to us are not always physically tangible in the strictest sense.
   ii. Our plans, independent of God, can sometimes prevent us from experiencing the truth of some of God's promises and potentials for our lives. Those fleshly plans can affect what we experience in the physical world in almost unlimited ways, because God usually doesn't tell us what will or won't happen in our futures.
   iii. We aren't always guaranteed to experience certain physical world results like Abram was.
   iv. Our occasional disbelief can seriously affect things God might have done through our lives; although we do not always know what those things are.

LESSON 6: GENESIS 12:1-4 (SARAI)

WHAT WAS Sarai's HEART DISTURBANCE?
   Not specifically recorded in Scripture.

DID Sarai SUBMIT TO THE LORD TRANSFORMING HER HEART AND MIND SO THE LORD COULD LIVE THROUGH HER?
   Whether or not Sarai's own knowledge of God, and whatever knowledge Abram may have shared with her, made a difference in her dependence on God is not clear from the Bible. Clearly though, she did go with Abram, but whether she argued against the move or complained continually or not is uncertain.

ONE PERSON'S EXPERIENCE
WHAT WOULD YOUR TYPICAL HEART DISTURBANCE BE IF YOU WERE Sarai IN THIS SITUATION OR ONE LIKE IT?

I'd feel upset because God didn't give me personal confirmation of His Promises and Abram is saying God wants to move me away from friends and family. When I'm upset, the thinking is, "God wouldn't tell him and not me too, so maybe God didn't tell him at all! God wouldn't do this."

DISCERN/OBSERVE:

Discern Fleshly Tendencies
1. The flesh tempts me to put my human relationships over my relationship with God.
2. The fleshly thinking is that being fulfilled by the people in my life means I am being fulfilled through Christ.
3. Fleshly thinking is that God would never want to do something through me that might separate me from the people in my life.

Discern Lying Belief
I am alone.

Discern and Feel the Truth of Your Identity in Christ
In Christ, I am NEVER alone! I feel satisfied and calm because You really are with me! I feel sad but in a good way because You are showing me that I need YOU more than I thought and I didn't discern that before. I feel thankful because You never left me and never will. I feel safe and fulfilled because You are my first family and best friend! I feel trusting because You don't give up on me.

Discern What The Lord Would Seek to Change in You to Transform Your Heart Disturbances So You Experience the Peace of God.
God would want to change the fleshly preference to stick with the familiar and *always* be around people I like. "Starting over" in human situations doesn't mean starting over with God. The Lord definitely is telling me that it is more important to embrace the preference to have Him live through my life no matter what. After all, if He ever has me move, there might be other people He wants to connect me to and reach through me. Most important though, is Christ is always with me.

Discern Possible Steps of Faith; Observe Things About Your Life, Spiritual Battles, and What to Expect in Trials.

1. I'd have to take the step of faith to embrace the fact that God is to be my fulfillment, which means being supportive of what the Lord is doing through Abram (by moving) and not just reluctantly going along with Abram.

2. Another step of faith is to let the Lord's presence within me be real. I need to seek Him out more by spending some one-on-one time with Him daily. To me this means giving Him credit for the blessings in my life, and not just being happy that I've been blessed. My relationship with the Lord needs strengthening so the flesh isn't getting me to focus only on human relationships.

3. The Spirit is showing me that it is important not to become too attached to things, my lifestyle or plans. Plus, God doesn't always reveal everything at once; faith is always a factor. The flesh can really influence me if I'm not open to God changing me, and making His plans into my plans.

4. Having relationships with people is important and needed – it isn't inherently bad. However, the flesh might definitely try to use my enjoyment of people to drive me to weaken the resolve of others in following God should His plans take them away from me or me from people I'm used to having in my life.

5. What stands out to me is the tender issue of roles. Whether I like it or not, this lesson shows that God sometimes tests a wife's willingness to be changed by Him in the course of her following God living through her husband. While there are a lot of touchy issues that can be associated with that thought, the bottom line for me is that a woman's dependence on God has to be very strong, and it is important that she discern God's will and let Him select her husband. It is really important to have a husband whose own listening-to-God is solid and well established!

LESSON 7: GENESIS 12:10-20 (SARAI)

WHAT WAS Sarai's HEART DISTURBANCE?
Not specifically recorded in Scripture.

DID Sarai SUBMIT TO THE LORD TRANSFORMING HER HEART AND MIND SO THE LORD COULD LIVE THROUGH HER?

The Bible isn't clear whether Sarai even had a trial in this situation. To be fair to Sarai, she had to have been convincing as a "single woman," at least on the outside. Was Sarai secretly miserable? It is usually hard to hide it when we are miserable. However, when Pharaoh recognized that Sarai wasn't actually "available," it was because of the disease in his house. So, Sarai's behavior didn't give away Abram's deception! This seems to support the idea that if Sarai had a trial, she actually did let God transform her and live through her.

DISCUSSION QUESTIONS:

1. Why is God watching over Sarai while she is with Pharaoh? When Sarai is with Pharaoh, she is letting God fulfill her role as a wife by having her act in support of her husband Abram, who had clearly made up his mind to lie to Pharaoh.

2. What are Sarai's roles?
    a. Follower of God. She must be obedient to her God-given role as wife. God is clearly permitting this situation happen to Sarai. It would be important for her to discern how He would want to live through her in the situation, and take steps of faith from a place of peace and acceptance – not necessarily happiness, but certainly not resistance either!
    b. Wife. Obviously Sarai may have sought to provide input to Abram's idea of lying to Pharaoh, but ultimately her role is to follow in support of his decision as leader of the family.

3. Is Pharaoh's action (to take Sarai into his home to "date"/marry) appropriate or inappropriate? Pharaoh's desire to seek to marry Sarai is appropriate, in the sense that he's allowed to marry a single woman, which he believes is true about Sarai. However, God sees that Abram has not told the truth about Sarai, so God alerts Pharaoh to the issue by bringing "serious diseases" upon his family. While that is an undesirable way to be "alerted," it seems to support the idea that neither Abram nor Sarai were doing anything that would reveal Abram's lie to Pharaoh! Once Pharaoh realized something was wrong with the situation concerning Sarai, to have

continued to pursue Sarai after that might have been fatal for Pharaoh and his family!

4. How are Abram, Sarai, and Pharaoh each responsible before God? Abram, Sarai, and Pharaoh are all responsible before God, but each in a different way based on their roles and whether they let God live through them within their roles.

5. Is Sarai a victim of Abram's decision to lie to Pharaoh saying she is his sister? She may or may not appear to be a victim depending on two perspectives:

   a. Her own perspective independent of God. If she had similar heart disturbances like we did (the authors' small group), then she may have seen herself as a victim. But, if she let God transform her, however hard that may have been, then she may have been very content to let God live through her in her role in support of Abram's lead. The Bible doesn't say what she felt. It shows that she followed Abram's lead, and Pharaoh didn't figure it out by her attitude or behavior (to some extent she allowed herself to be viewed as "single woman").

   b. Our perspective. When we put ourselves in Sarai's shoes, we may view her as a victim because we can't imagine *not* feeling victimized ourselves, if we in the same position. The disturbances we experience in our hearts warn us to discern what God would want to change in us in order to experience His peace toward letting God live through us, as opposed to focusing on being victimized or mistreated.

ONE PERSON'S EXPERIENCE
WHAT WOULD YOUR TYPICAL HEART DISTURBANCE BE IF YOU WERE Sarai IN THIS SITUATION OR ONE LIKE IT?

I'd feel unloved, humiliated, angry and distrusting of Abram because it isn't right that my husband should put me, as a married woman, in a position to be approached as a single woman.

DISCERN/OBSERVE:
Discern Fleshly Tendencies

1. The flesh says that God living through me (by following Abram's lead) means I have to pretend I'm somebody I'm not.

2. Fleshly thinking is that I should stay upset and keep not trusting Abram because he is messing up.

3. Fleshly thinking is that God wants to use me to correct Abram.

Discern Lying Belief

In this situation, I believe the Spirit is revealing that the Lying Belief is I can't be at peace with God's plan to live through me because in the previous trial (going along with Abram to move without knowing where we are going) God was working to change me so that He could live through me as a supportive wife. For me, this trial is a repeat of that.

Discern and Feel the Truth of Your Identity in Christ

In Christ, I can be at peace with You living through me! I feel peaceful and confident because You are showing me that this trial is just another where You are strengthening me in You. I feel thankful because You helped me discern Your truth about me in Christ. I feel joyful because You are using me! I feel free and light because You are helping me resist old fleshly junk!

Discern What The Lord Would Seek to Change in You to Transform Your Heart Disturbances So You Experience the Peace of God.

God would want to change the fleshly point of view that I'm godly enough and God doesn't need to change me. The truth is, God is teaching me that He must live through me to make me a godly wife, who can follow my husband's lead even if my husband makes mistakes.

Discern Possible Steps of Faith; Observe Things About Your Life, Spiritual Battles, and What to Expect in Trials.

1. The step of faith would be to put my whole heart into doing exactly what Abram asked of me, based on the role God has given me in the relationship.
2. I need to be careful in trying to predict what God might and might not want to do through me. Abram assumed God wouldn't protect his life, unless he "used his own brain" to solve his problem. That, in itself, was a problem given that God made the Promises He did. It shows me that I need to really be aware of God's counsel to me in my own trials, and to submit accordingly.

ANOTHER PERSON'S EXPERIENCE
WHAT WOULD YOUR TYPICAL HEART DISTURBANCE BE IF
YOU WERE Sarai IN THIS SITUATION OR ONE LIKE IT?

I'd feel justified (in an angry way) in viewing Abram's actions as wrong and his followership of God as weak because it seems Abram is merely looking out for himself and not me.

DISCERN/OBSERVE:
Discern Fleshly Tendencies
1. Fleshly thinking is that if I was good enough, then Abram wouldn't be putting me in this position.
2. Fleshly thinking is that I am justified in resisting Abram's leadership when I think it is off, and that it is OK to judge others.
3. Fleshly thinking would try to get me into a fight with Abram.

Discern Lying Belief
I am not good enough.

Discern and Feel the Truth of Your Identity in Christ
In Christ I am good enough! I feel loved because You are showing me how to let go of being judgmental. I feel free and calm about that too! I feel confident because You are showing me that the burden of handling my life is one You will shoulder for me. I feel safe because nothing will happen to me that You don't know about or allow to happen. I feel honored because You are using me to shine toward others.

Discern What The Lord Would Seek to Change in You to Transform Your Heart Disturbances So You Experience the Peace of God.
God would want to change the fleshly thinking that Abram ought to face the danger instead of putting me in a bad position. God would want to change my thinking and expectations so that they center on Him and whatever He wants to do through me.

Discern Possible Steps of Faith; Observe Things About Your Life, Spiritual Battles, and What to Expect in Trials.
1. A step of faith is that I need to conduct myself as Abram says while remembering that God is greater than Abram, who even makes mistakes.

2. Another step of faith is that when Abram and I are talking, I must let the Lord speak through me so that I am not being judgmental and angry. This step of faith also means that my only expectation is that God do whatever He wants in this situation, once Abram makes his decision. Then it is about letting God live through me and make me be the wife He wants me to be, leaving the outcome all up to the Lord.

3. In trials, I need to be specific in my communication with God about the questions I have. Doing so helps me focus more intently on my part in discerning God's response, even when He says, "Hey, just trust Me and don't fear how things will turn out!" I can see from this trial that sometimes part of taking faith steps involves letting go of judgments about someone else not doing their part right. Even in marriage, I have to trust God more than my spouse! We all make mistakes.

LESSON 8: GENESIS 13:1-11 (ABRAM)

WHAT WAS Abram's HEART DISTURBANCE?
1. V. 8 – Abram's desire was to avoid quarrelling with Lot.
2. V. 8 – Abram's desire was to end the quarrelling among Lot's and his herdsmen.

DISCUSSION QUESTION: Ask yourself, "What would my typical heart disturbance be if I were *Sarai* and I found out Abram gave away the good land without consulting me?"
1. As Sarai, I'd feel doubtful because it seems that, to avoid conflict, Abram is going to let Lot have first choice.
2. As Sarai, I'd feel frustration because it seems that since Abram said he got the Promises from God, many times he does things that aren't showing me that I'm number one in his life.
3. As Sarai, I'd feel upset and angry because Abram seems to be indecisive and passive quite a bit and his inaction affects me.
4. As Sarai, I'd feel doubtful and skeptical of Abram's leadership because I'm not really sure he knows what he's doing and because many times he seems to act in weakness! I don't think God expects us to act weak. Those feelings make me think things like: Abram is

the leader, why does he want to let Lot choose the land he wants? Why did we stop on this less favorable land? Why does he (Abram) accept less? Why is Abram leaving the decision up to Lot when he is the leader?

DID Abram SUBMIT TO THE LORD TRANSFORMING HIS HEART AND MIND SO THE LORD COULD LIVE THROUGH HIM?

In this possible trial Abram applied his knowledge of God and let God live through him. That came from letting God transform him.

ONE PERSON'S EXPERIENCE

Having considered what Sarai might think about you (as Abram) giving away the choice land, then... WHAT WOULD YOUR TYPICAL HEART DISTURBANCE BE IF YOU WERE Abram IN THIS SITUATION OR ONE LIKE IT?

I'd feel alone because I may disappoint my wife again though I don't want (don't desire) to do so.

DISCERN/OBSERVE:

Discern Fleshly Tendencies

1. The fleshly thinking says that I acted independently of God (having Sarai pretend to be my sister), I messed up and so I need to make her feel included.
2. The fleshly thinking is that God would not live through me in a way that disappoints my wife.
3. Fleshly thinking is that my family shouldn't trust me to discern God's guidance, so consult them first.

Discern Lying Belief

In the trial about moving without knowing where we were going (pg 244, the first person's experience) the Lying Belief was that I wasn't good enough. God made it clear in that trial that discerning His will isn't about whether others are happy with me or not. This trial is a repeat for me – so it has to do with being at peace with the changes God has already made clear that He wants to make in me. The Spirit is showing me that the Lying Belief here is that I can't be at peace with God's plan for living through me.

Discern and Feel the Truth of Your Identity in Christ

In Christ I can be at peace with Your plan for living through me! I feel thankful because You are reiterating how much You are willing to handle things through me! I feel unencumbered because there is a continuity in how You are trying to transform me, and I'm excited about that! I feel exuberant and full of zeal because You are training me, Your child, in the way I should go!

Discern What The Lord Would Seek to Change in You to Transform Your Heart Disturbances So You Experience the Peace of God.

God is looking to change the fleshly point of view that if I know what steps of faith He wants me to take, then others will be happy with me. That isn't always true.

Discern Possible Steps of Faith; Observe Things About Your Life, Spiritual Battles, and What to Expect in Trials.

1. The main step of faith God is asking of me is to be willing to let Him live through me and let Lot decide about the land. This causes me to be dependent on the Lord!
2. Part of the way God is working to transform me in this trial is in accepting that I made a mistake by acting independently of Him (with lying to Pharaoh). Another step of faith would be to sincerely apologize to Sarai, if I hadn't already done so.
3. The Holy Spirit is revealing to me how much more concerned God is about a relationship with Him than my personal possessions and my own ways of doing things.
4. Satan causes problems in relationships first by causing me to experience problems in allowing God to change my heart. In a trial, when I want what God wants me to want, I can be at peace and Satan can't get me to contribute to relationship problems in that trial. What God wants to do through me includes being willing to take big steps of faith that He helps me with.

ANOTHER PERSON'S EXPERIENCE

Having considered what Sarai might think about you (as Abram) giving away the choice land, then… WHAT WOULD YOUR TYPICAL HEART DISTURBANCE BE IF YOU WERE Abram IN THIS SITUATION OR ONE LIKE IT?

I'd feel anxious and concerned because I don't want (desire) Lot to become unhappy with me as there are other peoples in this land and at some point we may need to protect one another's family and herds from them.

DISCERN/OBSERVE:
Discern Fleshly Tendencies
1. The fleshly tendency is to let Lot make the choice so I don't make him mad at me – this fleshly tendency is self-focused and based on the idea that I might need Lot's help later on. This fleshly tendency would also try to use the desire to not anger Lot as a way of showing Sarai I'm trying to be smart about future protection.
2. The fleshly thinking is that I have to be wise on my own because God expects me to figure things out on my own sometimes.
3. The flesh says it is OK to play the game so I survive today and then God can use me later.

Discern Lying Belief
I don't have enough.

Discern and Feel the Truth of Your Identity in Christ
In Christ I have everything I need! I feel calm and burden-free because You can take the action needed through me. I feel relieved because I don't have to look out for me as if You aren't looking out for me. I feel grateful because You are fine with me leaning and depending on You. I feel humbled because You have shown me, once again, how to let You transform me into Your image.

Discern What The Lord Would Seek to Change in You to Transform Your Heart Disturbances So You Experience the Peace of God.
God would be working to change the fleshly point of view that I should let Lot make the choice of land because I have to look out for myself. By embracing that change, the emphasis is on *why* I'm letting Lot pick first. The point isn't to try to handle things on my own and work to be prepared for the future, but to let Christ live through me in the moment and trust the future to Him.

Discern Possible Steps of Faith; Observe Things About Your Life, Spiritual Battles, and What to Expect in Trials.
1. A step of faith is to let Lot pick the land he wants, but from the reality that it isn't me letting him pick, rather it is the Lord living through me to let him pick.
2. Once Lot made his choice, a step of faith would be to talk both to my family and to my herdsmen. I would need to tell them that we are seeking to be good stewards of whatever land the Lord has let us have. I would remind them of His blessings and would let them see my trust in the Lord, so they too might trust Him more.
3. We all experience problems that need solving, but solving them has to demonstrate us depending on the Lord. Christ can help me do this without arguing and quarrelling with others. I can depend on God even when others *do* lose their sense of peace. Christ living through me is an example of faith in Him, especially when the chips are down.

LESSON 9: GENESIS 15:1-16:3 (ABRAM)

WHAT WAS Abram's HEART DISTURBANCE?
Genesis 15:2, 16:3 – In the first trial, Abram wanted (desired) an heir because he didn't have a son. In the second trial, Abram agreed to sleep with Hagar because he desired a son, even though getting one might not be through Sarai.

DID Abram SUBMIT TO THE LORD TRANSFORMING HIS HEART AND MIND SO THE LORD COULD LIVE THROUGH HIM?
1. In the first trial, Abram sought the counsel of the Lord. That came from letting God transform him. Through Abram, God lived Abram's knowledge that God is to be trusted and will provide a son when the time is right.
2. In the second trial, the knowledge Abram had of God and His plan did not keep Abram from acting independently of God. Abram was willing to try to have an heir via Sarai's plan. In short, while Satan isn't specifically mentioned in the passage, the power of sin twisted Abram's knowledge that God would *give* him a son. This fleshly influence caused Abram to think he knew everything he

needed to know to make a decision about Sarai's suggestion, independent of God.

DISCUSSION QUESTION:

What would your heart disturbance be if you were **Sarai** and Abram refused your plan?

1. I'd feel frustration because I'm older, barren and it is highly unlikely that, at my age, I'll have an heir. I'd feel anger if Abram refused my plan.
2. I'd feel as though I'm not good enough because I'm thinking, "What's wrong with me?" "Why can't I have a child?" I would feel unloved if Abram refused my plan with Hagar.
3. I'd feel very disappointed, maybe even despair, because I'm thinking, "Why has God prevented my pregnancy for 10 years?" I'd feel flat mad at Abram if he didn't support me in having a child through Hagar.

ONE PERSON'S EXPERIENCE

WHAT WOULD YOUR TYPICAL HEART DISTURBANCE BE IF YOU WERE Abram IN THIS SITUATION OR ONE LIKE IT?

I'd feel doubt and uncertainty because maybe I haven't taken the right steps of faith and the delay in having a son is punishment from God.

DISCERN/OBSERVE:

Discern Fleshly Tendencies

1. The fleshly thinking is that if I don't get what I want or feel I deserve, then I'm being punished.
2. The fleshly thinking is that I'm sinful and God is angry at me.
3. The flesh makes me want to act independently of God so I get what I want and don't feel punished.

Discern Lying Belief

I'm not good enough.

Discern and Feel the Truth of Your Identity in Christ

In Christ I am good enough and He loves me! I feel so clear-minded about this situation because while You discipline me to have faith in You, You do it out of love not out of punishment or reprisal! I feel loved because You know I need Your love and Your help, and You are willing to give it to me! I feel so thankful that You are my Father and are always with me. I feel empowered because You aren't trying to break me down but are trying to lift me up in my identity in YOU!!

Discern What The Lord Would Seek to Change in You to Transform Your Heart Disturbances So You Experience the Peace of God.

God would want to change the fleshly opinion that He is punishing me so I realize He's asking me to have faith in Him and to continue to let Him live through me, however that goes! By accepting that change, I can see that God is telling me not to use the power I have to get a son because that means I'd be acting independently of Him and not trusting Him in this situation.

Discern Possible Steps of Faith; Observe Things About Your Life, Spiritual Battles, and What to Expect in Trials.

1. The step of faith God is asking of me is to simply sit down with Sarai and tell her that I love her and God too much to try to have a son this way (with Hagar). By letting the Lord center me in my identity in Him, no fear or anger would come out, just love, patience and understanding. That's the Lord living through me.
2. When I don't discern the Spirit, in a moment of doubt, I don't have the ability to exercise true faith (trust) on my own.
3. Just like Abram, when I fail to take steps of faith and/or discern God's counsel clearly, I add to or strengthen fleshly beliefs and patterns in fleshly behaviors.
4. The flesh often tries to get me to control or want to control God's timeline or simply wish it was different. When I can't change God's timeline, the flesh wants me to doubt and lose faith.
5. When Satan's initial attack fails, he will often attack again, but from another direction, by using some other aspect of the external situation.

ANOTHER PERSON'S EXPERIENCE

WHAT WOULD YOUR TYPICAL HEART DISTURBANCE BE IF YOU WERE Abram IN THIS SITUATION OR ONE LIKE IT?

I'd actually feel better once I started thinking that Sarai's logic makes sense because, from a certain point of view, that thinking gives me the idea that having a son through Hagar may be OK with God and I like that idea!

DISCERN/OBSERVE:
Discern Fleshly Tendencies
1. The flesh says that if I feel good about an idea, it is because the idea is a godly one!
2. The fleshly thinking is that if I don't take the chance to have a son, then I'm being defeatist and thinking I don't deserve it.

Discern Lying Belief
I'm not good enough.

Discern and Feel the Truth of Your Identity in Christ
In Christ I am good enough! I feel thankful because You work to save me from fleshly thinking and doubt! I feel grateful because You can handle things better than I can. I feel released because I don't have to take on the burden of trying to make Your will happen. I feel confident because even when I am tempted by "good things" Your Spirit can show me what is truly good from Your point of view. I feel safer because You desire to live through me and are willing to show me how to let that happen.

Discern What The Lord Would Seek to Change in You to Transform Your Heart Disturbances So You Experience the Peace of God.
God would want to change fleshly thinking. That would be a challenge because that fleshly thinking is causing me to have a "pleasant" heart disturbance (like Eve did), which feels like confirmation that the thinking is right! The fleshly thinking is that since I have heard the Lord clearly before (concerning Eliezer), then that means I don't have to take this new twist (Sarai's plan for getting a son) to the Lord for additional counsel.

Discern Possible Steps of Faith; Observe Things About Your Life, Spiritual Battles, and What to Expect in Trials.
1. One step of faith God asks of me is to take what Sarai has suggested to the Lord. But, based on what I've discerned from God's Spirit, I'd have to say, "No" to Sarai's plan. This would mean I need to be really patient with any concerns she has, and encourage her to seek the Lord's guidance for her too. This is a big

step of faith for me, but the Lord isn't going to tell her one thing and tell me another. This is about faith in Him living through me!

2. Just like both Abram and Sarai, I often accept cultural practices as the equivalent of listening to God.

3. Abram's example shows me that I can allow the Lord to help me overcome Satan's temptation in one trial and then turn right around and fall to his deceptions in the next trial by acting in the flesh! I have to take things to the Lord continually, but the hard part is continually discerning His counsel while remembering what He helped me discern about the issue before!

4. Though I might be in harmony in my role with someone else that does not mean my decision is in harmony with God. This can be true when I lean on fleshly thinking.

LESSON 10: GENESIS 16:1-6 (HAGAR)

WHAT WAS Hagar's HEART DISTURBANCE?

V. 6 – Hagar despised Sarai. Hagar wanted (desire – heart disturbance) to run away from Sarai because Sarai started mistreating Hagar after she despised Sarai.

DID Hagar SUBMIT TO THE LORD TRANSFORMING HER HEART AND MIND SO THE LORD COULD LIVE THROUGH HER?

Hagar did not seek God's will at the start so God could not transform her heart and mind *before* she first despised and then fled from Sarai. Any knowledge Hagar did have of God or about God leading her was set to the side. Hagar took things into her own hands.

ONE PERSON'S EXPERIENCE

WHAT WOULD YOUR TYPICAL HEART DISTURBANCE BE IF YOU WERE Hagar IN THIS SITUATION OR ONE LIKE IT?

I would not desire to be mistreated in the first place. I also wouldn't want to have to go out on my own in order to avoid being mistreated. I'd want (desire) Sarai to change and be nicer, and I'd want (desire) Abram to change and stand up for me more.

DISCERN/OBSERVE:
Discern Fleshly Tendencies
1. The flesh gets me to focus on the other person's faults.
2. Fleshly thinking is that I'm justified to show others their faults.
3. Fleshly thinking tries to get me to make others change.

Discern Lying Belief
  I am a good person and that is good enough.

Discern and Feel the Truth of Your Identity in Christ
  The truth of my identity is that only in Christ am I good enough! I feel released from the burden of judging others because Your desire is to transform me. I feel trusting of the changes You want to make in me because You love me and have my well-being in Your heart. I feel protected because You are greater than anyone and nothing can happen to me without Your permission. And I feel confident that even if others mistreat me, You are always watching over me. I also feel thankful because You see me in Christ and Your strength will handle all through me.

Discern What The Lord Would Seek to Change in You to Transform Your Heart Disturbances So You Experience the Peace of God.
  God would want to change the fleshly opinion that it is OK to control others in my life when I don't agree with what they are doing.

Discern Possible Steps of Faith; Observe Things About Your Life, Spiritual Battles, and What to Expect in Trials.
1. One step of faith is to focus on being pleased that the Lord can see why staying in a bad situation can be good. This would involve being willing to be mistreated, because it gives the Lord a chance to show love back – that would be impossible on my own, but by letting the Lord change my heart, He could do it through me.
2. Any past victories I may have experienced are really God's over the flesh. Those do not guarantee I will automatically discern God's will for me or let Him transform me when another trial comes along. I'm not godly on my own, so I need to focus on God changing me, not me trying to change others in the name of God. God seeks my cooperation and faith, not my opinions regarding what His will should be toward others.

ANOTHER PERSON'S EXPERIENCE
WHAT WOULD YOUR TYPICAL HEART DISTURBANCE BE IF YOU WERE Hagar IN THIS SITUATION OR ONE LIKE IT?

I'd feel questioning toward God because He isn't making "His servants," Abram and Sarai, change!

DISCERN/OBSERVE:
Discern Fleshly Tendencies
1. The flesh says to leave immediately and have my baby somewhere else.
2. The flesh tries to get me to be sarcastic and "whatever" when Sarai is being mean to me.
3. Fleshly thinking says it is OK to give Abram the cold shoulder.
4. The flesh makes me judge Abram and Sarai both for having me as a slave and then for getting me pregnant.

Discern Lying Belief
I am not good enough.

Discern and Feel the Truth of Your Identity in Christ
The truth of my identity is in Christ I am good enough! I feel thankful that I don't have to handle this problem because You can handle it through me better than I can. I feel safe because Your love can flow through me no matter what else happens. I feel grateful because You love me so much and want to use me to let Your love flow through. I feel trusting that You have the best plan, even though I don't know how things will turn out. I feel calm because You can work things through me so that I don't have to take the problems on myself.

Discern What The Lord Would Seek to Change in You to Transform Your Heart Disturbances So You Experience the Peace of God.
God would want to change the fleshly preference to experience only nice relationships instead of ones that have conflict. God would want to change the fleshly preference to run away! God would want to change my "righteously judgmental" attitude. I can see how the Lord would want to actually live an attitude of kindness and love through me.

Discern Possible Steps of Faith; Observe Things About Your Life, Spiritual Battles, and What to Expect in Trials.

1. I would have to take a step of faith to want what the flesh doesn't want – Christ living through me. In this situation, a step of faith would be to stay unless God made it clear I should leave. A step of faith would be to actually be willing to let the kindness of Christ flow through me and not be sarcastic when Sarai is being mean.
2. Another step of faith would be to love Abram and Sarai because clearly they are getting lost in their desire to have a child any way they can!
3. The Spirit is revealing to me that part of Satan's deception is to get me to "manufacture" truth, which basically manipulates God's truth into what I want it to be, but without discerning that I am doing that! Just because I have the power/skill to do something, this doesn't mean it's God's will that I use that power/skill independently of Him.

LESSON 11: GENESIS 17:1-18 (ABRAM)

WHAT WAS Abram's HEART DISTURBANCE? (i.e., as shown by his laughter)
1. V. 17 – Abram laughed at thinking it reasonable that he would have a son because he is 99 years old and Sarai is 90.
2. V. 18 – Abram desired to have Ishmael as the son God would bless because Ishmael was "a son in hand."

DID Abram SUBMIT TO THE LORD TRANSFORMING HIS HEART AND MIND SO THE LORD COULD LIVE THROUGH HIM?

Abram's knowledge of what God has said (and is now repeating) does not immediately transform his heart (as seen in V. 17-18).

ONE PERSON'S EXPERIENCE
WHAT WOULD YOUR TYPICAL HEART DISTURBANCE BE IF YOU WERE Abram IN THIS SITUATION OR ONE LIKE IT?

I'd feel a lack of trust and faith in God because I'm almost 100 and Sarai is 90, and God's promise of a son is almost 24 years old. I'd feel burdened because my family and servants will probably doubt this latest plan, as I've been saying that God made Promises to me for so long and none have been completely fulfilled.

DISCERN/OBSERVE:
Discern Fleshly Tendencies
1. The fleshly thinking is that when others are not happy with me then I'm not doing what God wants to do through me.
2. The flesh wants me to behave in a way where I avoid doing anything that upsets others who are close to me.
3. The fleshly thinking is that God wouldn't ask me to take a step of faith that might cause my family to be upset.

Discern Lying Belief

This trial is a repeat for me concerning God's will and how my family reacts. In a previous lesson's trial, the Lying Belief was I am not good enough. But, what the Spirit revealed to me about this directly applies to this trial situation. So, the Lying Belief here is I can't be at peace with God's plan for living through me.

Discern and Feel the Truth of Your Identity in Christ

In Christ I can be at peace with God's plan for living through me! I feel excited because You are strengthening me in my true identity in You! I feel confident that You are living through me. I feel thankful because again You are transforming me from the fleshly ways of thinking that lie to me about who I am in You!

Discern What The Lord Would Seek to Change in You to Transform Your Heart Disturbances So You Experience the Peace of God.

God would want to change a particular fleshly point of view. The point of view God wants me to have is not to view the resistance others may have toward me as something that "shouldn't" or "mustn't" happen. Christ is to be my sole source of approval! God would want to change my point of view so I'm willing and motivated to take to Him any challenges others might throw at me.

Discern Possible Steps of Faith; Observe Things About Your Life, Spiritual Battles, and What to Expect in Trials.
1. The step of faith is really clear to me. Like before, I need to sit down with the people involved and be honest about what the Lord

has laid out before me. Being centered in my true identity in Christ, the Lord will live through me with a lot of patience and love as I help them embrace what the Lord does through me.

2. I can see now how important it is to recognize how the flesh has "gummed up" the works before; i.e., by discerning the Spirit's revelations about fleshly patterns/control issues, etc.

3. When "wait" is God's step of faith for me, I must watch out for the flesh to try to get me to take action or "speed up" God's goals.

ANOTHER PERSON'S EXPERIENCE

WHAT WOULD YOUR TYPICAL HEART DISTURBANCE BE IF YOU WERE Abram IN THIS SITUATION OR ONE LIKE IT?

I'd feel powerless because I have little control. God is saying He's going to control the whole thing in spite of all the "human aspects" like age, timing, and the promise of so long ago, and I'd feel uncertain because I can't see how it will all happen.

DISCERN/OBSERVE:

Discern Fleshly Tendencies

1. The flesh says that God's plan should unfold immediately, or at least relatively quickly.

2. The flesh says that I don't deserve to receive what God gives.

3. The fleshly thinking is that I'm supposed to make things happen in my life, but with God's help.

Discern Lying Belief

I don't have enough.

Discern and Feel the Truth of Your Identity in Christ

In Christ I do have enough; I have everything I need! I feel patient because Your word is good, and my life shows me You are true. I feel trusting because You are transforming me and my heart and mind need that. I feel confident because You are in control and it is better that I'm not. I feel grateful because once again You are showing me that You love me.

Discern What The Lord Would Seek to Change in You to Transform Your Heart Disturbances So You Experience the Peace of God.

God would want to change the fleshly thinking. Fleshly thinking tends to try to get me to focus on what typically happens or what is likely to happen. That kind of thinking does not help me to prepare for the unusual, i.e., the miracle of God living through me. Embracing that change would help me strongly believe in God fulfilling the promise of me having a son with Sarai.

Discern Possible Steps of Faith; Observe Things About Your Life, Spiritual Battles, and What to Expect in Trials.
1. The first step of faith is to take the steps of faith the Lord gave. That also means letting the Lord's patience and love flow through me as I share that with my family and servants.
2. Another step of faith is to focus more on my one-on-one time with the Lord, not just in the morning, but throughout my day. If the flesh can lead me to have a knee-jerk reaction like Abram, then it just shows that I'm overlooking doubt that is stewing somewhere in my head and heart. I believe the Lord would have me take steps to believe in what His Spirit reveals to me more regularly. That could be as simple as remembering and clinging to what He is changing in me and wanting to do through me throughout the day. It could also include giving Him credit for the blessings in my life as they happen. It would also include thanking Him for being with me whenever little annoyances of life pop up! I think the main thing is to seek to be more open to His presence in daily living.
3. This lesson shows me that "taking God at His word" requires submitting to Him changing my heart and mind on a regular basis.

LESSON 12: GENESIS 18:1-15 (SARAH)

WHAT WAS Sarah's HEART DISTURBANCE?
V. 12 – Sarah felt inadequate (worn out) because of her age.

DID Sarah SUBMIT TO THE LORD TRANSFORMING HER HEART AND MIND SO THE LORD COULD LIVE THROUGH HER?
Sarah's own knowledge of God, and whatever knowledge Abraham may have shared with her, didn't get her to allow God to transform her heart and mind in this trial.

ONE PERSON'S EXPERIENCE
WHAT WOULD YOUR TYPICAL HEART DISTURBANCE BE IF YOU WERE Sarah IN THIS SITUATION OR ONE LIKE IT?

I'd feel afraid because the promise of a son has been such a long wait that it hurts to have hope that it will come true.

DISCERN/OBSERVE:
Discern Fleshly Tendencies
1. The fleshly thinking is that this "having a baby" talk is so old it's ridiculous. The flesh wants me to say, "Whatever!"
2. The flesh says that if God was going to bless me with a child, He would have done it by now.
3. The fleshly thinking is that if I was a better person, or if Abraham was a better person, then God would have blessed us by now.

Discern Lying Belief
I am not good enough.

Discern and Feel the Truth of Your Identity in Christ
The truth is that in Christ I am good enough! I feel valued because You understand me and simply ask that I trust You. I feel loved because You have watched over and blessed me. I feel encouraged because You seek to live through me and bless others through me. I feel patient because Your timing takes all things into account, including what is best for me!

Discern What The Lord Would Seek to Change in You to Transform Your Heart Disturbances So You Experience the Peace of God.
God would want to change a fleshly attitude. The fear of having hope after waiting so long is essentially a fear of being vulnerable before God. All that comes from the flesh and it has to do with me not being in control of what will happen or when. In seeking to change this attitude, the Lord enables me to submit to Him with a whole heart so that His love and patience flow through me to bless both me and others.

Discern Possible Steps of Faith; Observe Things About Your Life, Spiritual Battles, and What to Expect in Trials.
1. The big step of faith is one of letting the Lord bless me with the opportunity to serve Him in whatever way He sees fit. So this step

of faith includes being sensitive to God's Spirit more in daily living. I mean, not just in the times that bring me pleasure, but in the times the Lord asks me to trust and be faithful to Him. I want Him to see me as His willing servant, who allows Him to work through me to handle things that might be very uncomfortable or unsettling to others. In this way, this step of faith leads opening my heart to a continual attitude of faith and thanksgiving.

2. When it comes to believing or disbelieving, trusting or distrusting, each of these things happen one trial at a time. The present trial is the main one that counts. Past victories in Christ do not guarantee how I will respond to a trial in the present. The good news is that times in the past when I fell to the flesh do not mean I am locked into that again, if I depend on the Lord in my present trial!

3. V. 12 (Sarah's perspective of herself and her heart disturbance) shows us that a negative self-thought can be an indicator of a heart disturbance.

4. While Satan is not mentioned in this situation, Sarah's heart disturbance, in the form of being down and leading her to laugh reflects Satan's influence and involvement in this trial. This happens to me sometimes because I'm not submitting myself continually to the Lord and His ways and timing!

ANOTHER PERSON'S EXPERIENCE
WHAT WOULD YOUR TYPICAL HEART DISTURBANCE BE IF YOU WERE Sarah IN THIS SITUATION OR ONE LIKE IT?

I'd feel worried or disappointed in a way because, due to my age, I don't have the energy for a baby now, and I can't imagine having to try to keep up with a two year old, let alone an infant!

DISCERN/OBSERVE:
Discern Fleshly Tendencies
1. The flesh says that the timing for having a baby is all wrong, not natural, and God wouldn't do that to an older mother.
2. The fleshly thinking is that my limitations are from God in the first place and He isn't going to remove them.
3. The fleshly thinking is that having a child at this point is more of a punishment than a blessing.

Discern Lying Belief

In a previous lesson (with Abram), the fleshly sense of being punished by God came up. The Lying Belief was I'm not good enough. This lesson is Sarah's situation, but the heart disturbance is mine. I think the Lord is bringing up an area of transformation I discerned from His Spirit before. The Lying Belief is that I can't be at peace with God's plan to live through me.

Discern and Feel the Truth of Your Identity in Christ

In Christ I can be at peace with God's plan to live through me! I feel grateful again because You aren't trying to punish me, You are trying to strengthen me by living through me! I feel calm, but excited too, because You will enable me to handle what You do through me! I feel special because You love me and are not giving up on me. I feel free because You have this situation and in You my hope is fulfilled, and You will shine through me every step of the way as I leave all things to You!

Discern What The Lord Would Seek to Change in You to Transform Your Heart Disturbances So You Experience the Peace of God.

If God chose to wait until I was older before charging me with a responsibility that requires the energy of a younger person (like having a child), then God would want to change a very strong fleshly perspective. The fleshly perspective is that part of the purpose of having a child is to be young enough to enjoy all the many things parents like to enjoy as a child grows up. God would want to change my perspective to be less concerned about how much energy I have available to do what I want with my child. The perspective He would want me to embrace is to orient more on dependence on God and the fact that God will live through me the energy to serve Him in raising a child that He intends to use in His service. Wanting to do things with my child isn't wrong, but it can be if I embrace a sour fleshly perspective because I'm not getting all that might have been.

Discern Possible Steps of Faith; Observe Things About Your Life, Spiritual Battles, and What to Expect in Trials.

1. The step of faith is to embrace the perspective of "OK, if you give me a child, I can't do this, but You can!" To me this is about embracing the perspective that I am His servant; after all, my child

is really a gift from Him – it's His child! The Lord will enable me to do just fine.

2. This lesson gives another good example that knowledge of God's truth and plan is not enough to change our hearts.

3. Once I recognize I am in a trial, it could help if I said to myself, "In this moment I must acknowledge God's truth about who I am. If I don't, untruth will likely be expressed in my life through fleshly action or inaction."

LESSON 13: GENESIS 18:16-33 (ABRAHAM)

WHAT WAS Abraham's HEART DISTURBANCE?

V. 22-32 – Abraham did not want Sodom destroyed (the way he asks God to spare Sodom seems to infer it is because Lot and kin were living in the city). The Bible does not specifically record any heart disturbances Abraham felt about not going into Sodom to assist Lot.

DID Abraham SUBMIT TO THE LORD TRANSFORMING HIS HEART AND MIND SO THE LORD COULD LIVE THROUGH HIM?

Abraham returned to his home and did not seek to get involved with God's plans for Sodom. Abraham's actions showed that he allowed God to transform him so he could embrace that Lot was completely capable of drawing on the full power and support of God.

ONE PERSON'S EXPERIENCE

WHAT WOULD YOUR TYPICAL HEART DISTURBANCE BE IF YOU WERE Abraham IN THIS SITUATION OR ONE LIKE IT?

Though I realize that God sent two angels into Sodom and that they are fully capable of assisting Lot and his family, I'd feel guilty because the thought of not going to assist Lot personally seems wrong; it doesn't seem like a godly fulfillment of the idea of helping and loving others. I wouldn't want (don't desire) my family to be harmed, even if they aren't living for God.

DISCERN/OBSERVE:

Discern Fleshly Tendencies

1. The flesh says it is not wrong for me to warn or save family when they are in trouble.
2. The fleshly thought is that Lot's situation is my fault because the only reason Lot is in Sodom is because we split up due to the land not sustaining both our herds (Genesis 13:1-11).
3. The flesh says I need to try to protect Lot and family because I might need their help one day.
4. A fleshly tendency is to always be a rescuer; it makes me feel good about myself because I have a need to be needed.

Discern Lying Belief

I am not good enough.

Discern and Feel the Truth of Your Identity in Christ

Only in Christ am I good enough! I feel trusting because You love me (and everybody else) so much You sent Your Son to die for me! I feel trusting also because You are seeking to transform me yet again, and You are focusing me on that good thing! I feel secure because You know way more about what is going on than I know. I feel clear-minded and focused because Your goal is to help me stay centered in You. I feel grateful because You are consistent in Your guidance to me and You are always trying to save me from the power of sin and acting in the flesh!

Discern What The Lord Would Seek to Change in You to Transform Your Heart Disturbances So You Experience the Peace of God.

God would want to change a fleshly perspective. The fleshly perspective that comes up for me is that it is morally wrong not to get directly involved in a family member's life if they are facing an issue of life or death. As a result of that perspective, the flesh would be trying to get me to not even question whether God wanted me involved, I'd just do it. I've always wanted my priorities to be God first, family second, work third. The Spirit is revealing to me that the flesh tends to lead me to jump to family being first. The flesh would get me to assume God would not want my family to be harmed, even if they were "less righteous" than they ought to be. So, that must mean that sometimes the flesh influences me to think that "familiness" *is* godliness, when that isn't always true!

Discern Possible Steps of Faith; Observe Things About Your Life, Spiritual Battles, and What to Expect in Trials.

1. A step of faith is to seek out what God wants to do through me first, before I react and start getting involved. While I may not know what God is intending to accomplish in the lives of others, His Spirit tries to help me discern what God wants to do through me in a given trial. Sometimes I have to entrust others to the Lord! I believe it is important not just to pray that God will be with someone (because He always trying to do that), but to pray that the person will open their heart and be sensitive to what God is seeking to communicate to the person.

2. Clearly, being at peace about having to stay out of a family member's trial may not necessarily be the same as being happy, but it certainly isn't about being discontent towards God's plan either.

3. The peace of Christ isn't about tolerating painful stuff while remaining fearful of how God seeks to transform me. That is hard to see when some trials last for a while. In other words, I might experience the peace of Christ about a situation in the morning and then in the evening the fleshly thoughts and concerns come back. Waiting to find out the outcome of a situation may seem like one trial, even though it takes several days to wrap up. I would probably be better off to look at it as a series of repeating trials that deal with the same changes that God seeks to get me to embrace. Each day presents a new trial in the sense that each day I must take steps of faith to allow for God's transformation process in me, as though it were the first time.

4. When today's situation is bad, Satan sometimes gets me to question a step of faith I took before. Even though I may have to go through the transformation process regularly with God, I don't want to allow the flesh to eventually get me to violate what God is doing through me. At the same time I must be certain of God's will for me.

LESSON 14: GENESIS 19:1-8 (LOT)

WHAT WAS Lot's HEART DISTURBANCE?
V. 2, 3, 6-8 – Lot wants (desire) to protect the two angels.

DID Lot SUBMIT TO THE LORD TRANSFORMING HIS HEART AND MIND SO THE LORD COULD LIVE THROUGH HIM?
The Bible does not make it clear whether Lot's action was an action of sin against God or not. It is not clear whether Lot let God transform his heart and mind throughout this trial.

DISCUSSION QUESTION 1: Was the cultural obligation of protecting a visitor in the home absolutely right (godly)? Does that mean Lot didn't need to seek God's counsel on how to fulfill that obligation, or did Lot have the responsibility to seek God's counsel regardless?
1. We can't assume that what God wants is always what we are inclined to want at the start of a trial. God has been known to tell men and women to do things that are clearly not what we'd normally want to hear, nor are they things the flesh thinks of as reasonable. For example...
   a. God told Noah to build an ark with the faith that it would flood 80+ years later (Lesson 4).
   b. God told Hagar to stay with Sarah, who was being mean to her, and Abraham, who was not supporting her (Lesson 10).
   c. God did not give Abraham permission to personally go to Sodom to warn his nephew and family of the impending disaster (Lesson 13).
2. Generally speaking it would be wrong for Lot to allow the two men (angels) to be sodomized.
3. Generally speaking it would also be wrong for Lot to allow members of his family (in this case the two daughters) to be raped.
4. The bottom line is that Lot had to discern what steps of faith God had for him.
5. Something else to consider is that the obligation to protect visitors to one's home *at any cost* (if that were the extent of the obligation) was cultural. Just because a practice or custom is cultural doesn't make it OK with God. Put differently, protection of visitors was an

obligation that the world embraced; a worldly obligation, although a respectful one. Lot had a responsibility to discern whether fulfilling that obligation is *always* the step of faith God wants of *him* regardless of the circumstances.

6. Just because a trial might unfold very rapidly, and I have little time to discern God's Spirit, that doesn't mean I'm not responsible for doing so. God wants to help me get better at discerning what His Spirit seeks to reveal to me. God wants to help me submit to Him as He works to transform me. And, God wants to help me see through Satan's deceptions quickly. This doesn't mean "having good intentions" is all that it takes to not act in the flesh.

7. Sometimes I want a certain outcome to a trial so much that the flesh convinces me to think that working toward that outcome will be right in God's eyes. The Spirit is revealing to me that I sometimes act independently of the Lord counting on the forgiveness He's given me. That logic is of the flesh.

8. In the end, it really isn't important for the Bible to specify whether Lot acted independently of God or not, because ultimately that was between Lot and God. The story of Lot's trial helps me see that I must continually open my heart and be sensitive to discern God's counsel in hectic, complex trials. That is between God and me.

DISCUSSION QUESTION 2: When we experience the peace of Christ concerning how He is trying to change us and what He is trying to do through us, how do we act and how do our hearts feel?

1. When the peace of Christ is in my heart, I put renewed, strong energy into fulfilling the task, no matter what it takes.

2. When I experience the peace of Christ, I really go after whatever step(s) of faith He asked of me. And, I don't look back, because I am confident about letting God do whatever He wants to do through me.

3. I persevere and don't quit on the steps of faith God gives me.

4. I have a "can do" attitude toward the steps of faith God wants me to take.

5. I embrace the task of giving up desires for things or results that the flesh tries to use to move me in a direction independently of God.

6. When I experience the peace of Christ, I let the Lord help me exercise self-discipline.

7. When I experience peace of Christ, I may not always be "happy," but I have a strong sense of certainty about the steps of faith God wants of me. I am motivated to take whatever steps He wants.

ONE PERSON'S EXPERIENCE
WHAT WOULD YOUR TYPICAL HEART DISTURBANCE BE IF YOU WERE Lot IN THIS SITUATION OR ONE LIKE IT?

I'd feel doubt because I persuaded the men (the angels) to stay at my house and their presence has brought down the men of Sodom on us. I'd feel worried because my mind is interpreting the fact that we are under attack as meaning I have lost my connection with God. I'd also feel guilty because I can't protect my family.

DISCERN/OBSERVE
Discern Fleshly Tendencies
1. The fleshly thinking is that this is happening because God has abandoned me.
2. The flesh says I am on my own now (without God) so it is up to me to figure out what to do next.

Discern Lying Belief
I am alone.

Discern and Feel the Truth of Your Identity in Christ
In Christ I am not alone! I feel calm and accepting because You ARE with me and I am Yours to do with as You will. I feel loved because You are changing me in this trial so that You can live through me. I feel serene because You have designed this moment for a very important purpose. And I feel thankful because You chose this moment to live through me for Your glory.

Discern What The Lord Would Seek to Change in You to Transform Your Heart Disturbances So You Experience the Peace of God.
God would want to change a fleshly perspective. God would be trying to get me to focus on the trial from the perspective of letting Him live through me as His instrument, but not so much with a focus on being the father/husband – He is THE Father! God entrusted my family into my care, but they are His children. He can

live through each of His children as He wills. In letting the Lord change the fleshly perspective, He can live through me as He wills.

Discern Possible Steps of Faith; Observe Things About Your Life, Spiritual Battles, and What to Expect in Trials.

1. A step of faith would be to act on the perspective of "whatever is Your will Lord," so that He can live His peace and love through me in the situation, however that ends up going. This is how my family needs to see the Lord in me in this moment. There comes a time when God will take us home. We don't usually like to think that way, but if my life really is His life, then I have to embrace the perspective that the moment can come at any time. This perspective of God's makes it hard for the flesh to tempt me to act independently of God by clinging to the very life God has given me in the first place! This trial reminds me to have the same kind of heart that the Christians had when they were being thrown to the lions in the Roman Coliseum.

2. Lot had little time to discern how God wanted to live through him in the moment. The same thing happens to me sometimes. I think at first God shows me lots of mercy and helps me because I'm not used to being open to Him. However, I also think He seeks to grow and transform me so that I become more used to the ways of His Spirit and become more centered in my identity in Him. It's like weaning a child off the bottle –I am the children being weaned so He can live through me always.

3. Sometimes I don't discern the power God is willing to make available to me in my trial. Often times His power won't flow through me unless I take the steps of faith God asks of me. The hard part is that God may also allow me to suffer in the trial and not deliver me from it so I can see how much I need Him. Only by faith in Him can I accept my suffering as Him transforming me.

4. We usually do not get to know the big parts of God's plan. In trials we have to allow Him to transform our hearts and minds and discern His steps of faith for us. Every act of righteousness requires we discern what God's Spirit reveals and roll with that, without knowing for sure what the outcome of the trial will be!

LESSON 15: GENESIS 19:30-38 (LOT'S DAUGHTERS)

WHAT WAS Lot's Daughters' HEART DISTURBANCE?
V. 31-32, 34 – Lot's daughters want to have children, and their father is the only man around by whom they can become pregnant.

DID Lot's Daughters SUBMIT TO THE LORD TRANSFORMING THEIR HEARTS AND MINDS SO THE LORD COULD LIVE THROUGH THEM?
Any knowledge that Lot's daughters had of God, of His deliverance of them, His mercy toward them, or His desire to lead their decision-making did not get accepted by them. They did not allow God to transform them and live through them.

ONE PERSON'S EXPERIENCE
WHAT WOULD YOUR TYPICAL HEART DISTURBANCE BE IF YOU WERE Lot's Daughters IN THIS SITUATION OR ONE LIKE IT?
I'd feel out of control because first my dad offered us to the crazy men in Sodom (Genesis 19:1-8), because now I am living in a desolate cave with nobody around, and because I lost my fiancé in the destruction of Sodom and Gomorrah.

DISCERN/OBSERVE:
Discern Fleshly Tendencies
1. The fleshly thinking is that when a person's life is bad, it is because they didn't take control when they should have.
2. The flesh says that if I don't take control then I will be victimized or taken advantage of in some way.
3. The flesh says that God would never want me to be in a bad situation. It says that God would not want me to enjoy things of life that normal girls get to enjoy.
4. The flesh thinking is that if I was good enough, God would let me have the things that are really important to me.

Discern Lying Belief
I am not good enough.

Discern and Feel the Truth of Your Identity in Christ

The truth is that in Christ I am good enough! I feel encouraged because You have watched over me, have delivered me, and are transforming me. I feel strengthened because You have a plan for me, which starts by letting You have the control of the life You've given me. I feel satisfied and understood because Your mercy is great and You can make my life count for You! I feel humbled because I did not realize how much change You saw that I need. I feel thankful because You love me, have not given up on me, and are seeking to live THE life through me!

Discern What The Lord Would Seek to Change in You to Transform Your Heart Disturbances So You Experience the Peace of God.

God would want to change the fleshly point of view that I have been victimized even though I'm still alive. God would also want to change the fleshly point of view concerning my purpose for living. His new point of view is about my purpose being His child and as an instrument in His hand for His glory. I am not victimized in Christ! His new point of view changes the view of being mistreated by God when I lost my fiancé. If it serves God's love through me, then He'll give me a family while I'm young, and if not, then He has another way of living through me. Whatever that looks like, it will be the most fulfilling experience I can have, for sure!

Discern Possible Steps of Faith; Observe Things About Your Life, Spiritual Battles, and What to Expect in Trials.

1. A step of faith would be to view myself as an instrument of the Lord. To me this means accepting that my life is really His. Only with that could I even be open to discerning that it is inappropriate for me to act to fulfill what the flesh thinks I should do. I don't see how anyone can figure out what "acting independently of God" could look like without first discerning the fleshly tendencies and then letting the Lord center their hearts in the truth of their identity in Christ!

2. You know, if God put me in a cave so to speak, that would be like experiencing a period in life where I am kind of by myself humanly speaking. What a great opportunity to meditate more on Him! This makes me think that another step of faith would involve letting the Lord reframe my point of view about losing my fiancé,

losing my mom and seeing my home destroyed. God is love, so letting Him reframe what has happened leads to allowing Him to show me that I have so much to be thankful for. That, in turn, takes the sting out of having to wait for Him to lead me out of this cave (a place with lots of alone time) and on to a new life He chooses to live through me.

3. Through this trial the Spirit is revealing to me that acting on fleshly thinking can lead to very big life complications, even though I may not see how at the time. Fleshly thinking WILL make sense, unless I am open to discerning what God's Spirit tries to show me about what's off in that thinking. This can't happen if I am not willing to seek out God's correction in fleshly thinking!

4. Lot's daughters learned from the people they lived around in Sodom and Gomorrah. Sometimes, as a parent, I cannot easily change what my children learn from others. This is why I need to teach them, by my example, how to let God change them.

5. God's Spirit is revealing to me how true it is in trials that taking control just because I can is often exactly how the flesh tries to get me to act independently of God!

6. When I think of how Lot's daughters had to allow God to help them resist the flesh, I come up with this: when I am trying to discern what God seeks to do or not to do through me in a trial, I must let the Holy Spirit remind me of my past experiences with the Lord, including things the Spirit has revealed to me before.

LESSON 16: GENESIS 20:1-13 (ABRAHAM)

WHAT WAS Abraham's HEART DISTURBANCE?
1. V. 11 – Abraham was afraid because Abimelech might kill him to get Sarah.
2. V. 13 – Abraham wanted (desired) Sarah to lie for him as a way of showing him her love for him.

DID Abraham SUBMIT TO THE LORD TRANSFORMING HIS HEART AND MIND SO THE LORD COULD LIVE THROUGH HIM?
Abraham's knowledge of God did not transform Abraham's heart and mind and strengthen him in a way that would keep him from

lying to Abimelech. This happened even after God specified His promise to give Abraham a son through Sarah.

ONE PERSON'S EXPERIENCE
WHAT WOULD YOUR TYPICAL HEART DISTURBANCE BE IF YOU WERE Abraham IN THIS SITUATION OR ONE LIKE IT?

I'd want (desire) to do the same thing (tell the white lie) that I did in Egypt because it worked there and I lived; after all, God said that soon we'd have a baby so I need to use my brain to try to be smart about staying alive in such dangerous situations.

DISCERN/OBSERVE:
Discern Fleshly Tendencies
1. The fleshly thinking is if I have the power to do something, then God gave me the prerogative to do that thing.
2. The flesh works to get me to look at undesirable life situations as if they happen because God doesn't love me.
3. The flesh says that God doesn't love me, and the proof is that my life keeps being threatened. The fleshly thinking says, "Not again" and "Why does this keep happening?"

Discern Lying Belief
I am good enough the way I am.

Discern and Feel the Truth of Your Identity in Christ
The truth is that only in Christ am I good enough! I feel humbled because the flesh tempted me to take Your forgiveness for granted, and You have saved me again! I feel thankful because You only ask me to surrender to You and You even help me with that! I feel safe and secure because there is nothing that can happen to me without You being aware. I feel valued because You love me and seek to live through me! I feel honored to let You use me to serve You.

Discern What The Lord Would Seek to Change in You to Transform Your Heart Disturbances So You Experience the Peace of God.
God would want to change the fleshly perspective that He will let me get away with certain things when it is really hard for me to change – sometimes He might, sometimes He won't. God's new

perspective for me is one of having the courage to let Him live through me, and to love Him enough to let Him be glorified in however that might need to go down.

Discern Possible Steps of Faith; Observe Things About Your Life, Spiritual Battles, and What to Expect in Trials.

1. One step of faith is not to act independently of the Lord. In this situations that means God wants me to face the potential dangers and unwanted situations. It means to focus on allowing Him to live through me so He is represented well.

2. Another step of faith is to apologize to Sarah. She's got to be worried I am going to act out of self-preservation again. I believe God would want me to take the step to tell her how much she means to me, and that I won't put her in such a position again by acting independently of God.

3. Like Abraham, I may have my reasons for doing what I do and say. But, that doesn't mean God isn't trying to respond through me with a trial in different ways that involve big steps of faith in Him, even though I don't know how the trial is going to turn out. The flesh tries to get me to justify having strong control issues, as if they are inherently godly.

4. When I have the power to do something and the Spirit makes it clear that doing so is of the flesh then sometimes I may look like I am being passive in a foolish or even downright self-destructive way. I see this in Abraham's trial because if I were in the same kind of situation, I might think I am behaving irresponsibly by strolling into Abimelech's territory, saying that Sarah is my wife, and then blindly trusting that God is going to protect us. Still, that is exactly what God wants to do through us sometimes; we just need to be able to discern from His Spirit when that is.

5. I often sin when I buy into fleshly thinking that distorts what I think others "should" do for me in the name of love.

6. I often think that God's will for me is to take things into my own hands when I cannot otherwise see how God will take care of me.

7. I often think, "God gave me a brain to figure out how to be wise and solve problems." God did give me a brain, but Satan's deceptions distort my thinking in trials. As a result, I sometimes justify the ways the flesh offers to solve my problems, even when they are actually more about me taking things into my own hands, independently of God, and asking Him to bless what I've chosen

and want to do independently of Him. When my actions fall in that category, and I am used to doing so for a long time, I usually don't really think about that. The Spirit is revealing to me that I must have some serious introspection time with Him.

8. I sin when I focus on the external situation, as opposed to my true identity in Christ.

9. Part of Satan's deception involves losing sight of the bigger picture of what God has done for me in the past (both in trials and in terms of other blessings and acts of grace)!

10. Being transformed by the Lord sometimes involves being willing to "lose" from the world's perspective.

11. I often fail to remember that God can work on me though unbelievers.

12. It is possible to "commit" our lives to the Lord and still fail be open to discerning what God's Spirit offers to reveal to us about giving our daily decision-making to the Lord in a trial.

DISCUSSION QUESTIONS:

1. What are some *similarities* between our trials and Abraham's?
   a. God asks us to trust Him by submitting to Him all of our expectations for how real-life situations and trials may turn out.
   b. Like Abraham, we have the responsibility to surrender to the Lord for Him to overcome Satan's influences on us in a trial.
   c. Like Abraham, God has made promises to us, which He will fulfill:
      i.   God says we can experience a relationship with Him.
      ii. God continually offers us counsel in our trials.
      iii. God says we're with Him now, and will be always.

2. What are some *differences* between our trials and Abraham's?
   a. God does not always guarantee us a particular external outcome to trials. With Abraham, God's Promises did guarantee that the external outcome of some of his trials would be a certain way (nobody could kill Abraham or Sarah because Abraham had to have a son other than Ishmael).
   b. Another difference between us and Abraham is that God doesn't always guarantee us that we will live for a certain amount of time or until certain things are accomplished in our lives. This difference means that, for us, living in the flesh in trials can lead to lots of pain for us personally. While God's

greater plan cannot be thwarted by us acting in the flesh, doing so can prevent us personally from having the most rewarding life in His service that He can make possible for us.

LESSON 17: GENESIS 21:1-11 (ABRAHAM)

WHAT WAS Abraham's HEART DISTURBANCE?
V. 11 – Abraham was distressed because what Sarah wants Abraham to do involves abandoning Abraham's son, Ishmael.

DID Abraham SUBMIT TO THE LORD TRANSFORMING HIS HEART AND MIND SO THE LORD COULD LIVE THROUGH HIM?
Abraham had knowledge of God, and in this trial he listened to God (V. 12). God transformed Abraham so he was willing to take steps of faith for God, even though it seemed to support Sarah's anger and go against the customs of the day (V. 14).

ONE PERSON'S EXPERIENCE
WHAT WOULD YOUR TYPICAL HEART DISTURBANCE BE IF YOU WERE Abraham IN THIS SITUATION OR ONE LIKE IT?
I'd feel angry because clearly Sarah's motives and attitudes are wrong, but she doesn't seem to want to submit to let God change her; that drives me nuts!

DISCERN/OBSERVE:
Discern Fleshly Tendencies
1. The fleshly thinking says God would never want me to follow what Sarah wants because that would mean I'm mistreating Hagar and Ishmael.
2. The flesh says not to speak with Sarah about her worries because while I may protect Hagar and Ishmael, I will probably alienate Sarah in the process.
3. The flesh says I'll never win because I'm not good enough.
4. The fleshly thinking is that God has abandoned me to this situation because I screwed up by sleeping with Hagar in the first place. The

flesh says I shouldn't have listened to Sarah (about having a son through Hagar) and so I shouldn't listen to her now.

Discern Lying Belief

I'm not good enough.

Discern and Feel the Truth of Your Identity in Christ

In Christ I am good enough! I feel connected and loved because You promised not to abandon me and I believe You! I feel lighter and free because You are showing me that I don't have to figure this out on my own. I feel relieved because Your solution is always right and I don't have to fear abandoning You because of what others might say about You living through me. I feel thankful because, again, You are transforming me so that You can live through me! I feel peaceful and calm because You've revealed to me how the flesh is trying to deceive me.

Discern What The Lord Would Seek to Change in You to Transform Your Heart Disturbances So You Experience the Peace of God.

God would want to change a fleshly perspective about this whole thing. The flesh gets me to resist doing what someone else wants when they are all worked up like Sarah seems to be. That resistance can affect my relationship with God by leading me to act independently of God, on my own. In this way, the flesh is trying to tie me to the other person's heart disturbances, and that is a heavy burden. Sarah may not have the kind of heart God wants her to have in this trial, but God's Spirit has revealed that the Lord is seeking to change a fleshly perspective so I don't embrace it. The Lord can transform my heart and thinking if let the Lord live through me. So even though the Lord might live through me in a way that looks like I'm doing what Sarah wants done, the Lord living through me happens for a completely different reason than Sarah's reasons. The Lord never abandons me, and I had to embrace His perspective to feel my connection with Him again. In submitting to the Lord and letting Him change the fleshly perspective, the Lord also reveals to me that the cultural custom of always looking out for one's servants and their children doesn't bind Him. God may have me go against normal cultural thinking for His purposes!

Discern Possible Steps of Faith; Observe Things About Your Life, Spiritual Battles, and What to Expect in Trials.

1. A step of faith for me would be to talk with Sarah, tell her I love her, and to tell her what the Lord has revealed to me. This would include gently reminding her that we must not act in fear – the Lord has this situation in hand.

2. Another step of faith would be to speak with Hagar and Ishmael about what the Lord has said to me. I would let the Lord live through me to try to encourage them, and to remind them that the Lord will be with them always. I would have to probably talk father to son with Ishmael about letting the Lord live through him as well. If Ishmael were open, I would take a step of faith to assist him in discerning what God's Spirit might reveal to him about not acting independently of God.

3. The Spirit is revealing to me that *sometimes* God may want to do things through me that on the surface seems to support someone else's fleshly actions and motives. It all depends on the situation, and I think it is super important to discern whatever the Spirit will reveal about how God seeks to transform me in the situation at hand.

4. To have faith, I have to believe. Why is it hard? It's about giving control to God versus trying to maintain control myself.

LESSON 18: GENESIS 21:1-16 (HAGAR)

WHAT WAS Hagar's HEART DISTURBANCE?

V. 16 – Hagar is in great pain, she's crying, and she doesn't want to see her son die. She is afraid they will die because they have run out of water.

DID Hagar SUBMIT TO THE LORD TRANSFORMING HER HEART AND MIND SO THE LORD COULD LIVE THROUGH HER?

Hagar did not seek to let the Lord transform her initially. Even though she had knowledge of God and His promise to her 14 years earlier, she wasn't taking steps of faith for God initially. She continued to believe that she and Ishmael would die. She was not overcoming fleshly lies and fears by believing in what the Lord had already revealed to her.

ONE PERSON'S EXPERIENCE
WHAT WOULD YOUR TYPICAL HEART DISTURBANCE BE IF YOU WERE Hagar IN THIS SITUATION OR ONE LIKE IT?

1. I'd feel a lot in this trial situation! I'd feel angry because I am actually being victimized and mistreated; that feeling would be very strong, maybe even rage because it's not like I just *feel* like I'm being wronged, it's not just my perception, the mistreatment is actually happening. This makes me feel right in judging Abraham and Sarah as being bad people.
2. I'd also feel unsupported by God because I'm wondering, "Why would God tell me to go back to a bad situation only to be completely abandoned later on?"
3. And finally, I'd feel worried because I don't know what is going to happen to Ishmael and me! That would make me feel guilty and have self-doubt because maybe I didn't correctly understand God's guidance to me 14 years ago.

DISCERN/OBSERVE:
Discern Fleshly Tendencies
1. The flesh gets me to focus on the other person's faults.
2. Fleshly thinking in this trial makes me look at what God is allowing to happen as being wrong, unacceptable and all bad!
3. Fleshly thinking tries to get me to doubt what God revealed to me before.

Discern Lying Belief
In the other lesson of being in Hagar's trial (pg. 264, the first person's experience), the Lying Belief for me was that I am a good person and that is good enough. That trial was directly related to this one for me, so the Lying Belief here is that I can't be at peace with God's plan for living through me.

Discern and Feel the Truth of Your Identity in Christ
In Christ I can be at peace with God's plan for living through me, and I'm excited about that! I feel hopeful and relieved because You are transforming me again! I feel encouraged and blessed because

You revealed to me that You have a plan to live through me. I feel thankful because Your Spirit has reminded me again not to forget things You've taught me before – You don't abandon me! I feel strengthened because I don't have to handle the situation on my own, You are offering to live through me in it, making all Your strength available.

Discern What The Lord Would Seek to Change in You to Transform Your Heart Disturbances So You Experience the Peace of God.

God would want to change a fleshly attitude in this kind of trial. The fleshly attitude tempts me to believe the only thing that matters is the external disaster I'm facing and what Sarah and Abraham have done to me. As a result, that attitude says my experiences SHOULD be more pleasant! That expectation is not a reality in spiritual warfare. This world has bad things happen *because* Satan is in it and because we are all being called to fight spiritual battles with God in our hearts! The fleshly attitude clouds my thinking and causes me to forget things God revealed to me before, which in this case was about taking care of Ishmael. In changing that attitude, God reveals to me that He sees all and knows exactly what has happened and what is happening to me. God's new attitude for me causes me to accept that, while what is happening to me would not be the way I'd like things to happen, God still has a plan which includes steps of faith that I get to take with Him in this trial.

Discern Possible Steps of Faith; Observe Things About Your Life, Spiritual Battles, and What to Expect in Trials.

1. Steps of faith include acting with God's different attitude for me by being certain that God has something for me, even in undesirable situations. In living through me, God can enable His new attitude to come out so that I leave Abraham and Sarah with my head up and with a grateful heart. God can live through me to be a good example to Ishmael, so that he doesn't lose heart.

2. Another step of faith is to focus on what the Lord wants to do through me. This takes the fleshly attention off of judging others, like Abraham and Sarah.

3. The Holy Spirit is revealing to me that it is very important to remember the previous guidance He revealed to me. Remembering the Spirit's previous revelations to me implies that I must remain

open to discerning Him in each of my trials. When I see what Satan is trying to do in this trial involving Sarah, Abraham and Hagar, the Spirit opens my eyes to the fact that I *am* a participant and new creation in the Lord, whether it feels that way at the start of a trial or not. My heart must be open to discern what God's Spirit would reveal to me about a given trial. If I don't discern Him in today's trials, the flesh has an easier time of making my sense of God's direction in future trials to be unclear, scary and misguided.

LESSON 19: GENESIS 21:22-32 (ABRAHAM)

WHAT WAS Abraham's HEART DISTURBANCE?
 Not specifically recorded in Scripture.

DID Abraham SUBMIT TO THE LORD TRANSFORMING HIS HEART AND MIND SO THE LORD COULD LIVE THROUGH HIM?
 If Abraham experienced a trial, he definitely let God transform his heart and mind because he accepted responsibility for the fact that he had dealt falsely with Abimelech in the past. As a result, God was able to live Abraham's knowledge of God through Abraham in this trial with Abimelech.

ONE PERSON'S EXPERIENCE
WHAT WOULD YOUR TYPICAL HEART DISTURBANCE BE IF YOU WERE Abraham IN THIS SITUATION OR ONE LIKE IT?
 I'd feel upset because I don't want (don't desire) to be criticized today just because I made a mistake yesterday.

DISCERN/OBSERVE:
Discern Fleshly Tendencies
1. The flesh makes me reluctant to accept correction or criticisms.
2. Fleshly thinking focuses my attention on comparing myself to others.
3. The flesh says it is OK to judge others when I feel I'm being judged.

4. Fleshly thinking is that I love God and want to live for Him so God doesn't need to change me.

Discern Lying Belief

The Holy Spirit is revealing to me that this situation is a repeat of an earlier one for me (this person is referring to Lesson 3 with Cain – first person's experience pg. 237). In that situation, the Spirit revealed that the Lying Belief was I am good enough the way I am. I know what God was wanting to transform in me back then and the same is true here, so here I believe the Spirit is saying the Lying Belief is I can't be at peace with God's plan for living through me.

Discern and Feel the Truth of Your Identity in Christ

In Christ I can be at peace with God's plan for living through me! I feel humbled because again I need You to transform me into who I am in You. I am thankful You have helped me avoid the knee-jerk reaction of judging others! I feel comfortable because You helped me discern that this trial is a repeat for me and You are strengthening me in Your new attitude for me. I feel peaceful because You are showing me that there is no shame or anything to fear in You teaching me to remember I'm not perfect when I act independently of You. I am so grateful You are saving me from the flesh yet again!

Discern What The Lord Would Seek to Change in You to Transform Your Heart Disturbances So You Experience the Peace of God.

For me to be at peace, the Spirit is revealing to me that God again is working to transform a fleshly attitude. In the face of criticism or implied criticism, that fleshly attitude tends to drive me to resist someone bringing up one of my past mistakes and it tempts me to point out their faults! When that happens, the fleshly attitude is, "If you forgave me, why do you keep remembering the mistake and bringing it up?" I'd have to let God shift that to an attitude of acceptance.

Discern Possible Steps of Faith; Observe Things About Your Life, Spiritual Battles, and What to Expect in Trials.

1. A step of faith would reflect taking responsibility for what I've done before, even when I didn't have a bad intent. It also includes

accepting that, when I've sinned against others, it sometimes takes time for them to heal or trust again. The step of faith involves letting God live humility through me.

2. God is always aware of what I do and why I do what I do. I am not always aware, because I don't always seek to discern whatever the Spirit might reveal to me about a trial!

3. Abraham accepted responsibility for his poor reputation. Sometimes that is really hard for me to do because it is so humbling. Satan wants me to fail to not be open to discerning what the Spirit reveals about my shortcomings because that makes it easier for the flesh to come out. The result is that I don't always quickly discern what the Spirit reveals about a fleshly sense of identity versus my true identity in Christ.

4. What I saw in Abraham's example is that his step of faith involved making a binding treaty that required *him* to acknowledge and remember his past wrong against Abimelech. When I seek God's counsel about behaviors and attitudes He wants to change in me, I will work to be open to the Spirit showing me some similar techniques.

5. Sometimes, like Abraham, I need to recognize that God is actually working in places where I think God is being excluded. When I judge others in such broad terms, Satan can use that to blind me to the fact that God works in many ways that I will miss out on seeing or appreciating when I don't discern His Spirit.

6. Sometimes unbelievers function in ways that are godlier than I am as a believer. My personal relationship with God is a big difference between me and unbelievers. But, it seems to be more condemning against me when unbelievers are able to demonstrate self-discipline and people-skills that should come more naturally to me based on who I am in Christ.

7. I think that it is important to observe that the offender (Abraham) initiates the treaty. I think this lesson's passage shows the following to be true about reconciling:

   a. The OFFENDED can work to forget the offense and trust the OFFENDER *when,*

   b. The OFFENDER lets the Spirit remind him of his own offense so as not to repeat it.

   This is a two-way "treaty;" each has a responsibility.

LESSON 20: GENESIS 22:1-10 (ABRAHAM)

WHAT WAS Abraham's HEART DISTURBANCE?
Not specifically recorded in Scripture.

DID Abraham SUBMIT TO THE LORD TRANSFORMING HIS HEART AND MIND SO THE LORD COULD LIVE THROUGH HIM?
Abraham had knowledge of God and of what God wanted of him. If this was a trial for Abraham, he let God transform his heart and mind. Abraham was discerning and submitted to God in this very challenging situation.

DISCUSSION QUESTIONS:
1. How does taking steps of faith involve being willing to be detached? This lesson is another of many that show we must often detach from our external circumstances in order to open our hearts to trusting in God. Detachment doesn't mean we don't care about what is going on in life. It means we do care, but we care more about what God wants to do through us in life. When taking steps of faith to trust God, it often involves external sacrifice on our part. We have to want what God wants more than we want a particular outcome to a trial.
2. What would we need to be willing to embrace in order to be detached, wherever God is challenging us to do that in a trial?
   a. We have to be certain and sure of what He is seeking to transform in us, as well as what steps of faith He asks of us.
   b. We have to discern His Spirit. The two-way interaction of a relationship with God is what enables us to let Him act through us as He transforms us. We can't overcome Satan's attacks and transform our hearts on our own. We have to submit to let God help us!
   c. We must have a change of heart during trials, and we have to let God make that happen – but it doesn't happen very quickly with a resistant heart.
   d. We have to realize that the flesh wants us to choose less than the best (meaning anything less than dependence on the Lord). When we buy into the flesh, we often feel worse, or empty, later on.

ONE PERSON'S EXPERIENCE
WHAT WOULD YOUR TYPICAL HEART DISTURBANCE BE IF YOU WERE Abraham IN THIS SITUATION OR ONE LIKE IT?

1. In this trial, there is a lot I'd feel and be worrying about!! I'd feel doubt because I'm wondering, "Did I really understand God correctly? God wouldn't want me to take a step of faith that could kill Isaac."

2. I'd feel doubt because I'm wondering, "I'm just thinking God wants this because I'm actually a self-sabotaging person. Plus, how will I explain this to Sarah?! God said we should be fruitful and multiply, so it must be Satan telling me to sacrifice Isaac."

3. I'd feel resistant because my son isn't a toddler. He's old enough to understand how the offering works and he's not going to be chomping at the bit to lay down on the rock to be sacrificed. He's going to know what's going on!

DISCERN/OBSERVE:
Discern Fleshly Tendencies

1. The flesh says that I know God and I know that sacrificing Isaac isn't what God would want.

2. The fleshly thinking is that God blessed me with a son because God wants me to have what my wife and I want.

3. The flesh gets me to thinking that since God isn't doing this sort of thing with others then He probably isn't behind it in the first place!

4. The fleshly thinking is that God is behind me when I get all that I want in life.

Discern Lying Belief

This isn't what I wanted for my life!

Discern and Feel the Truth of Your Identity in Christ

In Christ I have everything I need! I feel empowered because You have provided everything I need to take the steps of faith You can help me with. I feel honored because You seek to live through me. I feel calm because Your desire to live through me scares the flesh. I feel thankful because Your will is so much more loving and grander than my own. I feel secure because You give me so much so that You can live through me.

Discern What The Lord Would Seek to Change in You to Transform Your Heart Disturbances So You Experience the Peace of God.

God would want to change a fleshly opinion about God. This fleshly opinion is that God would NEVER act in ways that I think He wouldn't act! In this way, the flesh tempts me to handle issues my own way, independently of God. The flesh leads me to take things into my own hands. As we've studied this trial, it has helped me to discern God's Spirit concerning this tendency of the flesh against Christ in me. The Spirit has revealed to me that there is a pattern in how the flesh gets me to live off of opinions that certain kinds of acts are self-sabotaging when actually they can involve steps of faith in the Lord. God has a plan. In letting God transform my opinion and let Him live through me, I feel a great sense of relief and certainty about the sacrifice of Isaac. The fleshly tendency would be to hold on to my son for myself and to put him on a pedestal above God in my life. Letting God transform that fleshly opinion puts that tendency where it should be: on the altar of God.

Discern Possible Steps of Faith; Observe Things About Your Life, Spiritual Battles, and What to Expect in Trials.

1. The main step of faith is about accepting that my life isn't mine, but His, and letting Him act through me accordingly! This means that this fleshly opinion that Isaac is mine isn't really fully true. I did nothing to make this miracle of Isaac to happen – if anything, I tried on my own a number of times without the Lord and messed some things up. If my life is His, then so is Isaac's life! The step of faith is to do exactly what God said, leaving the results to Him.

2. A second step of faith (if God somehow delivered Isaac) would be to talk with him about putting God first, even above me as Isaac's earthly father. I would be excited about working with Isaac on this so he might surrender to God in his life!

3. Abraham's actions demonstrate that he realizes how much God must be in charge of decision-making, no matter what the external circumstances look like, and no matter how things may turn out when we let the Lord act through us. God has accomplished what He promised Abraham 25 years earlier.

4. God's testing involves training me to submit and trust Him without being able to control the outcome of things. Some characteristics of that involve:

a. Embracing my knowledge of God and His steps of faith for me and letting Him live that knowledge through me in my trials.

b. Embracing the Lord's discipline to do what He says, even when doing so may appear to be unfavorable to me (servant attitude).

c. Embracing the Lord's discipline to learn from my past actions independent of God and from how the flesh has managed to lead me to act independently of God in other trials.

d. Having trust in God, and demonstrating that in steps of faith.

e. Having an acceptance of the fact that living for God is a deeply spiritual opportunity. It involves a number of areas: introspection, courage, detachment from "bad experiences," discernment, all through the Spirit of God Himself.

5. When I am being tested, whether I realize it or not, the flesh makes me fearful of worldly risks. It is really important to see each trial as a test and a training opportunity. If I don't do that, or if I'm not really willing to do that, then the following risks increase:

a. Risk that I won't discern (with the heart, not just mentally) that God's testing and Satan's temptations are both experienced during a trial. This is the nature of trials, but still, I often overlook it, which results in underestimating the importance of discerning God's guidance to me. That underestimation is the result of the flesh.

b. Risk that I won't actually let God live through me. Satan can drive me simply by getting my heart to be out of sync with God. So while sometimes I may do the "right" external action, I'm still acting independently of the Lord due to the lack of willingness to be transformed, because I'm afraid to be changed by Him.

c. Risk that I won't experience the true inner peace of God which He offers me during trials. This is the flesh. Often, though, I believe I am OK inside when, in fact, I am only being deceived by the flesh such that I do what I prefer to think God wants of me. That experience is not the same as the deeply fulfilling experience of God's peace during a trial.

6. What if God were trying to tell me to do something really big like He did with Abraham? What if He were doing so, but without words that I could hear? Would I be able to hear Him that clearly with my heart? Would it be strictly His responsibility to get the message across clearly to me, so that I knew for certain that it was

Him and I understood His instructions? Sometimes when we talk with another person, they don't *hear* us. Sometimes it's not that we aren't communicating clearly, and it's just that they don't *want* to hear what we are saying. If I don't want to do the same thing with God in one of my trials, then I have to really be sensitive to what the Spirit reveals about my fleshly tendencies and Satan's influences. That is a big deal!!

LESSON 21: GENESIS 22:1-10 (SARAH)

WHAT WAS Sarah's HEART DISTURBANCE?
Not specifically recorded in Scripture.

DID Sarah SUBMIT TO THE LORD TRANSFORMING HER HEART AND MIND SO THE LORD COULD LIVE THROUGH HER?
The Bible is not clear whether Sarah experienced a trial.

ONE PERSON'S EXPERIENCE
WHAT WOULD YOUR TYPICAL HEART DISTURBANCE BE IF YOU WERE Sarah IN THIS SITUATION OR ONE LIKE IT?
1. I don't want (desire) my husband to kill our child, or to even think that God might want that because I waited 25 years for a son. I'm not willing to lose my son now! Abraham is crazy and needs to be locked up; I'm calling 911!
2. I'd also feel mad, angry, and even rage because you (Abraham) are thwarting the very plan God has for this boy (Isaac) by planning to kill him.
3. I would also want (desire) Abraham to talk to me first because that would enable me to reason with him. It would give me a chance to change his plan or use whatever I could as leverage to prevent or motivate him to not follow through with his plan. I think Abraham needs my help and input!

DISCERN/OBSERVE:

Discern Fleshly Tendencies

1. The flesh says God wants me to fight Abraham.
2. The fleshly thinking says I'm not a loving person if I let something happen to Isaac.
3. The fleshly thinking says God isn't loving if sacrificing Isaac is really what He wants. The flesh then says this can't be of God, so it is OK to resist Abraham and not love him.

Discern Lying Belief

This isn't what I wanted for my life!

Discern and Feel the Truth of Your Identity in Christ

In Christ I am not alone! I feel loved because You are so much greater than me and yet You want to live through me! I feel so relieved because I don't have to be the defender, You are the caretaker of us all! I feel trusting because You are showing me that I need You so that Your love and peace can flow through me. I feel thankful because again You are showing me that my point of view is so painfully limited and Your point of view is so wonderfully loving and full of grace and mercy. I feel grateful because You have not given up on me and are connecting me to my true identity in You!

Discern What The Lord Would Seek to Change in You to Transform Your Heart Disturbances So You Experience the Peace of God.

God would want to change a fleshly point of view. The fleshly point of view that comes up for me is to have things be the way the flesh thinks they should be in order to be "good." That leads to wanting to know the reasons why it is supposedly "good" to sacrifice my son! I say "supposedly" because in this trial my first reaction probably isn't going to be "Oh goody, let's go please God by sacrificing the boy we waited all our lives for!" The flesh works to make me resist any discussion with Abraham unless it starts with God Himself telling me why this needs to happen! In letting God help me embrace His point of view, the Holy Spirit reveals that Isaac isn't my son, but the Lord's. I know that sounds naïve, but it's true. The Lord is looking for me to trust Him more than my husband. The Lord is looking to save me from the flesh, which tells me it's OK to be argumentative with my husband, Abraham.

The Lord's new point of view for me enables me to let Him live love through me towards my husband in the face of this huge issue. Anyone can harbor hate and anger in this situation, but only by letting the Lord connect me to my true identity in Him can He live love through me in such an incredible way. The Spirit also reveals to me that, based on how I've acted in the flesh before, the Lord is looking for me to take steps of faith that release Isaac to Him! The Spirit is revealing that I have been trying to possess what is actually God's!

Discern Possible Steps of Faith; Observe Things About Your Life, Spiritual Battles, and What to Expect in Trials.

1. Steps of faith would involve taking pride and full contentment in trusting God. God is looking for me to take steps of faith that demonstrate a sense of detachment. It's not that I wouldn't care about or love Isaac; it's just that living for God involves the trusting Him to live through me no matter what I face. The Spirit is telling me that this means I need to express sincere support for Abraham's step of faith in God. This also means that even if Isaac has to die, God's love must still pour through me toward Abraham. This can only be possible in letting God change me, but I'm willing for that!

2. In some trials the external part of the trial seems "bigger" than in other trials. This trial is like that because the external issue is about sacrificing Isaac. When the external issues seem big and more important to me, the flesh tends to try to make me jump immediately into doing something to produce the outcome I believe God *should* want. The flesh immediately wants me to take an action without really pausing to discern how my heart disturbance is connected to a spiritual issue God is addressing. I have to get in the habit of being open to the Spirit so He can help me discern what God wants to change and transform in me. The flesh gets me to assuming I have all the facts: externally and in terms of how I think God actually wants the trial to turn out!

3. When I first put myself in this situation, I didn't really see how the role as a wife played such an important part for me to be open to being transformed by God. The only thing that made sense was that the husband somehow had the responsibility to do or say something to help me be at peace. I think that (overlooking roles) is a reflection of Satan's attack in this kind of trial. Satan gets me

to looking outward at others, in this case at Abraham, instead of looking inward to God and the role God wants to live through me in the trial. That's big!

4. Many times I have fleshly reasons why I think something should be different in a trial. In business, it is good to communicate a lot so everyone is in harmony; on the same sheet of music. It is important to have solid reasoning for making the decisions we make. However, God often doesn't give me all of His reasons. He can make it clear what He wants to do through me, but that has to be accepted in my heart, even when I'd like more of His answers to "why?"! The real answer to why the trial is happening is so the Lord can transform me and center me more in my true identity in Christ! In trials, letting God live through me goes against fleshly thinking and is only understood by a heart centered in Christ. It is also understood by discerning what the Spirit reveals to me about what Satan is doing against Christ in me in a trial – that's important. In business, we communicate a lot so that we need less trust. With God, He communicates and reveals some things to me, but not to the point where no faith or trust is required on my part!

5. Sometimes in trials I over-communicate so that less trust is actually required! But, I don't catch that. It's like a politically correct way of having control issues! That model doesn't work in a trial where God is giving me just enough information about what steps of faith to take. He doesn't always tell me why, and He doesn't always tell me what the outcome of the trial will be if I let Him act through me. In this way, I see the importance of faith in my relationship with God! That really puts some things in perspective for me!

DISCUSSION QUESTIONS:

1. Think about the heart disturbance(s) you felt when you put yourself in this potential trial. Now, short of Abraham saying, "You're right, Sarah, God probably doesn't want me to sacrifice Isaac, so I'm not going to do it," is there really anything that Abraham can say to you to cause your heart to transform to peace? Why?

    a. No, there isn't anything he could say to me to cause me to feel better. The reason is because I don't want Isaac to be sacrificed! My heart's desire can't be changed by Abraham, only by God – and I must surrender to Him for that to happen!

b. There really isn't anything Abraham can say to me to make me feel peaceful because I really want to say things to *him* to change *his* mind, and to convince *him* that God doesn't want to sacrifice Isaac. That's really interesting to me because even though I know from the Bible that God did want Abraham to go to sacrifice Isaac, if it were happening to me, I wouldn't tend to believe it based on Abraham's word alone. I'd be expecting God to confirm directly with me about His desire for Isaac to be sacrificed! I don't think that's how God sees roles!

c. Abraham couldn't say anything to make it better for me other than, "OK, I won't sacrifice Isaac!" But if you think about it, Abraham had to have been concerned about a sense of loss too. Still, it would appear to me, at least initially, as if Abraham was off his rocker and didn't care, because he was already at peace with the idea of the sacrifice!

2. If you are not at peace about sacrificing Isaac, is your issue really with Abraham, or is it more of an issue with God?

a. The Bible doesn't record that God ever directly told Sarah the same Promises and guidance He told Abraham. The only time He comes close to telling Sarah about Isaac's birth is very indirect (Genesis 18:10-14). In that situation Sarah was listening to what the Lord, His two angels and Abraham were talking about. She overheard the Lord talk about a son for them. Even when Sarah laughed about it, the Lord did not address her, but Abraham.

b. I'd definitely be affected by God's plan, but it is almost as if God isn't seeking to confirm things with me *because* God is trying to transform me too, but by speaking to my husband. I think that for me it actually would be more of an issue with God, than with Abraham.

c. So for me to experience the peace of Christ, I would have to discern from the Holy Spirit that in my role as wife God is not trying to tell me what Abraham should do. The Lord is trying to show me how to let Him (the Lord) live through me. It seems that God would be challenging me to trust Him through whatever He is doing through my husband. Apparently God saw this as the thing to do with Sarah, whether I like the implications of it or not!

d. For me to experience the peace of Christ in this situation, I really don't need to hear anything from Abraham anyway. If I can't let the Lord transform me to I experience His peace in my identity in Him then my issue is really with God, in the sense that I am uncertain *because* God isn't choosing to speak to me directly. That could be interpreted as meaning God loves me less, but only if I see God's view of our various roles as being inappropriate.

LESSON 22: GENESIS 23 (ABRAHAM)

WHAT WAS Abraham's HEART DISTURBANCE?
1. V. 2 – Abraham was mourning, and he wept over Sarah because she had died.
2. V. 4 – Abraham desired some property for a burial site because he wanted to bury his wife.

DID Abraham SUBMIT TO THE LORD TRANSFORMING HIS HEART AND MIND SO THE LORD COULD LIVE THROUGH HIM?
From what we read in the Bible about this possible trial, Abraham let God transform his heart and mind, and God lived Abraham's knowledge through Abraham while he was not being treated fairly.

ONE PERSON'S EXPERIENCE
WHAT WOULD YOUR TYPICAL HEART DISTURBANCE BE IF YOU WERE Abraham IN THIS SITUATION OR ONE LIKE IT?
1. I'd feel sad, mournful and even stressed because my wife, whom I loved, died, yet at the same time I have to deal with negotiating this land issue and I don't want (desire) to do that while I'm mourning for my wife.
2. I'd also feel torn because I don't want (desire) to be the "bad guy" by calling out Ephron on his pretense of sympathy, yet at the same time, I don't want to feel like a doormat.

DISCERN/OBSERVE:
Discern Fleshly Tendencies
1. Fleshly thinking says it is best to do nothing if I might upset someone else by standing up for something.
2. Fleshly thinking says that if I was a better person, people wouldn't take advantage of me, or at least God would stick up for me.
3. Fleshly thinking says that I am better off asking someone else to handle the tough issues when I am not feeling up to it.
4. Fleshly thinking says to walk away from this land deal or just give in to Ephron to avoid conflict.

Discern Lying Belief
I can't do this (the land deal).

Discern and Feel the Truth of Your Identity in Christ
In Christ I am good enough and You can handle this issue through me! I feel lighter and more free because You are fully capable of handling the issue through me. I feel strengthened because You are helping me lay down the burden created by fleshly thinking! I feel hopeful because Your plan is better than the fleshly concerns and fears. I feel confident because Your love can flow through me as I surrender to You. I feel thankful because You are giving me the opportunity to experience You living through me and it is Your example that others will see in me!

Discern What The Lord Would Seek to Change in You to Transform Your Heart Disturbances So You Experience the Peace of God.
God would want to change a fleshly point of view. The fleshly view is that I shouldn't have to deal with handling the land issue while in mourning. God's new point of view is that I must let Him handle the land transaction as He sees fit through me. If I don't embrace God's new point of view for me, then I may do the right thing externally (not be confrontational with Ephron), but still be in turmoil on the inside and feel as though I am lacking. That heart disturbance is a warning that I am still embracing the fleshly point of view that it is all about me. God's new point of view takes me beyond fleshly selfishness and strengthens me in this situation!

Discern Possible Steps of Faith; Observe Things About Your Life, Spiritual Battles, and What to Expect in Trials.

1. Since God is allowing this situation with Ephron to happen, a faith step would orient on a point of view of serving God though the external cost may seem unreasonable from a worldly point of view. When I take that to heart, it almost seems easier to be at peace in this situation because it isn't about me being cheated. It is about Ephron being a taker, and that is between him and God.

2. Another step of faith is to let the Lord's zeal come through me instead of focusing on someone else's hypocrisy. In this way the Lord is helping me to demonstrate belief in His God's promise about the land eventually becoming the native land of my descendants. If I followed those steps of faith, I would find pleasure in seeing that a legal transaction, even at exorbitant prices, had the least chance of leading to dispute in later years.

3. In some situations, as with Abraham, I must trust God realizing that, no matter what, I may lose according to the flesh and the world. In those trials, Satan's attacks against Christ in me challenge me to avoid taking steps of faith the Lord asks of me.

4. While God says He'll look out for me and take care of me, that doesn't necessarily mean I'll never experience being cheated, lied to, taken from, etc. The point of these kinds of trials is to discern how God would respond through me to those trials.

5. Trials always present us choices. In Abraham's trial, he had to recognize that he really couldn't just accept the burial cave through a verbal gift anyway, because that could be disputed later. Once he recognized that he had to at least buy the cave, the issue of being ripped off almost became spiritually irrelevant for him. Perhaps in discerning this Abraham was able to resist the temptation to make the rip off an issue to be confrontational about. Truthfully, the only choice Abraham really had to make was whether to submit to how the Lord wanted to transform him and live through him. The external decision-making then really wasn't a burden Abraham had to carry. I'm glad the Spirit revealed this to me because the flesh often tries to get me to think that external issues are a reflection of me when they really are about God transforming me!

6. Roles are always important in discerning God's guidance in trials. I see this in Abraham's trial. Abraham subjected himself to the Hittites' laws. Part of his role was not only to secure the burial site, but to accept the fact that the Hittites' legal and commercial

systems were not set up to work in his favor in a worldly way. God's expectation was to do through Abraham what He must to secure the burial site in what would be the native land of Abraham's descendants, even though the Hittites were actually living there at the time. This is a big example of having faith in God's vision of the future, while being in the present.

7.   Sometimes God wants to speak up through me about an issue like He did through Abraham to Abimelech concerning the issue over the well (Genesis 21:22-32 – Lesson 19). The Spirit is revealing to me that at other times God wants to NOT speak up through me, which may require swallowing my pride and resisting a fleshly need to speak out. To me it is obvious that when it is the latter, the flesh tries to get me to lash out. I don't like being victimized or taken advantage of. Even when I try to avoid conflict, the peace of Christ can elude me because I feel so uncertain and uncomfortable with how things may turn out. Letting God transform those feelings requires a very real connection of faith in God. I have to remember what God is telling me to do or not do at each trial along my way in life.

LESSON 23: GENESIS 24:1-16 (CHIEF SERVANT OF ABRAHAM)

WHAT WAS the Chief Servant's HEART DISTURBANCE?
1.   V. 12 – The Chief Servant wanted (desired) success on behalf of Abraham.
2.   V. 14 – The Chief Servant wants (desires) the choice of Isaac's wife to be God's choice, because he wants to be sure God's kindness (favor) is upon Abraham.

DID the Chief Servant SUBMIT TO THE LORD TRANSFORMING HIS HEART AND MIND SO THE LORD COULD LIVE THROUGH HIM?
   In this possible trial, the Chief Servant was able to let God live the knowledge of his master (Abraham). The Chief Servant actually let God transform his heart and mind as best he knew how!

ONE PERSON'S EXPERIENCE
WHAT WOULD YOUR TYPICAL HEART DISTURBANCE BE IF YOU WERE the Chief Servant IN THIS SITUATION OR ONE LIKE IT?

1. I'd feel inadequate, trapped, and somewhat upset because Abraham wants me to find Isaac a wife from over 400 miles away, Isaac cannot come with me, and the wife-to-be, and her family, has to agree to this without even meeting Isaac.
2. I'd also feel very uneasy and stressed because the task is so huge. There are too many variables and unknowns for me to be assured Abraham and Isaac will be happy with my decision. I'd want them to be pleased with my decision and with me, because I want to have a good relationship with them.
3. And lastly, I'd feel worried and uncertain because I'd be wondering whether it is right for me to be asking God for a sign of what to do, versus having the kind of heart that has faith in the Lord without signs.

DISCERN/OBSERVE:
Discern Fleshly Tendencies

1. The flesh says this task isn't fair and that it is OK to feel I have been wronged by Abraham.
2. The flesh says that Abraham should be handling this situation, or at least letting Isaac deal with it. They shouldn't be putting this on me.
3. The flesh says to do whatever is easiest for me, since this responsibility shouldn't be mine in the first place.
4. The fleshly thinking is if Isaac or Abraham aren't happy with my decision, then, "OH WELL!" The flesh says it is OK to be mad at them and blame them. If they don't like my decision, then say, "You should have done it yourself!"

Discern Lying Belief

I really work at being a good person and that is good enough.

Discern and Feel the Truth of Your Identity in Christ

Only in Christ am I good enough! I feel humbled because You have revealed to me that I cannot handle this; only You living through me can make this be Your will. I feel a renewed sense of confidence that You will take care of this issue as I submit to You.

I feel relieved because You are taking the burden because You love me. I feel grateful to be able to be part of this to see You at work!

Discern What The Lord Would Seek to Change in You to Transform Your Heart Disturbances So You Experience the Peace of God.
God would want to change a fleshly point of view. The flesh tries to convince me that I have to figure out the solution. By embracing the Lord's new point of view for me, I can be certain that figuring out the solution is God's issue and not my own. If I want God to live through me, then it isn't up to me. I have to embrace the point of view that God's help is real, it is good to *have* to trust God, and I just need to not act independently of Him. God's point of view for me also helps me embrace the fact that only God knows the woman for Isaac. My job is to make sure that I don't unduly influence the woman or the situation – I have to keep out of the way and not fall to being tempted to influence anything.

Discern Possible Steps of Faith; Observe Things About Your Life, Spiritual Battles, and What to Expect in Trials.
1. The first step of faith is to conduct myself as the messenger in this trial. The Lord wants me to observe and extend an opportunity to whomever God shows me. The ultimate decision is up to the woman and God. Part of this step of faith is to NOT say anything that could influence the woman, even if I feel really good about her as being "the one!"
2. Another important step of faith God would want from me deals with continuing to let God live through me when I return back to Abraham with a woman for Isaac. Once God shows me the wife-to-be, she, Abraham or Isaac may experience trials and disagreements in the future. That doesn't reflect on me personally. In my future, I will have to continue taking steps of faith for God, even though others may later question the decision God made through me. The Holy Spirit is revealing to me that God's steps of faith for me involve being detached from the outcome of the trial and never taking it personally if things don't always go perfectly in the future.
3. The Chief Servant probably had his job because he had good judgment and initiative. In this trial, he discerned a test that was actually fairly specific, and which made it harder for the flesh to lure him into "making things happen" on his own! Making the

choice of a wife based on his own judgment would clearly have been what Satan wanted him to do. Whether he thought in terms of Satan or not isn't the point; he knew that there was definitely a wrong way to approach decision-making in this trial. The Chief Servant discerned that the spiritual issue for him was about being assured that his own judgment was not what he used to make the decision. He wanted God to make the decision. God isn't going to give me physical signs each time I need His direction. So, a big part of my responsibility in discerning the direction God wants to take through me involves steps of faith that go against the flesh and Satan's temptation. I have to avoid making a judgment from the flesh, because Satan works to influence my judgment. Like the Chief Servant, when I am in a trial, I am being given a mission that is spiritually above my head, but the Holy Spirit reveals to me that God wants to succeed *through me to bring Him glory!*

4. Sometimes, like the Chief Servant, I have to be patient. The main temptation the Chief Servant had to avoid was acting independently of God. When trials come up for me, I must take a pause to discern God's Spirit so He can show me how to stay out of being an obstacle to the Lord living through my life.

5. Another aspect of the Chief Servant's trial was that he had a long journey to make to get to the area of Abraham's relatives. While the Chief Servant may have wanted to hurry up and find the wife in order to get through his trial, again he had to be patient. Sometimes, for different reasons, I too have to wait for some amount of time before it is time to take the steps of faith God asks of me. During that waiting period, Satan can attack me and keep my mind and heart stirred up. If I don't fully embrace the transformation God seeks to make in me, I will have many worries, concerns, etc. that try to get me to take fleshly action – action independent of God! That almost seems normal in life! But because God can transform me, my new normal in the Lord can actually be about being at peace during the waiting. That is a deep level of faith in God, and I'm glad He revealed this to me!

REFERENCES

Feelings 101: Pain to Peace 2nd Edition, William J. Clark, Jr. with CH (COL) William J. Clark, Ret., 2013, Keys To Understanding Life Series

from the *Living The Transformed Life In Christ* series/curriculum

> *Living Life From A New Source (book one)*, Bill Loveless, Christ Is Life Ministries, 2010

> *Do You Know Your True Identity? (book two)*, Bill Loveless, Christ Is Life Ministries, 2011

> *Being Transformed (book three)*, Bill Loveless, Christ Is Life Ministries, 2011

> *Living From The Overflow of Christ (book four)*, Bill Loveless, Christ Is Life Ministries, 2011

Oxford American Dictionary, 1999, Oxford University Press

The Exhaustive Concordance of The Bible, James Strong S.T.D., Ll.D., Macdonald Publishing Company, ISBN 0-917006-01-1

The Macmillan Bible Atlas, 1968, Macmillan Publishing Co., Inc.

The Rest of the Gospel, Dan Stone and David Gregory, Harvest House Publishers, Eugene, OR 2000

Word Pictures in the New Testament, A.T. Robertson, Broadman Press, Nashville, TN, 1930

Darcey and the Grasshopper

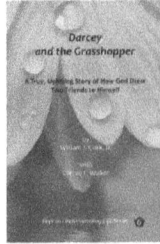

www.SecretHeartOfChristianity.com

This is a fun and light read for young adults and up!

A true, inspirational story of friendship, hope, learning to love... and finding God. If you are looking for something that'll pull you in – this'll do it for you.

God does amazing things all the time – we just gotta pay attention... and have faith.

Religious Origins of the Middle East Crisis, 2nd Edition

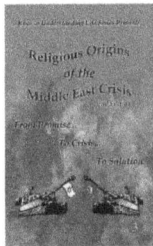

www.ReligiousOriginsMiddleEastCrisis.com

This book is specifically designed to be a simple resource to educate Christians on what is going on in the Middle East and why.

Chapter 1 covers key events starting with Abraham (c. 2000 B.C.) and moving to the present day.

Chapters 2 and 3 are packed with reference material to help the reader understand the identity, belief system, and "vision" of the 3 different faiths involved in the crisis.

ABOUT THE AUTHORS

The father and son team combine a variety of experiences including formal theological education, creating spiritually intimate fellowships and teaching powerful personal transformation skills possible in Christ. From their home in Texas, they help others learn how to enjoy the enriching and interactive life of being a disciple of Christ.

Learn more about the authors by visiting their website:

www.KeysToUnderstandingLife.org